SWEATSHOP CAPITAL

SWEATSHOP CAPITAL

—

PROFIT, VIOLENCE, AND SOLIDARITY MOVEMENTS IN THE LONG TWENTIETH CENTURY

Beth Robinson

DUKE UNIVERSITY PRESS   DURHAM AND LONDON   2025

© 2025 DUKE UNIVERSITY PRESS
All rights reserved
Project Editor: Bird Williams
Designed by Matt Tauch
Typeset in Alegreya and Antique Série Regular by
Westchester Publishing Services

Library of Congress Cataloging-in-Publication Data
Names: Robinson, Beth (Beth Diane), [date] author.
Title: Sweatshop capital : profit, violence, and solidarity
movements in the long twentieth century / Beth Robinson.
Description: Durham : Duke University Press, 2025. |
Includes bibliographical references and index.
Identifiers: LCCN 2025006496 (print)
LCCN 2025006497 (ebook)
ISBN 9781478032793 (paperback)
ISBN 9781478029335 (hardcover)
ISBN 9781478061526 (ebook)
Subjects: LCSH: Anti-sweatshop movement—United States—
History—20th century. | Sweatshops—United States—History—
20th century. | Consumer goods—United States—History—20th
century. | Capitalism—United States—History—20th century.
Classification: LCC HD2339. u6 r63 2025 (print)
LCC HD 2339. u6 (ebook)
LC record available at https://lccn.loc.gov/2025006496
LC ebook record available at https://lccn.loc.gov/2025006497

Cover art: League of Women Shoppers picket outside
Ohrbach's Department Store during the 1934 strike.
Courtesy of Nora Mitchell Sanborn.

CONTENTS

ABBREVIATIONS · vii
ACKNOWLEDGMENTS · ix
PROLOGUE · xiii

Introduction · 1

1 "The Struggle Has But Begun": The Labor Feminism of the Progressive Era · 13

2 "Don't Overlook Any Channel for Publicity": The Solidarity of the Popular Front · 47

3 "Settle the Case, or We'll Be in Your Face": The Worldview of the Global Justice Movement · 77

4 "Amazon Crime": The Omnipresence of the New Global Assembly Line · 109

Conclusion · 149

NOTES · 159
BIBLIOGRAPHY · 193
INDEX · 211

ABBREVIATIONS

FKP · Florence Kelley Papers, Manuscripts and Archives Division, New York Public Library

FMC · Fromkin Memorial Collection, Golda Meir Library, University of Wisconsin-Milwaukee, Milwaukee, WI

JLOP · Jessie Lloyd O'Connor Papers, Sophia Smith Collection of Women's History, Neilson Library, Smith College, Northampton, MA

LFPC · Lectures of Frances Perkins Collection, Kheel Center Labor and Management Microfilm Collections, Catherwood Library, Cornell University, Ithaca, NY

LWSP · League of Women Shoppers Papers, Sophia Smith Collection of Women's History, Neilson Library, Smith College, Northampton, MA

MCBP · Mary Cornelia Barker Papers, Manuscript, Archives, and Rare Book Library, Robert W. Woodruff Library, Emory University

NCLR · National Consumers' League Records, Manuscript Division, Library of Congress, Washington, DC

PWTUL · Papers of the Women's Trade Union League and Its Principal Leaders, Schlesinger Library, Radcliffe Institute, Harvard University, Cambridge, MA

RCLM · Records of the Consumers' League of Massachusetts, 1891–1955, Radcliffe Institute, Harvard University, Cambridge, MA

WGRPC · Walter Goldwater Radical Pamphlet Collection, Special Collections Library, Peter J. Shields Library, University of California-Davis, Davis, CA

ACKNOWLEDGMENTS

This book is about the immense, often-unseen labor that is behind every production. I am deeply grateful to the extraordinary network of people who helped me as I tried to make sense of this history. I will never know most of them—the workers who manufactured my computer, or who sewed my clothes, or who cleaned my conference hotel room—but this book would not exist without them, and I hope that it honors their work.

I began this project at the University of Wisconsin-Milwaukee, where I was fortunate to benefit from the department's generous pedagogical and financial support. I am indebted to my committee: the late Michael Gordon, Merry Wiesner-Hanks, and Carolyn Eichner, who questioned and challenged me and provided intellectual support. I am especially grateful to Rachel Ida Buff and Robert Smith, each of whom not only read every page multiple times, but also exemplified how to be both a public scholar and an engaged parent.

I have been lucky to learn from so many teachers who nurtured my curiosity. I am particularly indebted to Julie Willett, who first introduced me to women's history at Texas Tech University and encouraged me to pursue graduate school. At the University of Alabama, Carol Pierman, Jennifer Purvis, and Rhoda Johnson gave me the tools to apply a feminist lens to my scholarship and teaching. While there, I also benefited greatly from the many conversations about southern women's history that I shared with Ethan and Angela Brooks-Livingston, and from the independent study courses on women's labor history that Lisa Lindquist Dorr and Lynne Adrian generously offered me, without compensation, even though they were outside of my program. I am further indebted to many professors at the University of Wisconsin-Milwaukee, who taught me inside and outside of the classroom: including Amanda Seligman, Winson Chu, Joe Austin, Margo Anderson, David Hoeveler, John Schroeder, Aims McGuinness, and the late Steve Meyer, as well as those already mentioned.

This book was born out of my own work as an anti-sweatshop activist, and I have enormous appreciation for my friends in the struggle. My thanks to Dana Schultz, Kevin Suemnicht, Kyle Schulz, Kristin McCrory, Brian Averill, Jay Burseth, Dawson Barrett, and others who worked on the "Sweat-Free UWM" campaign. Their creativity, tenacity, and nerve pushed me to write our experiences into a long trajectory of labor activism. Their continued work as teachers and organizers is a testament to the transformative experience of campus activism. I am also grateful to Ann Zielke, Trevor Smith, and Lindsey Resnikoff for helping me think deeply about solidarity and working-class histories.

In that same spirit, I owe additional thanks to Jenny Chan, Chelsea Connor, Kshama Sawant, Li Qiang, David Reilly, and the late Katherine Copeland for granting me interviews. I learned much about organizing, courage, and solidarity from each of them.

I was incredibly fortunate to be hired by the Humanities Department at Texas A&M University-Corpus Christi, where I finished this book. I have learned and continue to learn so much from my students, and it is a pleasure to work with them. I am also particularly grateful to have had senior colleagues who recognize that scholars wear multiple hats: Thank you to Peter Moore, Sandrine Sanos, Robert Wooster, Anthony Quiroz, David Blanke, and Glenn Tiller. Thank you for being friends as well as colleagues: Eliza Martin, Jen Brown, Adam Costanzo, Michael Jin, Chrissy Lau, Lucy Sheehan, Scott Johnson, Kelly Bezio, Carolina Ortega, Allie Kelley, Rory Huang, Bonnie Soper, Lisa Comparini, and Jenny Sorensen. An extra heartfelt thanks to Claudia Rueda, who seamlessly embodied many roles—colleague, friend, yoga partner, and mentor.

The workers and activists in this book all fought to improve their lives and their communities. They also left behind records by documenting their stories and sharing them with labor journalists, graciously allowing future historians (and activists) to learn from their experiences. For helping me find those stories, I am indebted to the archivists, librarians, and student workers who graciously accommodated me during research visits. I owe more than I can express to the workers at the Special Collections Libraries and Archives at the Universities of Alabama, California, Davis, California-Santa Cruz, Florida, Washington, and Wisconsin-Milwaukee; Wellesley, Vassar, Allegheny, and Smith Colleges; San Francisco State, Emory, Cornell, Bloomsburg, and Kansas State Universities; Birmingham and New York Public Libraries; Alabama State Archives; Wisconsin State Historical Society; American Textile History Museum; and Library of Congress. At

TAMU-CC, the Frantz Endowment and Haas Professorship enabled me to complete this book. I am grateful for the assistance of Marti Beck, Amanda Hartlaub, Mari Alexander, and Anji Peralez.

Many colleagues and friends read portions of this work, offered helpful feedback, and cheered me along, including Melissa Terry, John Terry, and Joe Walzer. Landon Storrs and Karen Cox each read early chapters. Kathryn Kish Sklar and Thomas Dublin provided me with the first opportunity to publish my work, and I am forever grateful for how generously they shepherded me through the process. I also extend special thanks to Rosemary Feurer, Clara Potter, and Catherine Cocks, who worked with me on earlier versions of this project.

The editors at Duke University Press have been so wonderful to work with. I am grateful to Gisela Fosado and Alejandra Mejía for their enthusiasm, support, and patience. Many thanks to the reviewers of the manuscript for their careful comments, especially Eileen Boris, who read multiple drafts and offered generous support within her vast network.

Many people made my life better simply by being present. I was lucky to combine research trips to New York with visiting my oldest friend, Katie Bell, who generously hosted me. I also owe thanks to Christine Robbins, Sangmi Lim, Melissa Mizesko, Autumn Burkett, Inger Harvey, Jenny Lee, Eva Lopez, Kellyn Pfeffer, and Sarah McClung for organizing brunches, dinners, family camping trips, and birthday parties. Behind every working parent is a band of caregivers—family, teachers, and dedicated workers. I owe immense gratitude to Maureen Charleston and the other Montessori teachers, whose support allowed me to balance my roles as both a scholar and a mother.

Lastly, I would like to thank my amazing family. My parents, Don and Joan Robinson, have encouraged me every step of the way. They taught me to value curiosity, education, community, and family, as well as paid and unpaid labor. I am lucky to have my brothers, David and Michael, in my life, along with their families. Thank you to my parents-in-law, Phil and Aline Barrett, for cheering me on, asking thoughtful questions, telling jokes, and pouring wine. And thanks as well to the extended Robinson, Adkison, and Barrett families for being so supportive.

I could not have written this book were it not for Dawson Barrett, who always believed in it. He read and edited more drafts than I can recount, while also doing more than his fair share of household chores. My gratitude for him has no bounds. And finally, I want to thank Genora and Henry, who have been hearing for years that I want to finish my book. They are a daily reminder of what is important.

PROLOGUE

"UNIVERSITY APPAREL MADE IN SWEATSHOPS." Two decades ago, my friends and I used sidewalk chalk to write that slogan all over our college campus every few weeks. Our school's bookstore overflowed with branded merchandise, and, like our classmates, we showed pride in our community and our studies through the trademarked images on hats, shirts, and bags. Presumably, few of our fellow students had ever wondered who made their clothes or where they were made. When we began researching that question, however, we quickly reached an uncomfortable conclusion.

Today, the situation is demonstrably worse. Only the slightest curiosity is enough to uncover that the overwhelming majority of the clothing, technology, and household items that surround us are products of brutal, exploitative working conditions. From our phones, to our shoes, to our transportation, we are customers and workers in a sweatshop economy that squeezes its profits from people working long hours, under dangerous conditions, and for poverty wages. Awareness of this horrifying reality, and our role in it, does not have to lead to despair or apathy, though. It can also lead to action, as it did for my friends and me—and as it did for the thousands of workers and activists in this book. The pages that follow reflect a long history of sweatshop workers engaging members of the public, helping them see barely hidden realities, and inviting them to join movements for change.

Perhaps unsurprisingly, college students were often among those who answered that call, and universities were spaces of both activism and education. My own political awakening began in college as the Bush administration was leveraging the tragedy of September 11 into a devastatingly bloody and expensive war, a global campaign of torture, and a crackdown on American protest. I felt powerless, as it became clear to me that the world did not work how I had been taught. I committed to learning more about militarism, sexism, racism, and classism—and how they were connected. I wanted to know what was really going on.

After falling in love with a women's history course, I interned at a local rape crisis center and decided to pursue a master's degree in what was then called Women's Studies. I began thinking more deeply about power, privilege, and political organizing, and I researched a thesis on women textile workers in the Deep South. My first oral histories were attempts to learn more about my own grandmother's experiences in an Alabama hosiery mill in the 1930s. At a disadvantage because she was left-handed, her coworkers pitched in to help her meet quotas—an act of solidarity from women who were already exhausted from working long hours at intense speeds. In this history, I saw connections to the present not just in these women's lives and working conditions, but also in their impulse to go against the grain and to fight for one another. It made me feel less powerless—like there was a place for me in a proud tradition.

When my friends and I began chalking on our campus about the labor conditions that produced our branded clothes, we were told by administrators that, for legal reasons, they could not pledge to support more stringent standards in foreign factories. Publicly, they brushed off our demands as merely "symbolic" and offered assurances that they were just as concerned about sweatshop labor as we were. We found out through open records requests, though, that behind their strategically dismissive responses were emails voicing great concern about our campaign, which grew to include petitions, mud stencils, rallies, a "sweat-free" fashion show, and a campus appearance by factory workers—as well as all of the sidewalk chalk.

After two years, the administration finally relented and pledged its support. We won, and for several years afterward, the campus bookstore kept a sign on its door announcing that all university licensed apparel was "certified sweatshop-free." Long after rain and snow had washed our own messages away, hundreds of students a day were prompted to think about clothing and working conditions. The claim on the sign, however, was, at best, an oversimplification. Tackling the misery baked into the global economy was a much bigger, and more complicated, problem than a handful of college students could hope to solve with a box of chalk. We were not alone, though. It was a start, and I was proud to act in solidarity with garment workers around the world—and with other students, at my own school and at dozens of others nationwide.

Among the many lessons that I learned from that campaign was that our actions mattered, even when the people in power said that they didn't. This book, I think, offers a similar lesson. It was born, in part, out of my own feelings of despair as I learned about the working conditions that produced my clothing—and the computer on which I am writing this, for that matter. One of its themes is the often-surprising power of solidarity and collective action, and it is meant specifically for students, teachers, and organizers—that is, for people who want to learn this history, to build on it, and to change the way the world works. Though certainly not a complete history of American capitalism or of sweatshops, it provides glimpses into four major historical moments (including the present), centering the experiences of workers and anti-sweatshop activists and showing both the evolution of the American sweatshop economy and some of the many ways that people have tried to fight back against it.

The struggle between marginalized workers and powerful employers has long been an uneven fight. It is, of course, ongoing. Right now, just as at many points in the past, solidarity with workers starts with concern and a commitment to make a change. And, for what it is worth, the movements in this book were largely built by people like you and me.

INTRODUCTION

In January 1999, attorneys for American activist organizations filed three class-action lawsuits on behalf of thirty thousand garment workers in Saipan. They accused more than forty retailers and factories of conspiring to deny workers their basic human rights through indentured servitude, sexual harassment, and forced abortions. As disturbing details about the working conditions in Saipan's billion-dollar garment industry emerged, critics drew parallels to the notorious sweatshops that had plagued New York a century earlier. Sweatshops, it seemed, had returned to US soil, albeit nearly eight thousand miles west of New York in the Commonwealth of the Northern Mariana Islands. During the early twentieth century, labor activism and government regulation reshaped mainstream working conditions in the United States, but the garment industry—and its sweatshops—had repeatedly relocated in search of exploitable labor. In Saipan, for example, though the clothing that they made carried labels reading "Made in the USA," garment workers were not protected by US labor laws.[1]

The sweatshop déjà vu of the 1990s—the Saipan lawsuit and several other scandals—was emblematic of the American garment industry's long history of abuses. Among its long-held practices, now popular across many industries, was a structure that separated retailers from the workers who produced their goods, simultaneously incentivizing sweatshop working conditions while insulating clothing companies from any of the unpleasantries. Instead of hiring garment workers directly as employees, the retailers—for the factories in Saipan, these included The Gap, Tommy Hilfiger, and Target—instead offered short-term contracts to manufacturers who competed with one another to offer the lowest bids. The winning factories were those who could continually recruit the most desperate and marginalized workers—typically young women and children—and force them to work for the longest hours, at the lowest wages, and in the cheapest, and often most dangerous, settings. The working conditions could be extreme, and even illegal, but, by design, they were of little concern to the retailers who enjoyed both low costs and the flexibility to move their contracts to other factories, even across borders.

Further fueling the industry's race to the bottom, apparel manufacturing was often a quick and cheap "startup" business. While large-scale operations, such as those in Saipan, might involve massive factories and sophisticated methods for recruiting—and abusing—workers, more basic, entry-level manufacturing required almost no capital investment: little more than a sewing machine, and even that cost could be—and often was—deducted directly from workers' paychecks. Apparel manufacturing also required minimal infrastructure. A fly-by-night sweatshop factory could easily be set up in the back room of an existing business, or, if space was cost prohibitive, workers could just be compelled to sew and iron in their own homes. In effect, apparel manufacturers—whether the factories in Saipan in the 1990s, or New York's Triangle Shirtwaist Company (the infamous site of the deadly 1911 factory fire)—operated as vices for clothing retailers, squeezing workers through exploitation, coercion, or brute force. Perhaps it is not surprising then, that conditions in this industry compelled critics to adopt the term "sweatshop" to describe its horrors.[2]

In the mid-nineteenth century, Charles Kingsley, an English priest and history professor, first used the term "sweated" to describe London's apparel workers, who rather than being paid weekly or hourly wages, were subcontracted by each piece they produced. This arrangement, in which a "sweater" paid workers a low, set price per garment, effectively guaranteed long hours of exhaustingly fast-paced work—and forced workers to donate any downtime to their employer for free. Horrifying to the period's onlookers, this arrangement is, of course, now the standard for many laborers, ranging from farmworkers, to hairdressers, to Uber drivers. By the late 1800s, British Parliament had formally identified "sweating" by: "1) an unduly low rate of wages, 2) excessive hours of labour, [and] 3) the insanitary state of the houses in which the work is carried on."[3] Working conditions in US textile and garment factories, where workers produced fabric and sewed it into clothing, mirrored those in England, and in the late nineteenth and early twentieth centuries, "sweatshop" became a stand-in for the excesses of the American industry, as well.

The uncomfortable similarities between the sweatshops of the 1990s and those of a century prior sparked a wave of media attention and solidarity activism in the United States, including from groups such as Sweatshop Watch and Global Exchange, which sponsored the lawsuits in Saipan. The scrutiny also drew feigned surprise, and promises of reform, from business leaders. Two decades later, however, the global sweatshop economy is no longer industry's dirty little secret. Child labor, poverty wages, widespread workplace injuries, and death are routinely connected to a host of household names, from SHEIN and H&M to Apple and Amazon. Revisiting the long history of sweatshops reveals both more consistency through the twentieth century—the 1990s as another chapter, not a return to an old model—and a wider historical lens. For example, we can consider the living and working conditions of laborers in Lowell, Massachusetts, in the early 1800s and in Shenzhen, China, two centuries later—each working long hours for low pay, sleeping in company-owned dorms, and producing goods for American consumers.

The textile mill owners in Lowell deliberately recruited young women to be their workforce, and they were some of the first women in the United States to earn wages. By 1840, the mills employed some eight thousand people, were valued at more than ten million dollars, and drew praise from all over the world for their efficiency. The millhands, referred to as "Lowell Mill Girls," worked upward of seventy hours per week in noisy, poorly ventilated buildings. Even on hot days, factory windows remained closed to prevent any disruption to the threads. When their shifts ended, the millhands retired to spartan company boarding houses, generally sleeping six to a tiny room with just three beds. These "corporate households," as historical archeologists Mary Beaudry and Stephen Mrozowski call them, would become common in the United States over the next century, particularly in extraction industries such as lumber and mining. But while housing was undoubtedly a benefit, as Beaudry and Mrozowski argue, the Lowell boarding houses also revealed a "corporate ideology that sought to control workers' lives without taking ultimate responsibility for them."[4]

Despite long work hours and around-the-clock surveillance from employers, Lowell workers created and participated in an active intellectual culture through lectures, reading groups, and lending libraries. In the 1830s, they began publishing their own essays, gossip, and poetry in a company-funded magazine, the *Lowell Offering*. Though likely at least partially self-censored, writings in the *Offering* nonetheless touched on the bleak conditions in Lowell, for example by including a tribute to two workers who died by suicide. Lowell workers also began publishing a more critical, independent newspaper, *Voice of Industry*, which featured topics such as wealth inequality, sexism, slavery, the Mexican American War, woman suffrage, and, of course, working conditions. In 1846, one millhand wrote of her sorrows:

> I stand and gaze from my prison walls,
> On yonder flowing river;
> The thought will rise, Oh, why did it spring
> From the hand of its Almighty Giver? . . .
> Do they flow to add to the miser's gold?
> Or to cheer and bless our race?
>
> Gently its sparkling waters roll,
> With grandeur, pride and grace,
> To seek their mighty ocean bed—
> Their final resting place.
>
> Emblem of Purity and Truth!
> Made from thy aim to turn—
> To sap the lifeblood from young veins,
> And fill the funeral Urn.[5]

Though desperation and misery were front and center, *Voice of Industry* also featured writings about the importance of solidarity and organizing. The articles in these publications were subtle protests, and the women who wrote and read them also organized some of the earliest large-scale labor strikes in US industry. In 1836, more than 1,500 mill workers walked out in protest of a wage cut. In 1845, two thousand women millhands signed a petition to the Massachusetts state legislature asking for a ten-hour workday. Despite mill owners' attempts to control workers' time and their bodies, the *Lowell Offering* and *Voice of Industry* showed that they could not control their minds.[6]

In twenty-first-century Shenzhen, more than 120,000 workers live and labor in the Foxconn campus' high-rise factories and dormitories. After twelve-hour—or longer—shifts in the factory, workers' limited free time is spent sleeping in shared bunk beds, their privacy limited to the makeshift curtains that they hang in their rooms. Sociologists Jenny Chan and Pun Ngai write that the self-contained Foxconn campus "facilitates flexible production [by] imposing overtime work, as the distinction between 'home' and 'work' is blurred."[7] Like their counterparts in Lowell, the workers at Foxconn are squeezed and controlled to produce profits both for manufacturers and for retailers.

The Foxconn workers, who make iPhones, Kindles, and video game consoles, also resist the all-consuming demands of factory work through writing. Xu Lizhi, for example, published thirty pieces—poems, essays, and commentary—in *Foxconn People*, the factory magazine. One poem, "Workshop, My Youth Was Stranded Here," describes the unique stress of a factory assembly line with high quotas:

> Beside the assembly line, tens of thousands of workers line up like words on a page
> "Faster, hurry up!"
> Standing among them, I hear the supervisor bark.
> Once you've entered the workshop
> The only choice is submission
> Watch it being ground away day and night
> Pressed, polished, molded
> Into a few measly bills, so-called wages.[8]

Another of Xu's poems, written in January 2014, points directly to feelings of despair:

> A screw fell to the ground
> In this dark night of overtime
> Plunging vertically, lightly clinking
> It won't attract anyone's attention
> Just like last time
> On a night like this
> When someone plunged to the ground.

That September, after failed attempts to find other employment, Xu jumped off a factory building to his death, four years after a string of high-profile Foxconn suicides. He left behind a poem entitled "On My Deathbed."[9]

Scholar Laura Hapke argues that the sweatshop is "as American as apple pie," and indeed, though certainly not unique to the United States, the great wealth of the American economy has consistently been produced by hyperexploited labor—from formally enslaved and indentured workers onward.[10] Like "slavery," the term "sweatshop" itself elicits a powerful feeling of historical horror. It conjures images of workplace dangers and the exploitation of desperate workers, typically already marginalized because of their age, gender, race, and immigration status. Over-reverence for its historical usage, however, can stifle labor justice efforts in the present.

American history textbooks generally follow the lead of Progressive Era reformers, using the term to describe the cramped tenements, oppressive temperatures, child labor, and disease of the late nineteenth and early twentieth centuries. In this narrative, American sweatshops were a moment of historically and geographically isolated missteps on the road to the country's post-slavery industrial greatness. In some ways, adopting this framework helps maintain the term's strategic value, as it can be used to expose modern injustices, such as those in Saipan, as historically out of place. However, today's US media typically reserve "sweatshop" for headline-grabbing tragedies that afflict workers from the Global South, perhaps inadvertently serving the interests of abusive employers. This limited usage establishes a progressive historical narrative—often repeated by sweatshop apologists—in which the United States has overcome its sweatshop problem, while other nations are simply still evolving. From this perspective, sweatshops are simply growing pains, and their critics just need to be patient—and, most important, take no action.[11]

Officially, the US government defines a sweatshop as "an employer that violates more than one federal or state law governing minimum wage and overtime, child labor, industrial homework, occupational safety and health, workers compensation, or industry regulation."[12] Though this description does not account for the existence of sweatshops prior to, or outside of, US labor laws and regulations, it does establish a clear standard. And, by this definition, many of the country's factories, warehouses, farms, retail outlets, and offices—throughout the twentieth century and today—are inarguably sweatshops. Major US employers, including Walmart, Amazon, and McDonald's, have repeatedly been accused of violating labor laws, and workers themselves have openly used the term to describe their jobs. In 2021, for example, New Jersey Amazon warehouse worker Courtenay Brown testified to the US Senate that she worked in a "high-tech sweatshop."[13]

Some scholars agree, arguing that the sweatshop existed, and exists, across industries, place, and time. Historian Leon Stein writes, "The sweatshop is a state of mind as well as a physical fact . . . the sweatshop, whether in a modern factory building or a dark slum cellar, exists where the employer controls most of the working conditions and the worker cannot protest."[14] Book titles like *Sweatshops in the Sun*, *Sweatshops at Sea*, *Suburban Sweatshops*, *Electronic Sweatshop*, and *White-Collar Sweatshop*, if nothing else, reflect the vast practice of labor exploitation—applying the term to agricultural, domestic, and office workers; merchant seamen; and electronics manufacturers. Pointing to twenty-first-century abuses examined later in this book, labor historian Ruth Milkman similarly describes Amazon's delivery system as a "sweatshop on wheels."[15] Though I am most interested in the through-lines connecting the garment industry's sweatshops throughout the twentieth century, I also look at how the term has been used more broadly, particularly by workers and anti-sweatshop activists in their efforts to improve working conditions.[16]

This book examines the pervasiveness of workplaces—whatever they are called—that are defined by marginalization, misery, unfulfilled hope, danger, and a lack of opportunity. For more than a century, these spaces have been built, maintained, and defended by business interests, and they have created massive individual fortunes and vast corporate empires. However, this is also a book about the people who routinely challenged those conditions. Specifically, I examine solidarity movements for worker justice across the "Long 20th Century"—in this case, the late 1800s through the present. These movements overlapped with labor activism, but they also represented something broader, which brought workers together with a variety of activist allies.

Unsurprisingly, throughout this long period, the most desperate workers in US supply chains were often women—particularly women of color and women with precarious citizenship status. Garment workers at New York's Triangle Shirtwaist Company, for example, were disproportionately young Jewish women from Eastern and Southern Europe. In Saipan, factories relied on temporary workers from countries including Bangladesh and the Philippines. Foxconn, too, sought young women, many of them migrants from rural parts of China. As numerous feminist scholars have highlighted, sweatshops, because they deliberately target vulnerable workers, are frequently linked to gender-specific abuses, such as sexual harassment and assault; forced birth control, sterilizations, and abortions; and decreased maternal health. In short, the sweatshop is a tool of exploitation, and it is often an expression of misogyny, xenophobia, and white supremacy—as well as greed.

Workers' allies in their struggles for justice were also usually women, generally with more means and privilege, like the attorneys of Sweatshop Watch. At the heart of these cross-class alliances has been an evolving feminist solidarity, which has, with varying degrees of success, challenged the immense power of capital in hopes of improving the lives of workers.

Women's solidarity in the long fight against sweatshops is the subject of some of the most important studies in women's and labor history. I join some of my academic role models—Annelise Orleck, Alice Kessler-Harris,

Landon Storrs, Kathryn Kish Sklar, and Eileen Boris, among others—in trying to understand this struggle and its significance to our collective past. Though I spent many hours in archives, this book does not offer many big, new discoveries about, say, members of the League of Women Shoppers in the 1930s or the Women's Trade Union League two decades earlier. Rather, it allows readers to see those activists through a twenty-first-century lens—to compare the infamous New York garment factories to today's Amazon warehouses, and to consider how both working conditions and resistance have evolved. Unapologetically, it looks to history for answers—or at least hope—as we confront a host of problems in the present.[17]

Anti-sweatshop activists, at many turns over the last century, used the limited means available to them—including strategically using the term "sweatshop"—to apply pressure to industry, consumers, and lawmakers. I examine how each side—advocates for workers and for industry—sought to outmaneuver their opponents' efforts to create landscapes that either brought reform to sweatshops or ensured that they could thrive. This fight, between powerful elites on one side, and seemingly powerless workers and their activist allies on the other, helps frame a narrative of the twentieth century that positions the middle decades as what some US historians are now calling "the Great Exception"—the brief, albeit problematic, moment of recognized workers' rights and middle-class opportunities.[18]

However, by focusing primarily on the struggles of workers who remained on the margins during that moment of possibility—which became the heyday of the American middle class—this book ultimately focuses on the rule, not the exception. It recasts the history of modern labor through the lens of the sweatshop, revealing not just why working conditions were so similar in New York and Saipan a century apart, but also where we might go from here.

The sweatshop may be "as American as apple pie," and the persistent reliance on an underclass of hyperexploited workers would seem to suggest that human nature—perhaps the greed of American consumers, in particular—drives purchasing habits that prioritize good deals, no matter the human cost. At least one study suggests the opposite, though. Conducted in 1995, 1998, and 1999, Marymount University's National Consumer Sweatshop Surveys consistently reflected Americans' desires to purchase ethically produced goods. They revealed that two-thirds of consumers—across all income levels—would avoid shopping at a retailer that they knew sold garments made in sweatshops, and 86 percent would pay more money for their clothing if they knew that the workers who made them enjoyed good living and working conditions. More than half of those surveyed also said that a "fair-labor label" would provide the greatest aid in helping them make their purchasing decisions. Perhaps little can be drawn from one study, and certainly consumer impulses ebb and flow over time. However, the study's conclusions may help explain why US business interests have been so focused on crushing anti-sweatshop activism over the last century and why, especially in recent decades, they have worked so hard to keep sweatshops out of the public eye—often behind barbed-wire fences.[19]

One of the themes of this book is consistency, whether the use of centuries-old models of labor exploitation, or workers' use of poetry to carve out spaces of mental resistance. There have also been several significant moments when workers and activists engaged in collective action that challenged the idea that profit was more important than people. Tapping into wider discontent around economic and racial injustice, as well as concerns about the environment, these movements forced consumers to acknowledge and confront their relationships to sweatshop working conditions. They recruited broad segments of society to become allies in workers' fights for shorter shifts, higher wages, union recognition, and other demands. Sometimes, this meant joining picket lines. Other times, it meant contributing to strike funds. Still other times, it meant using their purchasing power in solidarity with workers in an attempt to "civilize capitalism."[20]

In yet another nod to historical constants, workers and activists a century apart also strategically targeted specific, high-impact days to maximize the influence of their boycotts, pickets, and other protests. Early twentieth-century campaigns, for example, directly appealed to an audience of middle-class and elite women by pointing out inconsistent experiences around Christmas. While holiday songs called on all to rejoice, the workers were unable to join in the celebration of the season due to the early mornings and late nights required by their employers. Activists in the twenty-first century, meanwhile, have asked consumers to refrain from purchases on specific days—Black Friday, Cyber Monday, Amazon Prime Day—to support workers' strikes, walkouts, and other actions and demonstrate public support for better wages and conditions. The point is not that nothing has changed over the last century, but rather that the past is not so distant.

The activist groups that I highlight in these four chapters used their members' privileges—including education, media savvy, personal and political connections, purchasing power, class, and race—to support workers during labor disputes, establish labor laws and independent monitoring of workplaces, and influence consumers to make ethical purchasing decisions. Navigating the disparities between workers and their allies was often challenging and messy, but, at their best, these organizations did not command or lead sweatshop laborers, but rather provided additional points of pressure on industrial and retail employers through elaborate boycotts, publicity, and strike support. As such, they are important models of feminist solidarity—of women organizing in support of themselves, their communities, and one another. They also show that people can work together against much more powerful political forces and, occasionally, win victories that make concrete improvements in the lives of working people. For example, in 2004, the workers in Saipan—whose lawsuit I mentioned at the beginning of this introduction—reached a twenty-million-dollar settlement with almost fifty US retailers and Saipan factories, upending conditions for workers and manufacturers—and setting the stage for the next conflict.

By the early 1900s, where chapter 1 begins, American industrial capitalists had experienced decades of expanding economic and political control. Though routinely confronted by workers, their power and influence were immense. In chapter 1, "'The Struggle Has But Begun': The Labor Feminism of the Progressive Era," I look at the Progressive Era alliances of workers and activists in the National Consumers' League and the Women's Trade Union League, who together challenged the myths of capitalist meritocracy and pushed for change. Both groups offered support to sweatshop workers during massive garment workers' strikes and in the aftermath of the tragic Triangle Fire. With memberships that included both sweated workers and middle-class and elite reformers, I argue that these organizations were important examples of economic activism and feminist solidarity—models that were adopted and improved upon throughout the twentieth century. Deriving strength both from their relative privilege and their practical understanding of workplace realities, they organized strike-relief funds, picket-line support, and soup lines to feed striking workers. They also agitated for worker-friendly labor policies and workplace protections, using the imagery of the "sweatshop" as a catalyst for a new consensus on improved safety regulations. In response to this movement's successes, however, capital relocated garment factories en masse and orchestrated a return to the unquestioned laissez-faire policies of the Gilded Age.

During the Great Depression, the Popular Front, a new coalition of left-leaning students, union organizers, civil rights activists, artists, writers, clergy, workers, and consumers emerged to fight for better working conditions and to challenge white supremacy. In chapter 2, "'Don't Overlook Any Channel for Publicity': The Solidarity of the Popular Front," I highlight the League of Women Shoppers, a key organization in that coalition that engaged in a range of creative protest in support of striking workers. With a membership of twenty-five thousand and chapters throughout the country—including in the US South—the group's slogan, "Use your buying power for justice," broadcast its intent to use members' shopping dollars to influence the outcome of various work stoppages and protests. The group was flashy—its members included famous Hollywood playwrights and actors, as well as First Lady Eleanor Roosevelt—and bold. It organized boycotts, pickets, and fashion shows, and it expanded the use of the term of "sweatshop" to industries beyond garment work. By the late 1930s, though, the group and the broader movement began to unravel under extreme political pressure, as the American Right reframed civil rights and labor agitation as threats to national security.

Chapter 3, "'Settle the Case, or We'll Be in Your Face': The Worldview of the Global Justice Movement," examines the return to prominence both of anti-sweatshop activism and of the American public's awareness of sweatshop labor. As a series of scandals exposed the working conditions of the global, "free trade"–era economy of the 1990s, anti-sweatshop groups, including Global Exchange and Sweatshop Watch, worked to turn public awareness into concrete change through lawsuits, pressure campaigns, and other protests. Activists faced many of the same challenges as their counterparts in earlier eras, but they also had to adapt to an industry that was increasingly mobile and global, and that often relied on contracted factories in foreign countries—far away from US consumers.

Chapter 4, "'Amazon Crime': The Omnipresence of the New Global Assembly Line," addresses the current moment, the 2010s and 2020s, in which a massive global supply-chain, climate change, the internet, and now the Covid-19 pandemic have upended the lives of workers and consumers alike and complicated the lines between them. Increasing numbers of workers have joined what some call the "precariat"—a class of laborers with few rights and even less job security due to subcontracting, temporary contracts, and the absence of benefits. They notably include day labors, seasonal hires, adjuncts, and, more recently, workers in the app-based "gig economy." I argue that the growing masses of precarious gig workers are essentially an expression of an old identity—the sweatshop worker, who, like an Uber driver, has often been paid per piece and treated as contractor rather than an employee. In this chapter, I explore the working conditions of companies like Amazon, Apple, and Foxconn, as well as worker and community resistance to these behemoths.

In each chapter of this book, women play significant roles, both as workers and as activists. Though expressed more explicitly at some times than others, this is a book about feminist solidarity—about movements that confronted not just the unchecked power of capital, but the power of patriarchy specifically. In one example in the pages that follow, a judge tells a group of women that instead of picketing, they "should be home knitting."[21] In another, nearly a century later, a woman objecting to sexual harassment from coworkers is told by factory supervisors that she needs to learn how to take a joke.

Women's solidarity was central to the cross-class alliances in these groups, between the most vulnerable workers and members of the self-described "comfortable class."[22] While not the only impulse driving these movements, their implicit and explicit feminism routinely drove them to push beyond the boundaries of traditional labor organizing and gender norms. For example, in addition to organizing around wages and hours, anti-sweatshop activists at times also targeted unfair hiring practices, deportations, and sexual violence. Likewise, while boycotts and other selective purchasing activities fit neatly within mainstream American gender norms for married women at the turn of the last century, activists in these movements, including college students and professionals, also challenged those limitations by confronting police and orchestrating media coverage.

The rise and fall of American anti-sweatshop movements through these periods and these chapters is the devastating history of the many horrors of the sweatshop economy, as well as the inspiring history of those who have dared to confront it. It is a history that connects us, in the present, to people in the distant past and to people all over the world.

1

"THE STRUGGLE HAS BUT BEGUN"
THE LABOR FEMINISM OF THE PROGRESSIVE ERA

In the fall of 1909, members of the Consumers' League of New York handed out as many as fifty thousand flyers and postcards to holiday shoppers, encouraging them to buy their presents early, rather than waiting until Christmas Eve or Christmas Day. The effort was part of a nationwide campaign launched several years earlier by the National Consumers' League (NCL), an activist organization dedicated to improving the lives of workers by changing the purchasing habits of women shoppers.[1]

Like seasonal "temp workers" a century later, department stores in the early twentieth century hired additional employees to help with the holiday rush—often expecting them to work upward of ninety hours per week during the shopping bottleneck of mid-to-late December. The literature produced by the NCL publicized the many hardships that the clerks, mail carriers, and delivery drivers, as well as the stores' ten- to fourteen-year-old "shop girls" and "errand boys," endured during the holiday season. Mirroring department stores' own ad campaigns, NCL chapters in Buffalo, New York, and Columbus, Ohio, produced cards adorned with holly and Santa Claus, alongside slogans like "An eleventh-hour shopper changes a merry Christmas to a weary Christmas" and "Your best Christmas gift will be shopping done before December 15."[2] In 1912, the NCL even distributed its own version of the holiday classic, "The Night Before Christmas," linking cruel conditions for workers with the consumption habits of the elite. The group's "The Week Before Christmas" began:

> 'Twas the week before Christmas, and all through the town
> The shopgirls and packers were fast breaking down,
> While women of leisure lay soft in their beds,
> And visions of purchases danced in their heads.[3]

From the pages of *Good Housekeeping* to the Vassar College student newspaper, consumer activists exposed the brutality of the laissez-faire economy and promoted responsible shopping habits as an antidote. Hoping to establish a new approach to American consumerism, they prioritized workers' rights over shoppers' convenience. Members of the NCL also worked closely with local merchants and store owners to offer incentives for early shopping. For example, several New York stores rewarded November purchases by holding the charges until January. As the NCL swarmed shoppers with its flyers and postcards, New York garment workers, who sewed the clothes that would end up on department store shelves, were also busy—picketing their employers.

During the Progressive Era of the early twentieth century, the NCL was part of a broad movement to fight sweatshop working conditions. While workers confronted their bosses throughout the supply chain, the NCL applied outside pressure, by making ethical shopping a mainstream concern even among supposedly "nonpolitical" women. The women who joined the NCL and another organization called the Women's Trade Union League (WTUL) were committed to cross-class solidarity, a more overt defiance of prevailing norms than was offered by many other Progressive Era groups. Workers of the period were not only up against employers, but also the notions that individualism and capitalism were morally good and natural. The US Supreme Court, state and federal laws, and mainstream public opinion supported "Liberty of Contract," the idea that government regulations and union contracts violated an individual worker's freedoms and rights. Without strength in numbers or established rules, workers were largely at the mercy of their employers, who had free reign to pay low wages and demand long hours, to allow dangerous and unsanitary conditions, to hire private guards to put down strikes, and to use the power of all three branches of the US government as they saw fit.

Many of the other women's groups of the period focused their efforts on philanthropy, education, and racial uplift. The NCL and WTUL mobilized support for working women in their efforts to gain union rights and to increase government regulations on industry. While employers used "Liberty of Contract" principles to isolate workers as individuals, the NCL and WTUL brought to working women's collective fight the additional weight—and relative power—of middle-class and wealthy American women. By the 1920s, both organizations had joined picket lines, played direct roles in changing labor laws, and made political connections that reached all the way to the White House.[4]

———

In the decades following the US Civil War, the country underwent an immense economic transformation. By 1880, most of the country's laborers were employed in nonfarming work—in manufacturing, construction, and transportation. From the mines to the factories, and on ships and trains everywhere in between, the work was incredibly dangerous. At the turn of the twentieth century, roughly thirty-five thousand American workers were killed in industrial accidents each year, while more than a million suffered from burns, mangled and amputated limbs, "scalping" from hair being caught in machines, and other horrible injuries. While mass-casualty disasters, such as collapsing mines and exploding factories, were not uncommon, most accidents were just routine occurrences for the growing industrial working class. They were part of the daily reality for all but the wealthiest Americans. When employers set working conditions according to their preferred "Liberty of Contract" standards, the results were a nightmare for workers.[5]

As bleak as Gilded Age life was for nominally "free" American workers, schemes such as debt peonage and sharecropping trapped many others—especially African Americans and immigrants—in even deeper cycles of exploitation. In the supposedly post-slavery US South, the "new" economy relied on the continued exploitation of Black workers, using legal loopholes, such as convict leasing, to ensure a cheap—and expendable—workforce. The death rate for Black men in Alabama's convict leasing system in 1873, for example, was around 25 percent. These men were held in chains, under armed guard, and worked to death to increase the wealth of Southern barons of agriculture, extraction, and industry. Similarly grim death rates accompanied the building of the nation's railroad system, which connected growing industrial centers and linked them to remote coal mines and oil fields. Perhaps most infamously, an estimated 20 percent of the Chinese immigrant workers who helped build the country's 1,911-mile transcontinental railroad were killed in the process—in addition to being scapegoated, assaulted, and race-baited by xenophobic white Americans.[6]

Across all forms of wage labor, hours were brutally long, and employers' policies often stretched them even further. For example, Agnes Nestor, a glovemaker in Chicago, worked sixty-hour weeks, but factory owners paid per garment, rather than hourly. To make ends meet, Nestor and her coworkers routinely took home additional sewing at the end of the workday, blurring the lines between their work and home lives. In many industries, workers were also required to live in, and pay for, company-owned housing, bolstering their bosses' profits even when off the clock. According to Nestor, her employers further "whittled away at [the workers'] weekly pay," deducting money for replacing sewing needles and for rent on their sewing machines. Additionally, workers were subjected to strict rules that prohibited them from talking with one another on the shop floor and during breaks. The often-petty harshness of the US industrial economy also produced severe inequality. As historian Steve Fraser notes, while most American wage earners worked sixty-hour weeks to earn less than eight hundred dollars a year, "about 4,000 families owned as much wealth as the remaining 11.6 million."[7]

In the final decades of the nineteenth century, the American garment industry expanded rapidly and came to epitomize the sweatshop. The setting varied, but whether the work was done in a crowded factory or in cramped tenement housing, it was grim and characterized by long hours, low pay, and little hope. Child labor was common, as were injuries. As a symbol, the sweatshop appeared to be at odds with the possibilities and promise associated with the United States. As such, reformers became increasingly uncomfortable with working conditions, especially for women and children. The term "sweatshop" served as a shorthand, so that when an employer was accused of sweating his workers, it was immediately clear that their workplace was brutal and exploitive—most likely, a garment factory employing women and children.

With little government regulation, the American economy of the period was also incredibly unstable, marked by frequent recessions and crashes that led employers to order wage cuts and lay-offs for workers who had no effective social safety net. In 1877, the first national labor walkout started in response to such a crisis, quickly spreading to cities throughout the Northeast and the Midwest. After state militia in Pittsburgh killed twenty strike supporters and wounded twenty-nine others (including women and children), federal troops were used in other cities to crush the railroad workers' strike—setting an important precedent of using the US military to aid employers. In the decades that followed, police, state, and federal soldiers, hired thugs, and private militia routinely attacked and killed striking workers and labor organizers, making the names of towns like Homestead, Pullman, and Ludlow synonymous with capitalist violence. For workers, the violence of the period was ubiquitous, both in the shop and against their efforts to improve their working conditions.[8]

Officially, most American women at the turn of the century had little power. Few universities and professional schools would admit them. Good job opportunities were scarce and underpaid. Bad job opportunities were dangerous and paid even less, and only a few states allowed women the right to vote. However, women had campaigned for suffrage, abolition, temperance, and better working conditions throughout much of the nineteenth century, often relying on their own creativity to work around the legal and social restraints on their activities. The emerging movements of the Progressive Era drew on, and merged, several of those threads—often with women at the helm.

One such movement was for consumer reform. The turn of the twentieth century saw the emergence of a consumer economy, what the chair of the Wharton School of Business called "a new order of consumption."[9] A shift from bespoke (custom-made) manufacturing to the mass production of ready-to-wear clothing (meant to be purchased directly off the rack) led to the rise of department stores. Despite the formal and informal racial and class segregation common in the early twentieth century, department stores routinely brought women of different classes into close contact with one another, as middle-class and elite shoppers made their purchases from working-class "salesgirls." The gendered nature of shopping, meanwhile, created an opportunity for women to develop a reform movement that addressed some of the ill effects of mass consumption, while at least appearing to stay out of formal politics. With a foot in the door, however, the twentieth-century woman suffrage movement adapted the language of consumption and modern advertising campaigns, drawing comparisons between ethical consuming and responsible voting.[10]

By the early 1900s, American women were actively organizing to influence business practices and public policies regarding child labor, education, temperance, suffrage, sweatshops, birth control, and more. American women's experiences and goals, however, varied widely. Most women's lives revolved around work. Historian Dorothy Sue Cobble writes that the "labor feminism" that emerged from the era was rooted in working-class women's understanding that their gender shaped their experiences and opportunities, from their workplaces outward. They saw the labor movement "as the primary vehicle through which to end the multiple inequities" they faced.[11] For these women, feminism was expressed less as a long-term goal of absolute legal equality than as immediate action, specifically in the form of grassroots solidarity and collective power in the workplace.[12]

Within the period's diverse and growing movement for women's right to vote, there were organizations with clearly elitist and even white supremacist focuses, as well as those devoted to alliances across racial and economic lines. In 1907, Harriet Stanton Blatch, daughter of famed suffragist Elizabeth Cady Stanton, formed the Equality League of Self-Supporting Women, with the specific aim of attracting working-class women to the suffrage movement. At one meeting, member and celebrated labor leader Rose Schneiderman offered scathing remarks on wealthy anti-suffragists, noting, in a time of elite philanthropy, that wealthy women, in fact, lived on the charity of the working class. The Equality League also championed unions and equal pay for women teachers, who made up to 40 percent less than their male counterparts. This understanding of women's common cause across class lines was also an awareness that limitations on women's freedoms applied to their work and home lives, as well as to the ballot.[13]

In the late 1880s, a group of working-class women, notably including garment worker and labor organizer (and subsequent Equality League member) Leonora O'Reilly, met with prominent middle-class progressive activists, including Josephine Shaw Lowell, in what became the New York Working Women's Society. Dedicated to documenting labor conditions and advocating for reform, the group's work evolved into the New York Consumers' League. In the 1890s, under the guidance of Lowell, famed social worker and Hull House founder Jane Addams, and anti-sweatshop activist Florence Kelley, consumer groups in New York united with others in Illinois, Massachusetts, and Pennsylvania to form the National Consumers' League. The network quickly spread throughout the United States and to several cities in Western Europe. By 1909, the group boasted more than sixty chapters in nineteen US states and was present on the campuses of eighteen of the country's colleges, universities, and boarding schools. Harnessing the collective power of consumers, the group became a leading voice against child labor and sweatshop working conditions.[14]

The NCL chose "Investigate, Agitate, and Legislate" as its motto, reflecting the broader goal of Progressive Era movements to improve conditions for the poor by exposing corruption and creating laws to protect the nation's citizenry—but not to make radical change. Individual NCL chapters chose campaigns centered around the "local conditions which seem to most demand their attention."¹⁵ For example, when the Milwaukee chapter formed in 1900, it focused on the issue of Saturday half holidays. After five hundred women pledged to refrain from shopping on Saturday afternoons, chapter members visited sixty-two area stores to speak to managers, who all promised compliance. Thousands of Milwaukee clerks were thus able to enjoy Saturday holidays during the summer months. These extra hours off represented a tangible improvement in the lives of working people, and other branches of the NCL tried to emulate the campaign. Ultimately, the NCL envisioned much broader reform; for example, its constitution called for all workers to receive a "fair living wage."¹⁶

One of the group's areas of expertise was producing literature. This included not only Christmas shopping flyers, but also placing articles in newspapers and magazines, as well as making its own muckraking informational pamphlets. One, entitled "WRECKS," features the photographs and stories of child workers who had been maimed or killed on the job. For example, it notes, a six-year-old boy working for a newspaper publisher had to have his right hand amputated at the wrist after it was caught in a machine. Another child, a fifteen-year-old boy named "Joe," who worked at a hardware factory, had to have both arms amputated at his shoulders. Yet another, a seventeen-year-old girl working in a textile mill, caught her hand in a machine and was permanently disfigured and disabled. These were just a few of the many lives "wrecked" by dangerous workplaces. According to the pamphlet, over the course of one year, in just three US states, industrial accidents had killed thirty-nine children and permanently disabled another 919. Before listing NCL officials—including Jane Addams and honorary vice presidents representing numerous universities—the pamphlet concludes, "Prevention of such needless horrors is one of the main purposes of the National Consumers' League."¹⁷

While NCL literature often exposed horrors, the group's messaging strategy attempted to appeal to potential allies in a variety of ways. For example, longtime NCL leader Florence Kelley played to readers' emotions with a 1911 account of the young workers who filled hospitals after the busy Christmas season, due to exhaustion, rheumatism, and pneumonia. In step with other Progressive Era organizations and middle-class concerns, the NCL also appealed to consumers' sympathies and their self-interest, through their fear of infectious diseases. The group's cautionary tales warned readers against spreading scarlet fever and tuberculosis to their families and neighbors via garments made in unsanitary factories and tenement homes. Without guaranteed sick days, the group argued, workers could bring contagious diseases to work and transfer them to the clothing they touched, potentially passing diphtheria or other diseases onto the unsuspecting consumer. The NCL appealed first and foremost to women—as the caring mothers of children, as protectors of the health of their households, and as consumers. The group returned to this strategy, and these arguments, again and again.[18]

The NCL also offered practical solutions, in this case by encouraging middle-class consumers to purchase only goods that contained their "white label," which certified that those goods were made under "clean and ethical conditions."[19] Offering guidance to chapters starting white label campaigns, the NCL advised that a committee should be comprised of "two influential, persuasive women who have patience and leisure" and observe potential merchants for one year before adding them to the list.[20] After twenty years of work, the New York chapter boasted a "white list" of fifty-eight approved merchants. The group believed that if consumers valued their "white label," manufacturers could be motivated to seek it.[21]

Because women rarely held economic or political power, the NCL understood that it needed to gain access through peripheral power. The group strategically built links to powerful political elites, giving the organization publicity, prestige, and access. For example, the Washington, DC, branch publicized the appointment of five honorary vice presidents in 1912, including not only their names, but also a "claim to fame" for each—the head of the American Red Cross, the wives of Supreme Court Justices and members of Congress, and prominent society ladies. Though official Washington offered little to the American working classes, the NCL's reach extended all the way to the White House. Helen Taft, daughter of the sitting President William Howard Taft, volunteered as a guide and lecturer at the group's 1912 exhibit on sweatshops.[22]

Many members of the NCL, and most of its leadership, were among the first generation of college-educated American women and served as pioneers of social work and reform. Florence Kelley, who was hired to lead the NCL in 1899 and was its guiding force for thirty years, was born into a family of activists concerned with civil rights, women's rights, and economic justice. After graduating from Cornell University, she moved to Germany to continue her education, joining a student socialist organization and marrying a Russian socialist medical student. She also befriended Friedrich Engels and translated his *The Condition of the Working Class in England in 1844*.

Fleeing her husband's abuse, Kelley then returned with her three children to the United States, where she worked as a Chicago factory inspector and lived at the Hull House and Henry Street Settlement Houses for most of her adult life. Kelley—who was also a suffragist and civil rights activist—believed that literally everyone had the power to push for improved conditions for the working class. That power lay in the emerging role consumers would need to embrace in a burgeoning consumer-based, industrial economy. Through a mass movement of daily, individual actions, consumers could collectively pressure the highest levels of government and business. Kelley articulated what became an early motto for the NCL, "To live means to buy, to buy means to have power, to have power means to have responsibility."[23] Under her leadership, the NCL used that power and responsibility to challenge child labor and sweatshops through white lists of approved employers, exhibitions exposing sweatshop goods, and other creative forms of consumer activism.[24]

Paralleling the NCL's efforts, and with some overlap in membership, the Women's Trade Union League (WTUL) formed in 1903, and united wealthy, middle-class, and working-class women in efforts to increase women's participation in trade unions. It was modeled on a British iteration of the organization established in the 1870s. Like the term "sweatshop" itself, which had resonated in both US and European contexts, many anti-sweatshop efforts were also transnational. The WTUL in the United States was launched at an American Federation of Labor (AFL) convention, though the group received little support from the AFL, which prioritized formally trained, male workers at the time. Among the WTUL's first members were Leonora O'Reilly and Jane Addams, who had also supported the formation of the NCL.[25]

The WTUL opened its membership to anyone supportive of women organizing and joining unions. Reflecting the organization's desire to put leadership in the hands of working-class women, the executive board was deliberately designed to include a majority of women trade unionists and a minority of middle- and upper-class allies, or "earnest sympathizers and workers for the cause of trade unionism."[26] This policy is noteworthy, as it challenged common, paternalistic assumptions about working-class inferiority. Leadership of local chapters came from both wealthy reformers, such as Margaret Dreier Robins, who became president of the Chicago local and the national WTUL in 1907, and working-class union members, such as O'Reilly; capmaker Rose Schneiderman, who left the sweatshop for a salaried position with the New York WTUL; and Agnes Nestor, the

Chicago glovemaker, who served as president of the Chicago WTUL from 1913 to 1948.

The WTUL started with three branches in New York, Boston, and Chicago that grew out of close relationships with settlement houses, which were community spaces that offered support to immigrant and working-class women—and served as important hubs of reform activism. The WTUL expanded, primarily in the Northeast and Midwest, but the original three branches remained the strongest due to decades of labor organizing that had provided a strong infrastructure. The organization's dual commitment to feminist values and trade unionism set the WTUL apart from many other Progressive Era–reform organizations. While eliciting support from male-dominated unions, the group reached across class lines to organize women workers, lobby for labor legislation, support woman suffrage, and provide educational programs.[27]

The WTUL's actions reflected the creativity and flair of its members. Many employers during the period, notably including Henry Ford, provided their largely immigrant workforces with English language lessons, which also sought to indoctrinate male workers with preferred values, such as thrift, hard work, cleanliness, sobriety, Christianity, and identity as a provider for a family. The Chicago branch of the WTUL flipped this approach on its head to spread the "gospel of unionism." The group created its own English-language curriculum with nouns and verbs about working hours and conditions. One lesson, for example, focused on poor conditions for non-union members, with students repeating, "I am not a union girl. I begin work at 7 o'clock in the morning and I work until 6 o'clock in the evening. I get $1 a week."[28]

At a national organization meeting, members from California's WTUL shared some of their efforts to attract publicity. The group had been supporting striking laundry workers and waitresses, but court injunctions against picketing demanded innovation. In one case, banned from demonstrating themselves, unionists had instead placed a donkey bearing the sign "Unfair House" in front of a restaurant. The angry business owner took the animal to court, but the judge admitted that he "could not issue an injunction against a donkey."[29] Just as the WTUL and NCL activists found routes to political activity that defied social mores—and male union orthodoxy—they also found ways around a legal system that favored employers.

They were nonetheless limited by the political and social contexts of the early twentieth-century United States. The women of the NCL pursued non-electoral political strategies by necessity, but their efforts embodied an assumption that social problems, such as sweatshops, could be solved through science and applied government—and, in this case, by harnessing the emerging mass consumer economy. As historian Lawrence Glickman argues, "Progressives saw consumers as the representative citizens of the modern age."[30] Essentially, they believed that the evolution of mass production was an amazing feat, but one that required responsible citizens to tame its excesses.

The cross-class alliances of the WTUL, too, exposed both the opportunities for, and limitations of, women's solidarity during the period. As Eileen Boris and Annelise Orleck note, middle-class and wealthy "allies" offered working-class women much-needed financial and political assistance, in part to work toward the common goal of winning voting rights, but they also used their clout to try to steer workers' movements toward what they deemed more palatable and modest reforms. While sympathetic to the plight of children and women workers, wealthy women also had practical loyalties to an economic system that benefited them.[31]

Operating at the intersection of feminism and the labor movement, the WTUL enjoyed great collaboration, as well as significant tension, as members' priorities came in and out of alignment. Despite aspiring to promote working-class leadership through its official structure, the WTUL was constrained by the prevailing power dynamics and social norms of its time. New York, for example, was segregated along class and racial lines, and WTUL activists of all backgrounds had lifetimes' worth of assumed hierarchies that had been ingrained and reinforced by parents, communities, churches, and social circles. Money was also undeniably powerful, and individual wealthy women inevitably held outsized influence in the group. Attempts to curtail their dominance, while important, often mirrored Progressive attempts to reign in capital.

Though the results were mixed, NCL and WTUL efforts to bridge class and ethnic divides were noteworthy—cutting edge for the period. Their inabilities to organize across racial lines, however, were equally glaring. Some white Progressives, including Florence Kelley and Jane Addams, were founding members of the National Association for the Advancement of Colored People (NAACP), but even those sympathetic to racial injustice often reached paternalistic conclusions. As historian Elizabeth Lasch-Quinn writes, some leaders in the Progressive Era–settlement house movement believed that chattel slavery "had obliterated morality, family integrity, social organization, and even culture and civilization itself" among African Americans.[32] Addams, for example, differentiated between European immigrants and African Americans, believing that a long history of slavery and urban segregation had undermined family stability in the latter—creating greater barriers to social integration than existed for immigrants. While white reformers were active in the anti-lynching movement in the early twentieth century, it would be decades before the cross-class solidarity of the Progressive Era would extend to Black women workers in a meaningful way.[33]

These limitations and tensions notwithstanding, the NCL and WTUL built alliances of American women dedicated to fighting child labor and sweatshops at a moment in which few women had voting rights and even fewer had the kind of wealth that would allow them to influence elections or policy debates. In addition to numerous publications and dozens of local and seasonal campaigns, the two groups were key players in some of the period's most pivotal events, including garment workers' strikes in New York in 1909 and in Chicago the next year, as well as the aftermath of the tragic Triangle Shirtwaist Factory Fire in 1911. Both the Triangle Fire and strike in New York, known as the "Uprising of 20,000" have rightly received significant attention from historians, journalists, filmmakers, and even children's book authors. They provide respective examples of tragedy and defiance during the Progressive Era, and illustrate the possibilities and limits of solidarity, alliances, and semi-coordinated collective action. The conditions at the Triangle Shirtwaist Factory—which was considered "modern" for its time—meanwhile, speak to a broader point, beyond that place and period, about the dangers of workplaces in which profits are valued over the well-being of workers. Similar conditions and similar tragedies—which will appear throughout this book—followed capitalism throughout the decades. During the Progressive Era, in a moment with few regulations and almost no enforcement, the NCL and WTUL worked to increase both.

Despite growing participation in the industrial economy, few women workers belonged to unions or workers' associations at the turn of the twentieth century. Though women were not officially barred from membership in most unions, labor leaders of the period typically subscribed to the idea that women in factories and mills were temporary workers who would leave to be homemakers once married. As such, unions devoted their resources to organizing men, whom they considered breadwinners, and reserved leadership roles for them, even within women's organizations. Historian Ann Schofield notes, for example, that while 80 percent of the rank-and-file members of New York Shirtwaist Makers Union in 1909 were women, men held all the union offices and more than half of the seats on the executive board.[34]

The lack of support from union leaders, however, did not deter working women from collective action. In 1909, workers went on strike at several New York factories that manufactured shirtwaists, which were ready-to-wear button-down blouses that women wore with skirts. Twenty-three-year-old shirtwaist maker Clara Lemlich—whose family had immigrated from Ukraine six years earlier—famously gave an impassioned speech at a mass meeting encouraging an industrywide general strike, and within a few days, almost two-thirds of the workers in the city's shirtwaist industry had joined the "Uprising of 20,000." Lemlich, already a seasoned organizer after the rent strikes and food protests that rocked New York's Lower East Side, later recalled that while many workers at the meeting were angry and irritated by the labor and socialist leaders who spoke in vague terms about solidarity, she was the only one unafraid to speak up and demand action. The striking workers—mostly young Russian and Italian immigrants—had little experience with organized labor, though some, like Lemlich, had been active in rent strikes and meat boycotts. Top leadership in the AFL, meanwhile, was initially unsupportive, preaching moderation and patience, while trying to quash the strike. If labor leaders, and conservative reformers, were skeptical of the workers' power, shirtwaist company bosses took them much more seriously—expressing fears that the uprising might involve as many as forty thousand workers. They hired private security to violently break up picket lines, and police arrested more than seven hundred striking workers, mostly on trumped up vagrancy charges. Lemlich herself was arrested seventeen times, and police and other hired muscle broke six of her ribs. A judge, during sentencing, told one striker, "You are on strike against God and nature, whose prime law is that man shall earn his bread in the sweat of his brow."[35]

Whether or not the shirtwaist companies had "God and nature" on their side, they certainly had the advantage of money and resources—and the backing of the police and the courts. The bosses also took umbrage with even the suggestion that the striking workers' cause was just. In December 1909, Eugene Solomon, of the Associated Waist and Dress Manufacturers, sent a letter to Rabbi Stephen W. Wise, decrying the support Wise had offered strikers in a recent sermon. Solomon argued that garment factories featured "the best sanitary conditions," and that workers were both well-paid and only expected to work "a reasonable number of hours . . . from fifty-two to fifty-four hours per week."³⁶ Further, according to Solomon, the only item that manufacturers were unwilling to negotiate was the workers' demand for union shops, which he wrote, "if conceded, would destroy the liberty both of the employer and employe [sic] and subject them to the orders and control of irresponsible organizers and leaders."³⁷ This was unacceptable, Solomon continued, as "no business could be successfully or permanently conducted under such conditions."³⁸

Solomon's objection to unionization was not an isolated opinion. Five years earlier, the National Association of Clothiers, itself a collective organization, had formally committed to resisting workers' demands for outside unions and instead maintaining "open" shops. According to the organization's constitution, "The closed shop is an un-American institution; the right of every man to sell his labor as he sees fit and the freedom of every employer to hire such labor are given by the laws of the land."³⁹

The—apparently "American"—liberty promised by Liberty of Contract was each worker's right not to be represented by a union, despite the worker's own demand for union rights. In short, the nonunion, open shop was a freedom for workers that was defined by, and maintained by, their bosses. Solomon's claims that companies could not succeed if they recognized unions would be echoed by business interests again and again, as they opposed minimum wage laws and child labor bans—and, later, as they justified moving their factories to "right to work" states and then beyond the reach of US labor laws altogether.

In this context, the WTUL and NCL became important allies to the striking shirtwaist workers. The WTUL rented out meeting halls for workers and offered support with public relations and picket lines. Members organized food donations and meals, and they raised money for bail and strike relief. They then publicized the largest contributions to the strike fund in newspapers, naming donors and amounts, to show the support of philanthropists. Because custom dictated that married women go by their husbands' names, newspaper columns covering the strike were peppered with names of some of the most prominent businessmen in New York. This support for the strike, even if by proxy, shifted the dynamics between workers and bosses.⁴⁰

Employers, meanwhile, were eager to divide workers along religious, racial, and ethnic lines. By the early twentieth century, employers had begun to see Black workers—often banned from jobs by unions' own deliberately discriminatory practices—as a massive pool of strikebreakers, further stoking racial resentment and violence among the working classes.

In hopes of discouraging Black workers from helping bosses undercut the uprising, WTUL activist Elizabeth Dutcher, a recent graduate from Vassar and a socialist, accompanied two striking workers to a meeting at Brooklyn's African Methodist Episcopal Zion Church. Noting racism within organized labor—a point that Dutcher acknowledged—the meeting ultimately issued a resolution, both encouraging Black workers to resist factory owners' recruitment efforts and urging organized labor to develop more inclusive practices. In a further nod to how rifts among workers helped bosses divide and conquer, Dutcher had also expressed concern about possible "race warfare" involving Italian Catholics acting as strikebreakers against the heavily Eastern European Jewish workforce. The fear was largely unfounded in this case, though, for as one Italian union organizer pointed out, more than one thousand Italian garment workers were on strike and active on the picket lines.[41]

At the invitation of the International Ladies Garment Workers Union (ILGWU), the WTUL provided direct picket line support, voting to join the picketers three times per week for the duration of the strike. While many strikers had been arrested with little fanfare, when New York WTUL president Mary Dreier—Margaret Dreier Robins's sister—was arrested, the resulting media attention drew public sympathy to the workers' cause. Police immediately released Dreier when they realized who she was, but the public relations damage was already done. According to one account, a police officer asked her, "Why didn't you tell me you was a rich lady? I'd never have arrested you in the world."[42]

After Dreier's arrest, women who were even more socially prominent then joined or worked in conjunction with the WTUL to highlight the workers' struggle. Wives and daughters of wealthy industrialists, notably including Alva Vanderbilt Belmont and Anne Morgan, donated money, time, and "moral support."[43] Morgan joined the WTUL and used her connections with elite media to gain favorable coverage, telling the editors of the *New York Times*, "When you hear of a woman who presses forty dozen skirts for only eight dollars a week, something must be wrong."[44] Belmont, meanwhile, used her wealth to secure the release of arrested picketers, whose bail was set at one hundred dollars apiece. She even offered the magistrate the deed to her mansion as collateral that the strikers would appear before court at a later date. Belmont and Morgan also lent strikers their cars for an automobile parade. Driving down streets lined with picketers and supporters, the vehicles displayed signs including, "Thirty thousand shirtwaist makers have joined our ranks. We want shorter hours and higher wages" and "Votes for Women."⁴⁵ Wealthy backers, especially Morgan, have rightly been criticized for their later efforts to undermine the strikers' demands, but their early support was significant.⁴⁶

Among the WTUL's main priorities was combatting the violence and arrests that were targeted at picketing workers. Pointing out the disparity in power between well-connected bosses and desperate workers, the group released a statement criticizing the "great abuses [which] are safely practiced by the employers and their hired guards" and began recruiting their own pool of legal observers—women from Barnard College and men from Columbia University and the local Young Men's Christian Association (YMCA).⁴⁷ With an eye toward future struggles, the WTUL recruited young women at prestigious colleges for other roles, as well. As historian Stephen Norwood documents, students from Vassar, Wellesley, Barnard, and Bryn Mawr Colleges all traveled to New York to support the striking workers.⁴⁸ While in New York, these students were active in fundraising, speaking to crowds, picketing, and trying to protect workers from police violence—while also building support for the strike back at their schools. Back in Massachusetts, for example, the Wellesley student newspaper proclaimed its support for the striking workers, noting that many of them were "girls just our own age."⁴⁹

The NCL, too, reached out to women on college campuses. The group sent letters to Smith College's class of 1909, asking each student to join the fight against sweatshops. Of the twenty-one women who replied to the letter, six wanted to form a new chapter, six planned to join an existing chapter, and one was already serving on the Executive Board of the Consumers' League of Providence, Rhode Island. Four others, who held teaching positions, organized chapters at their schools. The national organization offered guidelines and suggestions for college students who wished to form chapters on their campus and formed a Special Committee on Colleges and Graduates. While many of the committee's efforts focused on recruitment in elite, Northeastern women's colleges, it also responded to inquiries from schools in Washington, DC; Birmingham, Alabama; and Menomonee, Wisconsin.⁵⁰

The strike overlapped with the NCL's annual early holiday shopping campaign, and the group worked to educate the public on the conditions in which their clothing was produced as well as where it was sold. In January 1910, in the middle of the uprising, the group organized an exhibit to connect popular clothing items with images of exploited laborers. According to the *New York Times*: "The photographs [were] pictures of certain tenement rooms on the east side, in which men, women, and little children [were] toiling for twelve and fourteen hours a day for a few cents a day.

The garments which accompany the photographs [were] made by these tenement toilers."[51] The display and the press coverage it received framed sweatshops as a moral issue—the exploitation of workers by greedy industrialists. By confronting middle-class and wealthy women with images of child labor attached to the garments that they could be wearing, the NCL also connected them to that exploitation by extension, as consumers. In addition to exposing the realities of unrestrained capitalism, the group offered women a solution—solidarity through ethical purchasing.[52]

As the strike wore on through the winter, many firms agreed to terms with their workers. Some wealthy WTUL members—specifically Anne Morgan—withdrew their support for a continued strike, believing that the workers were holding out for overly radical demands. When the Uprising of 20,000 was called off in February 1910, most workers had achieved some tangible gains, including a shorter workweek and four paid holidays per year. Perhaps more important, the strike empowered workers and activists, set the stage for future organizing, and developed a generation of labor leaders. Miriam Finn Scott, a journalist who covered the strike, wrote, "There has been a tradition that women cannot strike. These young, inexperienced girls have proved that women can strike, and strike successfully."[53]

Frances Perkins, who would soon become executive secretary of the New York Consumers' League, similarly marveled at the women's collective action, "Women are learning to stand together and realize their social responsibility to each other. Women have gone from the individual basis in the home to the social basis in the world."[54] The next step, Perkins predicted, was political equality through suffrage.

In the years following the strike, union membership in New York City increased eightfold, to a quarter of a million workers. The number of women in unions increased dramatically, mostly in the ILGWU, which then represented more than 80 percent of New York's shirtwaist workers. Historian Ann Schofield argues that the Uprising of 20,000 broadcast the "support and cooperation that trade unions could anticipate from New York's reform community." The alliances built that winter, Schofield notes, guided "labor upheaval and reform activity" through the New Deal two decades later.[55] Men in union leadership roles also began to see value in organizing women workers. The strike, which garnered significant media coverage, forced the public to pay attention to working-class women and their concerns. It brought the details of sweatshop labor from out of the shadows and into the consciousness of middle-class and wealthy New Yorkers. This shift was reflected by a much-repeated slogan, "We want bread, but we

1.1 Women on strike in Chicago, Illinois, 1911. Newspaper clipping from *Chicago Daily Journal*, Official Report of the Strike Committee by the Women's Trade Union League of Chicago, Collection of the Chicago History Museum.

want roses, too."[56] These labor feminists did not merely want better wages; rather, these women demanded a life worth living, with resources to enjoy leisure, art, poetry, nature, family, and friends.

Later that year, some forty thousand garment workers in Chicago, where factories were similarly wretched, went on strike for seventeen weeks, from September 1910 to February 1911. Workers' grievances included a 15 to 20 percent pay cut, abusive and insulting language by tyrannical foremen, and excessive and arbitrary fines deducted from their paychecks. According to Bessie Abramowitz Hillman, a Russian immigrant and sweatshop worker, "We all worked 90 to 100 hours a week for $8 or $9. Then we were threatened with a pay cut. It was too much for us so five of us girls started a fight to stop it."[57] Other garment workers reported being forced, during busy periods, to work beyond Illinois's legal limit of ten hours per shift and then being forced to stay at work all day for one hour's pay during slow periods. She also said that they were forced to work slowly in order to stifle their own production and wages, since they were paid by the piece. As one sign held by marching workers explained simply, "We are striking for human treatments."[58]

While the terrible conditions had led to frequent walkouts by individuals and small groups of workers, the 1910 strike was the first major labor dispute in Chicago led by a group of women. As the WTUL later noted, during the strike, "thousands of men and women, speaking many languages and believing diverse creeds, stood shoulder to shoulder . . . in their fight for a living wage, for just industrial conditions and the right to self-government."[59] The striking workers pled their case at meetings of reformers throughout the city, to the press, and even in saloons.[60]

Within weeks, the WTUL of Chicago, at the invitation of striking workers, contacted the United Garment Workers to offer its assistance. The union gratefully accepted and assigned the group to work with its strike committee. Chicago WTUL President Margaret Dreier Robins—whose sister had been arrested in the New York strike—began, along with Jane Addams and others, to organize a coalition of local professors, students, church members, and radicals to support the strike and put pressure on factory owners. Striking workers also met at Hull House, which Abramowitz Hillman later described as "a citadel of hope and strength."[61]

Katharine Coman, a Wellesley economics professor and chair of the WTUL Committee on Grievances, wrote an article titled "A Sweated Industry" for the WTUL monthly newsletter *Life and Labor*. In it, Coman highlights the factories' abuses and authoritarian management, including fines for breaking needles and for using too much soap when washing hands. She ends with a plea to "all those interested in the social welfare of their city" to support the strike and "secure . . . civilized industry."[62]

As the strike grew, employers began recruiting replacement workers from around the country, even converting floors of their factories into kitchens and sleeping areas to keep strikebreakers on site. Violent clashes between striking workers, police, hired thugs, and strikebreakers were common, and two workers, one strikebreaker, one company guard, and one bystander were shot and killed. Paralleling efforts in New York, women attending the University of Chicago and Northwestern University joined picket lines throughout the cold Chicago winter. As "society women," the students were less likely to be attacked by police or industry-hired thugs, and their presence shielded striking workers. However, Chicago activists also used this tactic in reverse to confuse police and achieve similar aims.[63]

In what became a national news story, dozens of "club women and society women . . . garbed as working girls" joined the picket lines, leaving police unable to separate them from the striking workers.[64] After being roughed up by mounted police, arrested, and taken to jail, the women presented their engraved calling cards and were released. Ellen Starr, who had founded Hull House with Jane Addams, told the press, "The only persons who were violating the law were the policemen, who treated us roughly and hurt dreadfully with their clubs some of the poor boys who we were leading peacefully past the shops."[65] WTUL picket committee chair Emma Steghagen, meanwhile, was told by police that she should "go home and wash your dishes."[66]

Undeterred, the WTUL promised additional picket support and announced that some elite Chicagoans had offered to open their homes to striking workers. Activists also raised more than seventy thousand dollars for strike relief. According to the WTUL's Strike Committee's official report, "out of about 750 individual contributions, about 470, or over three-fifths were contributed by women."[67] Many churches, clubs, and political groups donated significantly, with the greatest nonlabor contributions coming from a group of socialist women.[68]

In February, however, the strike was called off. While some of the workers had been granted modest concessions—a minimum wage, non-retaliation for strike participation, and the promise of a better-ventilated workspace—thousands returned to work out of desperation, with little to show for their sacrifices. But, much like the uprising in New York, the Chicago strike laid a "foundation for the organization of the entire trade," leading to the formation of the Amalgamated Clothing Workers of America.[69]

Despite the outcome of the strike, historian Sue Weiler argues that it represents one of the WTUL's "greatest historical successes." She writes, "Women allies in the community were observed on the streets aiding pickets and collecting relief and were recognized for their work behind the scenes. Working women also behaved in a fearless fashion as they put down their shears and seized their picket signs."[70] As in New York, women had demonstrated, collectively, their defiance and noncooperation with the rules of industrial capital through feminist solidarity.

The massive strikes in Chicago and New York allowed garment workers and their allies to expose the dangers of sweatshops, and they demonstrated to labor leaders and employers alike that striking women could not be easily dismissed. In her retrospective on the Chicago strike, Margaret Dreier Robins concluded, "The strike is over, but the struggle has but begun. . . . The promise of America has been freedom and opportunity. Religious and political liberty were won for us through suffering and death, and the struggle for industrial freedom will demand the same qualities of heart and mind, the same courage and devotion."[71] Less than two months after the strike in Chicago had concluded, "suffering and death" in the garment industry were once again on full display.[72]

On March 25, 1911, as the workday came to an end, a fire broke out on the eighth floor of New York's Triangle Shirtwaist Factory. Company management, on the tenth floor, safely escaped to the roofs of adjoining buildings. The hundreds of workers a floor below them, however, were effectively trapped. Mary Domsky-Abrams, a blouse operator, recalled, "The screams and sobs all around were deafening," as workers tried to flee the flames, and firefighters and police officers on the streets below scrambled in vain to try to help.[73]

The building was poorly constructed, poorly ventilated, and poorly maintained, despite its reputation as a modern factory. The factory owners, who had staunchly resisted workers' demands during the mass strike two years prior, had locked their workers inside, allegedly to prevent unauthorized breaks, theft, and union organizing. When the fire started in the top floors of the building, workers were unable to access the main stairs, and the brittle fire escape quickly buckled under their weight. Firefighters' ladders were too short, and their hoses were not strong enough to put out the flames. Many of the women escaped the fire by jumping to their deaths on the sidewalk below—to the horror of a growing crowd of onlookers. The fire, and the conditions at the Triangle Shirtwaist Factory, killed 147 workers, most of whom were young, Jewish women who had recently emigrated from Eastern Europe.[74]

Eraclio Montanaro witnessed the disaster from the street. "The firemen were helpless," he later recalled. As they attempted to catch those who jumped, "the nets were ripped from the hands. Many stooped and picked up the nets again with their hands bleeding. All around us we saw people covered with blood. I got sick and could not look any more."[75] Domsky-Abrams, the blouse operator, remembered that a group of men had attempted to make a human ladder to help girls escape the flames to a neighboring building, but they ultimately fell to their deaths, alongside those they were trying to rescue. Moved by their bravery, Domsky-Abrams said survivors "tried to kiss their bodies as they were being removed to the morgue."[76]

Esther Hochfield, twenty years old and recently engaged, had worked in the factory for three years—and had been one of the 1909 strikers. Her brother Max, who survived the fire, returned to the factory the next day to look for her. "We looked for her for a whole week," he said. "My sister was burned to death. She was so badly burned we couldn't identify her, but her boyfriend did."[77]

The Triangle fire tragedy was the logical conclusion to the unrestrained harshness and cruelty of sweatshop capitalism. Not only was it predictable, but the WTUL had effectively done so just months prior, when, following a fire in Newark, the group publicized the alarming results of its ongoing investigation into New York factories—"firetraps" where workers had reported doors "locked all day" and windows "grated to prevent their being broken."[78] New York Fire Chief Edward Croker later said that he had reported issues with the building's lack of fire escapes numerous times, including just a week before the tragedy.[79]

Conditions in the Triangle factory were neither unique nor secret. The strikes in New York, Chicago, and several other cities had long since exposed the dangers of the industry to working people, middle-class consumers, and government officials. The Triangle Fire's survivors and witnesses understood some of these same young women had targeted the same industry, including the same employers, during the uprising. Triangle worker Rose Sabran reflected, "Two of our demands were for adequate fire escapes and open doors from the factories to the streets. But the bosses defeated us . . . so our friends are dead."[80] The WTUL's Mary Dreier also condemned Triangle owners Max Blanck and Isaac Harris for their actions during the strike, noting that rather than recognize their workers' union, they had fired and replaced organizers—and hired thugs "to insult and beat" them on the picket lines.[81] Indeed, Blanck and Harris had been widely recognized as the most aggressive and violent resisters of the strike. Journalist Martha Bensely Bruere, also with the WTUL, further lamented that "the same policemen who had clubbed and beaten [striking workers] back into submission" were now responsible for putting their bodies into coffins "in wagonfuls."[82] It was a literal truth, as some police officers stood over the bodies of workers whom they had previously arrested.[83]

Distraught and angry, a coalition of labor, reformers, and Jewish organizations came together, determined that the appropriate response to the tragedy must include "three distinct phases—relief, protest, and prosecution."[84] In other words, after they mourned the dead, they planned to fight for accountability and lasting change. As Rabbi Stephen Wise, who had been criticized for his supportive sermon—and was a cofounder of the

NAACP—declared, "We don't want an outburst of charity for those who have suffered only to have the whole thing forgotten in short order."[85]

As factory owners tried to evade both legal and financial liability, the WTUL and several Jewish groups, including the *Jewish Daily Forward* and United Hebrew Trades, formed the Joint Relief Committee, which worked to raise funds to help survivors, pay for funeral expenses, and provide support for dependents. Describing the response, union activist William Mailly wrote, "It was a working-class calamity and as such it was the duty of a working-class organization which sought the advancement and improvement of all the waistmakers through the trade union movement to go to the aid of its brothers and sisters."[86] In cooperation with the Red Cross and several labor unions, the committee notified victims' family members, many of whom were in Europe, and provided aid, often in Russian rubles. The Triangle Fire is considered a pivotal moment in New York history, but the tragedy was felt on both sides of the Atlantic Ocean. Though not yet as global as the assembly line that would follow in the 1980s and 1990s, the sweatshop economy of this period, like the anti-sweatshop movement, was already transnational.[87]

After a daylong process of identifying the broken and charred bodies, the Joint Relief Committee arranged to bury twenty-one of the deceased workers. The bodies of six victims remained unidentified and were buried as "unknown."[88] The mayor promised the committee that a police escort would treat the funeral march with respect, and the city arranged for funeral services to include a Catholic priest, a Protestant minister, and a Jewish rabbi for the unidentified victims.[89]

Led by the ILGWU, the coalition of allies organized a massive funeral demonstration to honor the victims of the fire and to bury those still unidentified. Labor journalist Bruere's account of the funeral connected the Triangle Fire to the broader tragedy of the period's sweatshops:

> There have been no carriages, no imposing marshals on horseback; just thousands and thousands of working men and women carrying the banners of their trades through the long three-mile tramp in the rain. Never have I seen a military pageant or triumphant ovation so impressive; for it is not because 146 workers were killed in the Triangle shop—not altogether. It is because every year there are 50,000 working men and women killed in the United States—136 a day; almost as many as happened to be killed together on the 25th of March; and because

slowly, very slowly, it is dawning on these thousands on thousands that such things do not have to be![90]

The funeral march was an incredible undertaking, with a division from each of the four boroughs, and it included dozens of labor unions, including those for carpenters, waiters and bartenders, typographers, subway and tunnel constructors, musicians, and many kinds of garment workers. Arturi Caroti, on behalf of the WTUL, served as one of the assistant parade marshals. An estimated 250,000 working people watched the procession, which included as many as one hundred thousand marchers.[91]

With relief and protest underway, public outrage demanded prosecution, and factory owners Blanck and Harris were arrested and indicted on charges of first- and second-degree manslaughter. Despite workers' and experts' testimonies, however, they were acquitted and also received a large insurance settlement. Just as in the strike, the law favored the owners, though subsequent civil suits compelled the payment of a paltry seventy-five dollars for each victim. Blanck and Harris continued to operate outside of even the lax labor standards of the time. When Blanck was caught once again locking in workers in 1913, he received a small fine, as well as a judge's apology for the nuisance of having to appear in court. A few months later, authorities cited him yet again for fire hazards in his factory. He received only a warning. Despite a clear disregard for the lives of workers sweating—and dying—in their factories, business owners could count on the justice system to operate on their behalf. As one newspaper concluded, "Capital can commit no crime when it is in pursuit of profits."[92]

A week after the fire, Anne Morgan and Alva Vanderbilt Belmont hosted a meeting on behalf of the WTUL at the Metropolitan Opera House. A crowd of 3,500—including survivors of the fire, wealthy elites, reformers, politicians, and clergy—gathered to pay respect to the dead, support the living, and discuss how to win reforms that would ensure such a tragedy would not happen again. While many middle- and upper-class reformers framed the issue as one limited to fire safety alone, Rabbi Wise intervened, saying, "This was not the deed of God but the greed of man. This was no inevitable disaster which could not be foreseen. Some of us foresaw it."[93] As the meeting descended into chaos, WTUL leader Rose Schneiderman, a former garment worker who had been active in the Uprising of 20,000, went to the front of the Opera House to speak. Shaking in anger and condemning calls for only limited reform, Schneiderman said, "I would be a traitor to those poor burned bodies, if I were to come here to talk good fellowship. We have tried you good people of the public—and we have found you wanting."⁹⁴ Having known many of the fire's victims personally and having experienced the daily exploitations of the sweatshop herself, Schneiderman had little patience for those who expressed sympathy after the fire—but had considered the preceding strike's demands too extreme. Ultimately, the meeting ended with a resolution to send a committee of representatives to lobby the state government for change.⁹⁵

Various city and state agencies subsequently launched investigations into the fire's causes, presumably to clear their own offices of blame. Edward Croker, the New York fire chief, publicly decried the Building Department, whose officials denied the accusations. The WTUL also announced its own investigation, appointing twenty-five men and women to what became the Committee on Safety. Frances Perkins and Rabbi Wise were among those chosen—but no workers were. In the meantime, the WTUL continued investigating and reporting building code violations around the city, with limited success.⁹⁶

In November, months after the fire, the ILGWU organized another march, a parade of the "relatives and friends of the victims." Among their signs were the slogans, "Harris and Blanck Got Their $200,000; We Protest"; "Union Shops Mean Open Doors"; and "A Strong Union Means Sanitary and Fireproof Conditions in the Factories."⁹⁷ The Triangle Fire, while just one of many workplace disasters during the period, had a profound impact on those who survived it. Years later, Mary Domsky-Abrams, the Triangle blouse operator, reflected:

> That spring of 1911 we mourned our dead comrades, the victims of a society which was concerned only with the profits of an individual and not with the welfare of the many, of the working masses. The Triangle victims were martyrs in the fight for social justice, and the labor movement will always remember them as those who, with their young lives, paved the way for a better world with a more just society, a world free from exploitation, in which equal rights for all will be respected.⁹⁸

After witnessing the terrible conclusions to laissez-faire logic in action, many reformers committed themselves to what would become a decades-long project for government regulation for the common good. Eventually, these efforts would reach the federal level. Rabbi Wise, for example, later became an advisor to President Franklin Roosevelt. Frances Perkins, an NCL leader who arrived at the fire just as young women began jumping to their deaths, served as Roosevelt's secretary of labor.[99]

In the meantime, the NCL and WTUL, the New York and Chicago strikes, and the Triangle Fire coalesced in an anti-sweatshop push that began remaking working conditions in New York and beyond. While those responsible for the Triangle Fire were not held accountable, groups like the WTUL and the NCL continued their fight for workplace reforms. The WTUL asked factory workers to fill out a questionnaire detailing their working conditions, and then used the hundreds of responses it received as evidence to condemn industry and government, and to demand change. By the end of the year, the New York City Council had created a Bureau of Fire Prevention and tightened safety standards in its building codes. Knowing that such reforms could be abandoned or overruled in the future by business-friendly officials, the WTUL and NCL also set their sights on state-level standards to match.[100]

In June 1911, under pressure from reformers, the New York state legislature established the Factory Investigation Commission (FIC). Frances Perkins of the Consumers' League of New York, as well as Pauline Newman and Rose Schneiderman of the WTUL, served as investigators. The commission received support from Fire Chief Edward Croker, who testified about how future tragedies could be prevented. When asked if firefighters regularly found factory doors locked by employers, he answered, "Oh, yes, plenty of them . . . they pay absolutely no attention to the fire hazard or to the protection of the employees in these buildings. That is their last consideration."[101] Croker argued that passing safety standards alone would not be enough to compel the industry to obey, and that there would also have to be government monitoring and significant penalties. His years of experience fighting fires in factories had convinced him that businesses would not hold themselves accountable. This debate, over whether factory owners should be allowed to self-monitor or require outside policing, would continue for the next century.[102]

With public opinion and a sympathetic state legislature on their side, the FIC effectively gave anti-sweatshop activists government funding to investigate workplaces, hear testimony from workers, and draft progressive reforms. Despite opposition from business leaders, the commission helped push thirty-six new laws through the New York legislature—and reform the state's Department of Labor to provide enforcement. Perkins resigned her position as executive secretary of the Consumers' League of New York to pursue factory inspections full-time, and the state became a testing ground for worker-friendly policies. Two decades later, Perkins would champion many of them again at the federal level through the New Deal.[103]

Progressive activists also took their fight to the US Supreme Court. For decades, the court had been a consistent ally for the rights of businesses. In 1886, in *Santa Clara County v. Southern Pacific Railroad*, the court granted corporations the same constitutional protections as people, empowering businesses to contest even modest labor reforms. In 1905, for example, New York bakery owner Joseph Lochner challenged the state's sixty-hour work week law. Ruling in Lochner's favor, the court essentially used the 14th Amendment, which granted full US citizenship to the formerly enslaved, in order to argue that state and federal labor standards impeded an individual's freedom to enter exploitative contracts with employers. The result was that maximum hour laws and minimum wage laws were declared unconstitutional, in the supposed interest of workers.[104]

Three years later, the court heard a similar challenge in *Muller v. Oregon*. Like Lochner, Curt Muller was a business owner, and he sought to overturn his state's law that specifically protected women by capping workdays at ten hours. In this case, however, the court unanimously upheld the law, citing the "difference between the sexes."[105] To defend the Oregon law, NCL activists Florence Kelley and Josephine Clara Goldmark hired Louis Brandeis, the future Supreme Court justice. In true NCL fashion, Goldmark, who was Brandeis' sister-in-law, compiled evidence to demonstrate the link between working conditions and health. The "Brandeis Brief" included hundreds of sources that established the damaging impact of long hours and harsh working environments on women's abilities to reproduce, care for children, and lead healthy and moral lives. Kelley later said that Brandeis "was convinced that, if the social facts of industry could be presented to the courts of last resort, it might become possible for the United States to take its place among civilized nations."[106] Staking its argument on the human impact of laws, rather than just legal doctrine, the Brandeis Brief notably focused on maternal health, with lasting implications for gender-specific legislation. In its decision, the court noted, "The physical well-being of woman becomes an object of public interest and care in order to preserve the strength and vigor of the race."[107] However, the concern for future generations was not spread uniformly, since these laws only covered about one-third of wage-earning women, notably excluding many occupations primarily held by women of color.[108]

Among progressives, protective legislation was divisive. Several US states already had laws limiting hours for working women and children. A Massachusetts law dating from 1874, for example, established that "No woman shall be employed in laboring in a manufacturing or mechanical establishment more than ten hours in any one day . . . and in no case shall the hours of labor exceed fifty-eight in a week."[109] After the *Muller* decision, seventeen more states adopted similar statutes. But while ostensibly intended to improve working conditions for women, the results were not so clear-cut. Reflecting on the *Muller* case, Supreme Court Justice Ruth Bader Ginsburg later remarked that protective labor laws "were in many instances protecting [women] from better paying jobs and opportunities for promotion."[110] Indeed, male-centered labor unions often favored protective legislation because it prevented women from competing with their members. By 1923, three years after the 19th Amendment established women's right to vote, the issue came to a head. While many labor feminists continued to favor protective legislation for its tangible, if imperfect, improvements in the lives of working-class women, the National Women's Party moved in a different direction, by introducing the Equal Rights Amendment.[111]

In 1925, *Good Housekeeping* published a written debate between Mary Anderson and Rheta Childe Dorr on the topic of labor laws for women. Anderson was a member of the WTUL and the chief of the Women's Bureau within the Department of Labor. She had worked in Chicago factories after emigrating from Sweden as a teenager and was active in the 1910 strike. Dorr, meanwhile, was the editor of the Woman's Department of the *New York Evening Post*. She investigated labor conditions for women and children and wrote about elite clubwomen's activities.[112]

Both women had witnessed the dangers of sweatshops, but they had different ideas about the solutions. Dorr critiqued the Brandeis Brief for blaming women's poor health and wrecked bodies on the "single fact that women were working outside the home for wages."[113] She wrote that there were too many factors that made workingwomen's lives untenable, including sexism, poverty, and poor housing. Ultimately, she argued, "Unequal wages and bad factory conditions, and not special laws for adult women workers, are the things in which we all should interest ourselves. Sex has nothing to do with the case."[114]

While Anderson agreed with the need to create greater standards for all workers, she argued that women were impacted by low wages and poor conditions, which they endured on top of their "second shift" of cooking, cleaning, and child-rearing. Endorsing gender-specific legislation, she wrote:

> Men in general work under much better conditions than women, where they work at night they can sleep during the day, and there are in any event no such double demands upon their energies as upon the wage-earning wife and mother; and, though men's wages are too often very low, they are never, I think we can safely say, as low as women's. The ditch-digger, the coal-heaver—any of the very least skilled of men—draw a better wage than do thousands of skilled and semi-skilled women.[115]

Both Anderson and Dorr saw the ways that industrial capitalism and patriarchy worked together to disproportionally impact women workers, but their conclusions were different and represented a crack in the burgeoning feminist movement—one embodied by the unsuccessful 1923 Equal Rights Amendment campaign. The WTUL, the NCL, and most of the labor movement were in favor of protective legislation, which shielded working women from equal exploitation in the workplace. More affluent women, including Alva Vanderbilt Belmont, meanwhile, were opposed to policies that they believed kept them from having equal opportunities. In retrospect, whatever the theoretical merits of each side's arguments were, the bottom line was that the lived reality for working-class women—and men—was abysmal. And while both contingents claimed to represent the needs and wishes of the female working class, one side actively aligned itself with business interests. For example, in the *Adkins v. Children's Hospital* Supreme Court case, National Women's Party leader Alice Paul worked closely with employers' attorneys to overturn a 1918 minimum wage law for women and children in the District of Columbia.[116]

By the 1930s, much of the protective legislation became unnecessary as New Deal policy established nationwide minimum wages and maximum hour laws for most men and women. Later in the twentieth century, most of these laws were repealed or ruled unconstitutional for singling women out for unequal treatment. However, like the Progressive Movement more broadly, for the few decades between the *Muller* decision and the New Deal, protective legislation provided a regulatory foothold, building the case, if imperfectly, that government bore some responsibility to restrain capital's greediest impulses.[117]

―――

Groups such as the NCL and the WTUL were instrumental in exposing, and to some degree cushioning, some of the harshest extremes of industrial capitalism in the early twentieth century in the United States. By providing

THE LETTER OF THE LAW.

1.2 1912 cartoon showing an owner of a factory, saying to a visitor, "That's all right! You see, we put a label on all our goods guaranteeing that they aren't made in a sweat-shop." Samuel D. Ehrhart, "The Letter of the Law," illustrated in *Puck*, February 28, 1912, Library of Congress.

direct strike relief to working women and building economic and political pressure, they created avenues for thousands of middle-class and elite women to act in solidarity with sweatshop workers. They documented and publicized working conditions and supported efforts to change them. They recruited students from Wellesley, Bryn Mawr, Northwestern University, and elsewhere to join the fight by marching on picket lines, and they spread their message through flyers and in the pages of national media. Members also helped shape laws—for example, Frances Perkins, through New York City's Committee of Safety, and Florence Kelley, in the *Muller v. Oregon* case—at a time when women did not have voting rights in either of those states. In short, in concert with working-class women, these activists demonstrated their collective political power.

The modest successes of the 1910s, however, were short lived, and capital's response to the Progressives was swift and severe. For businesses wishing to escape the reach of organized labor and protective legislation for women and children, the US South, with its social deference for the elite, its culture of extralegal violence, and its desire to court industry, provided a haven. Few industries fled the Northeast more quickly than textiles.

In a 1919 pamphlet aimed at enticing northern textile manufacturers, Alabama Power, one of the state's most influential businesses, noted, "The mills in the New England States operated chiefly on a 48-hour basis, while the mills in the cotton growing states operated largely between 54 and 60 hours a week."[118] The pamphlet further boasted of the lack of labor strife in the South, proclaiming, "Probably the greatest factor in the development of cotton manufacturing in Alabama has been the presence of an adequate supply of native labor which cotton mill operatives have found to be particularly well adapted to the textile industry."[119] Politicians, boosters, and industrialists alike linked the southern population with "reliability, industry, tractability, and high intelligence."[120]

In the South, companies could pay hourly wages of two-thirds to half of those in the Northeast—and require longer work weeks. Throughout the early 1920s, hundreds of new southern mills opened each year. In 1923 and 1924 alone, northern investors spent an estimated one hundred million dollars buying and building textile mills in the South. In turn, manufacturers in the North used capital flight to push for deregulation. In the early 1930s, for example, Massachusetts mill owners pressured their governor to roll back a law prohibiting night work for women textile workers to "meet southern competition."[121] The local branch of the NCL lamented that a race to the bottom could bring sweatshops back to the state. They chastised the governor saying, "because we cannot compete with the labor conditions of the hill-billies [sic] we may drop down to their level of labor laws, [the governor] makes a pitiable confession of short-sidedness."[122]

In the aftermath of the Russian Revolution and US involvement in World War I, US industry also used the Red Scare to associate unions with Bolshevism and anti-Americanism—and to justify violently suppressing strikes. In 1921, a group of approximately two hundred business leaders met in Chicago and formally coined the term the "American Plan" to describe the open shop—a workplace that undermines unions by hiring nonunion workers. Their motto was, "Every man to work out his own salvation and not be bound by the shackles of organization to his own detriment."[123] Adapting a tactic from the NCL, some companies even used "patriotic," antiunion labels to designate that organized workers did *not* produce their products. Importantly, however, collective power was only deemed unpatriotic when it served the interests of workers. The thousands of individuals who joined business associations, such as the twenty-three-thousand-member American Bankers' Association, presumably did not view their united effort as "the shackles of organization."[124]

Capitalizing on a postwar downturn, business interests also used their economic power to further influence national politics and expand their own wealth. Industrialist and investment banker Andrew Mellon, for example, served as secretary of the treasury from 1921 until 1932. On his recommendation, Congress drastically cut income tax rates, much to the benefit of those at the top, such as Mellon himself. With investment booming, corporate profits skyrocketed from $3.9 billion in 1922 to $7.2 billion in 1929—before the eventual crash. Wealth inequality, in the meantime, reached stunning heights. While the top 0.1 percent of Americans held about 25 percent of the country's total household wealth, the bottom 90 percent of the country shared about 20 percent.[125]

Both the WTUL and the NCL continued their activism into the 1920s, but their appeals to the public's conscience were no longer mainstream. Their open invitations to wealthy women to throw their weight behind working-class women's causes became less appealing, as the Red Scare and its fear of communism reinforced class loyalties, racial loyalties, and political divisions. Backlash to decades of immigration from Southern and Eastern Europe coalesced in anti-immigrant propaganda and laws and fed the revival of the Ku Klux Klan (KKK). Rooted in white supremacy and religious xenophobia, the new KKK focused its efforts on immigration restriction and centering Protestantism within American public life. Within a decade, numerous states had banned foreign language newspapers, thousands of Americans had anglicized their names to remove any markers of their immigrant past, and Congress had passed new federal laws limiting immigration. Among the main targets were Eastern European Jews and Italian Catholics—the groups who had been so involved in New York's garment industry. No longer focused on Progressive values, the wealthy and middle classes were more interested in protecting American whiteness and American capitalism than protecting workers from sweatshops.[126]

Looking toward a more hopeful future, in 1921, the WTUL and NCL founded the Bryn Mawr Summer School for Women Workers in Industry, bringing together women from around the country and offering them training in labor activism. Mary Anderson—WTUL organizer, experienced factory worker, and supporter of protective legislation—called the school "the bridge across the gulf between purely practical experience and theoretical training."[127]

Located on the grounds of the elite women's college, the school admitted one hundred working women between the ages of twenty and thirty-five to an eight-week summer program. Each applicant was required to have at least two years of experience as an industrial worker and be able to read and write in English. In a limited but important step toward a more inclusive movement, the program also began recruiting and admitting African American women in 1926, predating the first Black student at Bryn Mawr College itself by a year. The selection of two African American women industrial workers from Chicago was noteworthy enough for the Black press to feature it as a "first."[128]

Most of the program's students had no formal education beyond age thirteen, and its faculty used a nonhierarchical feminist pedagogy to develop the women's talents as writers and speakers. Many returned to work at the end of the summer to take on leadership roles, such as shop steward, not only using their new skills but also, ideally, passing them along to others. The program's opportunities also extended beyond its classrooms. In 1921, for example, twelve of the program's students, including garment workers from Seattle, electrical workers from Cleveland, and glove makers from Chicago, accompanied Mary Anderson to meet President Warren Harding at the White House. That fall, alums also traveled to Chicago to speak at a conference about women and trade unions alongside WTUL President Margaret Dreier Robins. During its seventeen-year history, students in the Bryn Mawr Summer Program also heard lectures from well-known figures, including Margaret Sanger, A. Philip Randolph, W. E. B. Du Bois, Eleanor Roosevelt (a WTUL member since 1922), Walter Reuther, and Frances Perkins.[129]

Much like Tennessee's Highlander Folk School, which trained several generations of labor and civil rights leaders, labor schools like Bryn Mawr, Wisconsin Summer School, Brookwood Labor College, and Southern Summer School trained their students (and teachers) to be effective agents for social change. Instead of lamenting the terrible organizing conditions of the Red Scare's antiprogressive backlash, labor activists, including members of the NCL and WTUL, continued to work and build power for the next political opening. As historian Rita Heller writes, "In the politically quiet 1920s, the [Bryn Mawr Summer] School thus kept alive a commitment to peaceful social change, grooming many of its participants for the recharged world of FDR and serving as a bridge to the later era."[130]

The school served as a hub both for its students and for activists around the country. For example, in the 1920s, the Indiana League of Women Voters established scholarships to cover two students' tuition at the school, naming them after Mary Anderson in tribute. The American Association of University Women in Seattle, meanwhile, hosted a lecture as a fundraiser to send working women from the Pacific Northwest to Bryn Mawr.[131]

In addition to the work done at the labor colleges, veterans of the New York and Chicago strikes, such as Rose Schneiderman, Clara Lemlich, and Agnes Nestor; NCL leaders, including Frances Perkins and Florence Kelley; and religious leaders, namely Rabbi Stephen Wise, also continued their activism through the repressive 1920s, doing what Annelise Orleck calls the "painstaking labor in the shadows."[132] While union membership dropped significantly during this period, these activists continued to lay the groundwork for a moment when the national stage would be ready for mass movements around civil rights, labor rights, and a social safety net. During the Great Depression of the 1930s, political conditions shifted once again, creating an opening for a reinvigorated anti-sweatshop movement and the most successful era of labor organizing in US history. The NCL and WTUL were part of that effort, as were many of the women those groups trained, educated, and inspired—at labor colleges, on picket lines, and through early Christmas shopping campaigns.

2

"DON'T OVERLOOK ANY CHANNEL FOR PUBLICITY"

THE SOLIDARITY OF THE POPULAR FRONT

Though especially focused on the conditions in American garment factories, groups like the National Consumers' League and the Women's Trade Union League had also exposed the horrid realities of early 1900s retail work, finding "bad lighting, inadequate ventilation, [and] squalid toilet and lunchroom facilities," on top of "long hours, extremely low pay, brutal and humiliating discipline, fines for infractions of rules, and prohibitions on the use of legally mandated seats even when they were provided."[1] Public-facing department store clerks enjoyed a higher social standing than domestic, laundry, and factory workers, but they often received lower wages and worked longer hours. Women working in department stores were also expected to maintain their hair and makeup, manicured nails, and stylish shoes and dress with their own funds, drawn from their already meager wages. At the turn of the twentieth century, WTUL organizer Rose Schneiderman had worked for three years as a department store "salesgirl," before abandoning retail for better-paying factory work—much to her mother's chagrin.[2]

Despite numerous NCL and WTUL campaigns and an array of state and federal labor laws over the ensuing decades, an investigation of New York City department stores in the 1930s found that employers had broken at least four laws regulating sanitary conditions, including one that prohibited the common use of a drinking glass. According to one worker, "Sixty girls drink out of one glass."³ Little had changed, even in the era of the New Deal. Without enforcement, labor laws were of little value to working women, whether they were sewing garments in sweatshops, or selling those clothes to the public.

In this context, in December 1934, workers at Ohrbach's and Klein's department stores in New York launched what became a five-month strike, demanding a pay raise, a forty-hour workweek, and an end to discrimination for union activity. Striking workers employed a variety of creative tactics to disrupt business as usual. At Klein's, workers allegedly released mice, creating an unsanitary—and perhaps frightening—environment for shoppers. On another occasion, the union gave children balloons emblazoned with the slogan "Don't Buy at Ohrbach's!"⁴ When management tried to take them away, the children and their mothers protested with tears and shaming. In January 1935, striking Ohrbach's cashiers chained themselves to chairs at a Waldorf-Astoria gala attended by storeowner Nathan Ohrbach, New York City Mayor Fiorello LaGuardia, and 1,700 other guests. Sympathetic wealthy allies had provided their tickets and fine gowns, allowing the undercover activists to enter surreptitiously. At the opportune moment, they then revealed their true identities, telling the gala audience that Ohrbach could afford to donate thousands of dollars to charity only because he paid his workers so poorly.⁵

Despite their efforts, strikers were unable to shut down the stores, and the New York Supreme Court granted Ohrbach's an injunction that limited pickets. Whenever more than three workers walked on the line, police responded with violence and arrests. With the strike in peril, the Department Store Employees Union put out a call for immediate assistance.⁶

Two of the groups that responded offered to use their social standing to stave off the police. One was a group of Catholic nuns and priests who carried signs with blunt messages of divine backing, notably "God Supports the Strikers."⁷ The other was a group of activists wearing the garb of society ladies. During an unlawfully large picket in front of the department store in 1935, a Rolls Royce pulled up. Assuming that its passengers were wealthy patrons, police rushed to make a path through the picket line. Instead, the two women who emerged from the car announced that they were members of the League of Women Shoppers, and that they had come to join the protest. Their signs read, "This dress was not bought at Ohrbach's where 45 employees are locked out," and "Use your buying power for justice."⁸

The priests and nuns may have brought God to the fight, but the league brought celebrity and glamour. Over the course of the next decade and a half, spanning the Great Depression and US involvement in World War II, the League of Women Shoppers (LWS) mobilized more than twenty-five thousand middle-class and wealthy women in twenty US cities. Among the group's many famous members were actresses Peggy Wood, Stella Adler, and Frances Farmer, as well as fashion designer Elizabeth Hawes. As part of the period's Popular Front, the LWS wove popular culture with economic justice, providing social prestige and media attention to strikes and other campaigns across the country. Activists in the LWS were experts at attracting publicity, but their social status did not provide complete immunity, and LWS members were arrested regularly. In one notable case, a judge berated eight members, ages twenty-four to thirty, telling them they "should be home knitting" instead of picketing businesses.[9] Generally, however, police and company security balked at attacking the socialites of the LWS, just as they had with WTUL and NCL activists—allowing strikers and their allies to press forward.[10]

The 1920s and 1930s offered many new opportunities for American women. After decades of activism from suffragists, the 19th Amendment finally extended voting rights to most white women. Progressive Era reforms also included publicly funded schools for children and increased access to higher education for women. By the 1930s, women made up 40 percent of the US college population, with the majority attending coeducational campuses. LIFE magazine framed this access as uniquely American and "a magnificent comment on US civilization."[11] In 1919, reform groups also succeeded in pushing for a Women's Bureau within the Department of Labor, headed first by Mary Anderson and then by Frieda Miller—both key figures in the WTUL. Frances Perkins of the NCL, meanwhile, made history as the first woman member of a US presidential cabinet, becoming Roosevelt's secretary of Labor in 1933. Progress for women, however slow and incremental, seemed undeniable on many fronts.[12]

Unrealistic hopes that after securing the vote, women would then "purify the cities, abolish child labor, clean up politics, [and] end all wars," however, quickly unraveled.[13] Women's growing integration into American public life was not all "magnificent" accomplishments. Greater attention is focused on the "Rosie the Riveters" of the 1940s, but women also flooded into factories to produce war materials after the United States entered World War I in 1917. While suffragists from the National Women's Party picketed outside of the White House, others, like Carrie Chapman Catt,

2.1 League of Women Shoppers picket outside of Ohrbach's Department Store during the 1934 strike. Courtesy of Nora Mitchell Sanborn.

pledged to support President Woodrow Wilson and the war in exchange for his party's commitment to woman suffrage. Women proved not to be the pacifist influence that earlier suffragists had predicted and were instead integral to the gruesome war effort. Propaganda in the United States highlighted their efforts via the Red Cross, victory gardens, and factory work. In 1923, when the newly re-established Ku Klux Klan began accepting women as members, thousands enthusiastically welcomed the chance to become leaders in maintaining Christian white supremacy. The Klan's ranks ultimately ballooned into the millions, and its open hostility toward African Americans, Jews, immigrants, and organized labor was reflected in widespread violence and in the halls of government—notably including federal immigration restrictions.[14]

The rollbacks, polarization, and repression of the 1920s, though severe, were not complete departures from previous decades. Many precursors could be seen not just in the clashes between Progressive Era activists and their opponents, but also within movements themselves—including among women. For example, while disenfranchisement theoretically created common cause for American women, the suffrage movement itself was segregated, and many elite, white women joined it in order to uphold racist and classist structures of power—a goal that they ultimately achieved. For decades after the 19th Amendment's passage, poll taxes, literacy tests, and citizenship requirements prevented many poor women and women of color—including those ineligible for citizenship, such as Indigenous and Asian American women—from voting. Many African American families migrated north around World War I, but in 1940, more than three-quarters of the country's Black population remained in the Jim Crow South, where the voting rights of the 15th and 19th Amendments went unfulfilled.[15]

While Progressives had often been able to cross barriers of class in the suffrage movement, they had routinely sidestepped—and, at times, even embraced—segregation and racism in the interest of expediency, or out of conviction. One national suffrage organization, for example, officially supported "state's rights" in an attempt to mollify white Southerners. At a major national suffrage parade scheduled for the day before President Woodrow Wilson's 1913 inauguration, the "southern strategy" again sacrificed the inclusion, and dignity, of Black women—who were required to march at the back of the parade instead of with their state delegations. Even among Progressive activists who would not have considered themselves racist, prioritizing narrow reforms, such as suffrage and protective legislation, over racial equality ultimately undermined their moral authority—and their hopes of a more just society. The Popular Front, which emerged in the 1930s, carried the torch for some Progressive projects, but the movement did so with a far more expansive vision of solidarity, crossing not only class lines, but racial lines, as well.[16]

During the Great Depression, marriage, birth, and divorce rates all declined. More than half of wage-earning women worked more than fifty hours per week, and women's average annual pay was about half of men's. The percentage of women working outside of the home steadily increased throughout the 1930s, particularly for married women—somewhat controversially. As historian Alice Kessler-Harris notes, most American school districts at the time hired only single women as teachers, and half fired women if they got married. Illegal and self-induced abortions were common regardless of age, marital status, religion, race, or class—despite sensationalized media coverage that highlighted the deaths of young, unmarried women.[17]

The widespread hunger, homelessness, and desperation of the Depression ultimately made it a fertile moment for labor organizing and for building political momentum for New Deal reforms. At the same time, however, the context was also ripe for those wanting to take advantage of the desperation, including employers who were seeking cheap labor. In 1933, *Nation's Business*, a publication of the US Chamber of Commerce, published an exposé about new "variations" on the sweatshop, where girls worked sixty-four-hour weeks for $6.96—and were told to drink toilet water and eat their lunches surrounded by rat poison. "This sort of exploitation," the magazine warned, "is spreading, both geographically and into industries where it has never before appeared."[18] This trend captured some of the contradictions of the period. Federal reforms provided relief to many Americans, but their shortcomings—including deliberately leaving many other Americans out—set the stage for a massive clash between industry and the working classes.

The New Deal was a triumph for progressive reformers and the labor movement many decades in the making, but it produced mixed results for women. On the one hand, because they were already the worst-paid workers, minimum wage standards from the National Recovery Administration and, later, Fair Labor Standards Act, disproportionately benefited women. However, they did not apply to about half of wage-earning women. As political scientist Katherine Rader demonstrates, overlap between industry desires to keep down labor costs, AFL organizing priorities, politicians' preferences—and white supremacy—led to carve-outs that excluded millions of Americans, notably including agricultural workers and domestic workers, from many New Deal benefits. Further, New Deal legislation actually required employers in many industries to pay women significantly lower wages than men, and women faced major barriers to accessing New Deal jobs programs. Of the four million people employed by the Civilian Works Administration in 1934, for example, only three hundred thousand were women. Likewise, the Civil Conservation Corps employed and housed 2.5 million young men and just eight thousand women. To get those jobs, women had to be heads of households, and they were still paid less than men. The Works Progress Administration paid men five dollars per day and women just three. In short, despite some gains from the New Deal, most women wage earners continued to face discriminatory hiring practices and take home extremely low pay.[19]

Perhaps the clearest benefit for women during the Great Depression was in unionization, boosted by a 1934 strike wave and the passage of the 1935 National Labor Relations Act. The ILGWU, the union at the center of the 1909 Uprising of 20,000, counted only forty thousand total members in 1933. Within two years, though, that number had ballooned to two hundred thousand—almost half of them women—making it the third largest union in the AFL. Though most leadership positions were still reserved for men, the ILGWU boasted one woman vice president on its executive board—Rose Posetta, who had attended the Bryn Mawr Summer School for Women Workers in Industry. Generally, the Congress of Industrial Organizations (CIO), formed in 1935 as an alternative to the AFL, was much more dedicated to organizing women. Nationwide, between 1929 and 1939, the number of women in unions more than tripled—evidence of many struggles and many victories.[20]

The organizations that were formed during the Progressive Era continued to campaign for worker justice, but some, like the WTUL, saw their numbers and resources dwindling as the Great Depression began. Others shifted from labor organizing to policy change. The NCL, for example, focused on passing the Fair Labor Standards Act—the 1938 New Deal law that mandated a minimum wage and overtime pay. As the WTUL's influence declined, younger activists sought new avenues for participation in labor disputes, and they found it in the Popular Front—a loose network that included workers, union organizers, civil rights activists, students, artists, writers, clergy, and more. Famed playwright Arthur Miller, a student at the University of Michigan during the 1930s, wrote that while previous generations of college students spent their time at football games with

2.2 Striking women picketing a textile mill in Greensboro, Georgia, 1941. Jack Delano, Farm Security Administration, Library of Congress.

their fraternities, his cohort "thirsted for another kind of action, and we took great pleasure in the sit-down strikes in Flint and Detroit.... We saw a new world coming every third morning."[21] Though most of the demands of the period were politically moderate, the Popular Front, as a coalition of socialists and communists as well as New Deal liberals, was generally more left leaning than its Progressive predecessors. The movement adopted a broader understanding of solidarity—among workers and among women—and organized against unrestrained capitalism as well as fascism, white supremacy, and militarism.[22]

The labor movement, and the Popular Front more broadly, offered many Americans a hopeful alternative to the bleak misery of Depression-era poverty. Union membership was on the rise, particularly with the growing influence of the CIO, and excitement for the "new world coming every third morning" could be seen in events throughout the country. According to union organizer Beatrice Lumpkin, "[In 1937], the labor movement was exploding with the energy of hope. Conditions were ripe for a huge increase in union membership. Communist-led hunger marches to state capitals had aroused the fighting spirit of working families. The veterans' Bonus March to Washington, DC radicalized thousands more.... These struggles, and passage of fair labor laws, created a pro-union climate."[23] The period's many strikes, protests, and other clashes—thousands each year during the 1930s—included a massive strike by four hundred thousand textile workers that spanned from Alabama to Maine, as well as strikes by department store workers from Detroit, to San Francisco, to Orbach's and Klein's in New York. Militant workers, supported by socialist groups and the Communist Party (CP), organized citywide general strikes in San Francisco, Minneapolis, and Toledo in 1934, setting the stage for a more aggressive and democratic labor movement. This climate also fostered a more comprehensive approach to anti-sweatshop activism—one that examined and highlighted the exploitive conditions of workplaces far beyond garment factories. The LWS served as one of its standard bearers.

The LWS was formed in New York in late 1934 amid the strike at Ohrbach's. Chapters soon sprouted in cities all over the country, including Chicago, Washington, DC, Atlanta, Saint Louis, and Pittsburgh. The group produced a handbook that gave guidance to women who wanted to form their own chapters, offering a "how to" checklist for recruiting members, fundraising, and organizing successful campaigns. Its many suggestions included, "Don't overlook any channel for publicity." In addition to encouraging local chapters to build alliances with churches, trade unions, and civic organizations, the handbook also suggested drawing in supporters with "teas or evening parties" featuring prestigious hosts or guests of honor, at which LWS literature could be distributed. In 1939, the Saint Louis chapter took the advice to heart by hosting a public picnic and screening of a Charlie Chaplin film at a prominent local residence.[24]

Drawing inspiration from the NCL and WTUL, the LWS embraced a multipronged, consumer-driven strategy to improve the lives of American working people. The group organized actions and campaigns focused on pressuring employers rather than organizing women workers or fighting for protective legislation—tasks already being spearheaded by other organizations. While the LWS often worked hand-in-hand with other groups—referring to the NCL as a "sister organization"—their strategies for achieving worker justice were different.[25] When asked to explain what made them unique, the LWS offered, "Other consumer organizations are not equipped to function where immediate action is required in a labor dispute. They concern themselves primarily with legislative action or with quality standards and prices."[26] The LWS aimed to be responsive, confrontational, and class-conscious—and to stay in its own lane.

Like the WTUL, the group was action-oriented, and—at the request of workers—its members were a constant presence on picket lines, at protests, and in jail cells afterward. The group also raised funds for strike relief and provided grocery baskets for striking workers—as well as toys for their children—during holiday seasons. The LWS also had a research component that paralleled the work of the NCL. When contacted by workers in labor disputes, the group conducted careful investigations, attempting to interview both labor and management, before reaching any conclusions. Investigators then published their findings, along with action recommendations, in LWS newsletters. After members read the reports, members could choose, for example, to boycott a particular business, donate money to strike relief, walk on a picket line, or write a letter to the management.[27]

The LWS was particularly adept at producing propaganda that would reach the reader both emotionally and practically. The group readily used the term "sweatshop" and warned shoppers that, "Unless you KNOW where and how to buy, your dollar helps keep children overworked and undernourished."[28] The Chicago chapter used this hook for recruitment, inviting local women to a panel about the conditions in garment factories, featuring two union organizers, an employer, and a member of the LWS's investigating committee. The invitation reads, "Are cheap dresses necessarily made by sweated labor? That question, which has bothered all of us who are bargain-hunters by choice or necessity, will be answered at our next meeting."[29] As its target audience were women shoppers—many of them mothers—the language of child labor and sweatshops had a specific power, linking gender roles, ethics, and history. However, rather than merely guilt shoppers, the LWS tried to educate them on conditions in particular industries or at particular businesses and steer them toward actions that would benefit workers. Though paralleling the work of the NCL in many ways, as part of the Popular Front, the LWS more clearly advocated solidarity in a growing workers' movement—not just maternal obligation.

Borrowing from liberal New Deal arguments, the group also tried to link middle-class members' prosperity to blue-collar worker justice, reminding members that most Americans were economically vulnerable during the Great Depression. The LWS argued that if the wives of doctors and storeowners fought for better working conditions and wages for mill and factory workers, those workers, in turn, would have more purchasing power. In step with the general principles of the New Deal, LWS activists argued, in effect, that the economy was a collective pursuit—that a rising

2.3 "Have You Forgotten?" League of Women Shoppers pamphlet. League of Women Shoppers Papers, Sophia Smith Special Collections, Smith College.

tide would raise all boats. The Atlanta chapter explained that the mission of the LWS was "to utilize the buying power of the community for the purpose of raising the general standards of merchandising methods for the benefit of the whole community."³⁰ While its members were often relatively secure, the LWS also warned that comfortable conditions could also change if the United States did not shift to a more equitable distribution of wealth through union recognition, enforcement of New Deal standards, and ethical behavior from consumers.³¹

In addition to supporting workers by highlighting labor disputes publicly, the LWS also found ways for women to make changes in their own lives. Recognizing that women did between 85 and 90 percent of household purchasing, the group appealed to its members as ethical consumers, noting that even a low-income housewife could make a difference in the fight against "starvation wages and sweatshop conditions."³² For example, a number of locals worked on implementing the union label to designate which goods were made under fair conditions, including "no unsanitary conditions, no child labor, and no home work."³³ The LWS also worked with the NCL and WTUL on a survey to investigate goods sold in New York department stores, as an expansion of the NCL's white label campaign a generation earlier. The study found that, while some of the high-end goods bore a union label, "practically none" [of] the lower-end merchandise"

> **I AM A CUSTOMER OF THIS STORE**
> AND PROTEST AGAINST
> THE SALE OF BERKSHIRE STOCKINGS
>
> **BERKSHIRE EMPLOYEES ARE ON STRIKE**
> RESPECT THE RIGHTS OF LABOR
> AND THE
> DEMANDS OF YOUR CUSTOMERS
> **I have stopped buying Berkshire Hosiery**
> **YOU stop selling it.**
> ⬛357

2.4 League of Women Shoppers Calling Card. Jessie Lloyd O'Connor Papers, Sophia Smith Special Collections, Smith College.

contained the worker-friendly designation. With the belief that the union label was a guarantee for good labor conditions in sanitary environments, the three groups launched a joint campaign for the label in 1938.[34]

With characteristic pizazz and bravado, members of the LWS advocated for the label by leaving calling cards in stores that did not carry union-made products. One such card read, "I came in to buy union made crackers. [I] did not see the Bakers' and Confectioners' Union label. That is why I walked out. I will call again."[35] By leaving a card, they could show management that shoppers supported workers' right to belong to a union—and that there was a price attached to the decision to carry nonunion goods. The Los Angeles chapter encouraged its members to patronize union shops and buy union-made goods even if nonunion companies provided the same wages and conditions. They believed workers not only needed better wages, but also a seat at the table—a belief that would be echoed by workers in the twenty-first century.[36]

Many LWS campaigns were coordinated at the national level, but chapters operated autonomously, allowing each to focus on issues and disputes specific to its own community. In 1936, for example, members of the New York chapter picketed outside of a local beauty shop, wearing bath towels on their heads to draw middle-class customers' attention to poor working conditions in the salons. The Chicago chapter, meanwhile, supported a

Newspaper Guild strike against the *Chicago Tribune* in 1938, and the Hollywood chapter supported striking Disney animators during a labor dispute three years later. The Miami and Atlanta locals developed campaigns for safer, ethically processed milk, leading Miami members to organize a milk boycott in 1946. In short, LWS chapters maintained a constant wave of locally relevant activism.[37]

As much as the LWS focused on purchasing power and economic privilege, though, the group's strategy for countering the power of businesses and government was rooted in wielding prestige. The group actively recruited nationally recognized figures in politics, the arts, academia, and journalism. Aline Davis Hays, for example, had years of experience merging activism with creative pursuits. Before she was elected as the LWS's first national president in 1938, she had written a suffrage pageant performed at Carnegie Hall, organized an art show to be accessible to a working-class audience with free admission, and worked as a stylist and textile designer. Lillian Hellman, who served as the group's national vice president, was a prominent playwright and Academy Award nominee.[38]

Early letterhead for the group also carried the endorsements of women who, while accomplished in their own right, were also married to prominent men, such as Leonore Gershwin (Mrs. Ira Gershwin) and activist and scholar Mary Beard (Mrs. Charles Beard). The LWS's prestigious links to Progressive Era activism, meanwhile, included the backing of Louise Waterman Wise (wife of Rabbi Stephen Wise, who had been active in the aftermath of the Triangle Fire) and Mary Phillips Riis, the widow of famed photographer of child labor Jacob Riis. In 1935, LWS Acting Secretary Rebecca Ducker wrote to Ida Tarbell, the famous reformer and journalist, in hopes that she also would lend her name to the group's work. Though Tarbell declined, the group maintained the relationship, including by asking her to distribute strike support information to the Pen and Brush women's gallery the next year.[39]

The group's most important connection, however, was at the top, with First Lady Eleanor Roosevelt, who addressed numerous LWS meetings and featured the group's campaigns in her popular national newspaper column, *My Day*. Just as the NCL had done with Helen Taft, the LWS managed to gain indirect access to the White House.[40]

The LWS's association with celebrities and socialite-activists strengthened its actions, drew public attention, and served as a recruitment tool. Wealthier members also loaned out silk gowns, jewels, and mink coats for the picket lines, in order to draw attention from shoppers and journalists.

While media accounts somewhat disparagingly referred to them as the "Mink Brigade," just as they had to similar Progressive Era pickets, the LWS welcomed the attention. The group's status gave it the power to highlight labor struggles, as the national media often covered their participation on picket lines as a story in itself. One journalist quipped that "A Fifth Ave. picket line today had the Fifth Ave. touch" when members wore mink, imported tweed, and other luxurious fabrics while protesting in front of a Woolworth Department Store in November 1936.[41] In February 1940, *Time* magazine reported that seven members of the LWS—wearing evening wraps, jewels, and orchids—had emerged from a taxicab to relieve picketers in front of a New York restaurant. Perhaps unable to comprehend their motives, the owner attempted to sway them with champagne but was rebuffed. *Time* also noted that just five blocks away from the LWS-supported picket, AFL President William Green had crossed a separate picket line to enter a hotel.[42]

Despite courting press attention, the LWS also confronted media owners directly, for example by supporting a strike at the *American Mercury*, a prominent literary magazine, in 1935—a decision that would later contribute to the group's demise. Within a month of the LWS's formation, members were among fifty-two people arrested for "disorderly conduct" on the *American Mercury* picket line. Attorney Arthur Garfield Hays, who was the husband of LWS President Aline Davis Hays and general counsel to the American Civil Liberties Union, successfully represented all of those arrested. Not only did the magistrate dismiss the charges, she called for a "definite police policy toward demonstrations."[43] The LWS activists' tactics, both on and off the picket lines, emphasized workers' conditions and the unfair advantages given to employers through business-friendly laws and police support.[44]

The group's actions were extensive, moving in concert with the ubiquitous strike activity of the period. In New York, the LWS supported striking shoe store workers, who won union recognition in 1935 after the group reached out to customers. In December 1937, the New Jersey chapter issued a special bulletin updating members on a labor dispute at a local department store over the impending mass layoffs after the holiday rush. In July 1939, the Atlanta chapter responded to a call for assistance by striking clerks, drivers, bakers, and butchers at area supermarkets. The LWS asked its members to write letters to management, to advise friends to shop elsewhere, or to volunteer on the picket line. Several months later, the Atlanta chapter reported on the strike in the group's national newsletter, *The*

2.5 "Women Do 90 Percent of the Buying," League of Women Shoppers pamphlet. Jessie Lloyd O'Connor Papers, Sophia Smith Special Collections, Smith College.

Woman Shopper, boasting, "We say with pride that League of Women Shoppers Members [sic] do not cross picket lines."[45] So while the LWS used the language—and many of the tactics—of its predecessor organizations, its view of sweatshop exploitation was much broader.

Further, by framing shopping as a form of unpaid labor that women performed for their families—that is, not a leisure activity—the LWS treated every strike as a potential boycott and shopping itself as potential strike-breaking. In fact, during a 1934 department store strike in Milwaukee, LWS members arrived to the picket line, and marched through the store, carrying a banner that read, "Customers Are on Strike Too."[46] Investigating working conditions and honoring boycotts and picket lines added to this work—the labor of shopping and of solidarity. With thousands of strikes every year throughout the 1930s, applying this principle reshaped the landscape of consumer activity.

Of the organization's many projects, their campaigns in support of laundry workers and domestic workers are particularly illustrative. As major employers of women of color, both industries were dangerous and hyperexploitative—and largely operated outside the protections of labor laws or unions. During the Uprising of 1909, the WTUL had decried employers' exploitation of racial tensions, but had stopped short of organizing across racial lines. The LWS, however, worked directly with African American women on a range of campaigns. The group offered its support to unions and workers, but only as allies and never as would-be leaders. Recognizing the strategic—and moral—strength that came with language, the LWS and other Popular Front activists also used the terms "sweatshop" and "slavery" pointedly, not to downplay the past but rather as reminders that many American women continued to labor in horrific conditions.

―――

By the 1930s, the steam laundry industry employed more than 250,000 workers in urban areas, as middle-class Americans outsourced this time-consuming chore. The laundries were incredibly hot, and workers sustained burns as well as strained muscles from the repetitive motions. Machines generated dangerous levels of heat and steam, and few employers provided adequate ventilation. Workers reported temperatures as high as 120 degrees in summer months. Fumes from starch and other chemicals burned workers' skin. Workers in industrial laundries, the majority of whom were women, were also subjected to rampant sexual harassment from supervisors. Laundry work had served as an icon of degradation since the 1908 *Muller v. Oregon* decision that upheld the use of protective labor laws for women, and the industry remained resistant to union organizing in the decades prior to the Great Depression. New Deal legislation had included laundry workers, but owners consistently resisted applying minimum wage and maximum hour standards. The LWS labeled laundries a "sweatshop industry," citing unsanitary conditions, dangerous chemicals and machinery, long hours, low wages, abusive management, and racial and gender discrimination.[47]

Historian Jenny Carson writes that laundry employers actively sought out workers who were "structurally disadvantaged by their gender, ethnicity, race, and other variables" that is, workers whom they could pay poorly and work under brutal conditions.[48] In the period around World War I and the Great Migration, African American women steadily replaced European immigrants in many of those jobs. Following decades of openly hostile racial discrimination from industry, the National Urban League promoted this employment as a victory for Black women, an opportunity to finally gain an economic foothold beyond sharecropping and domestic work in the South.[49]

However, it is difficult to overstate just how dangerous the "opportunities" in the laundry industry were in the early twentieth century. In Pennsylvania, laundries were considered the leading source of industrial accidents. In just the first half of 1923, laundry accidents accounted for some 20 percent of the 66,256 workplace accidents reported. In 1920, a Kansas laundry boiler exploded, killing one young woman worker and seriously injuring several others, causing broken legs, cracked skulls, and "severe internal injuries."[50] The next year, another laundry explosion, in Minnesota, killed one worker and injured four more. In 1928, a laundry explosion in Indiana killed another four women. A year later, a Washington, DC, laundry leaked so much chlorine gas from its bleaching machine that two hundred workers were forced to evacuate. Despite firefighters wearing gas masks, four members of the rescue crew became too sick to return to work. From the cotton fields to the textile factories, and then to the retail outlets and laundries, the manufacturing and maintenance of clothing left a trail of suffering—of broken and dead bodies. The LWS's designation of laundries as a sweated industry was appropriate, though really the entire textile economy bore the defining characteristics of a sweatshop.[51]

In the case of the laundries, the industry had also been quite active in maintaining its sweatshop conditions. In 1936, on the heels of the US Supreme Court's *A. L. A. Schechter Poultry Corp. v. United States* decision, which sided with business owners and invalidated early New Deal regulations, the court then overturned New York state's 1933 minimum wage law for women and children in *Morehead v. New York*. The *Morehead* decision was another victory for business owners and, specifically, laundry owner Joseph Tipaldo, who had been arrested for illegally underpaying his workers. *Time* magazine reported that some fifty thousand dollars of Tipaldo's legal fees—more than a million dollars today—had been covered by the New York State Hotel Association, whose members were major laundry clients.[52]

The following year, laundry workers nationwide launched a wave of strikes and union drives. In March 1937, five thousand workers in Brooklyn went on strike demanding a twenty-five-cent wage increase. In June, a picket in front of a New Jersey laundry was broken up by firefighters, police, and private security with clubs and tear gas. That same month, more than four hundred striking laundry workers shut down a dozen dry cleaning plants in Washington, DC, demanding a forty-hour workweek and a minimum wage.[53]

In this context, the LWS published a sixty-two-page booklet called "Consider the Laundry Workers." Members Jane Filley, a writer, and Therese Mitchell, a photographer, spent a year researching the New York laundry industry, interviewing workers, and compiling facts about relevant labor legislation. Among the specific issues they confronted were employers' efforts to exploit racial tensions to their benefit. For example, one African American laundry worker said:

> In our laundry they had only white girls first. Then later they started taking on colored girls but this is the way they did it: a colored girl would come in and the boss said, "We can't take you on. The white girls don't want to work with you." The colored girl would start to go and he'd say, "I'll take you, but you got to work for less money than the white girls." They incited one against the other and later they cut the white girls, saying they could get colored girls cheaper.[54]

"Consider the Laundry Workers" encouraged readers to visit laundries to witness working conditions firsthand and, of course, to use their collective buying power to pressure bad bosses. Though the ultimate goal was unionization, the booklet also gave tips to ease conditions for workers in the meantime. Mondays were popularly known as "washday," creating an uneven workweek, with excessively long workdays on Sundays and Mondays and little work to do on other days of the week. Paralleling the NCL's early holiday shopping campaigns, the LWS encouraged its members to be more flexible with their washdays, thus preventing a weekly bottleneck.[55]

Publication of "Consider the Laundry Workers" received widespread national media coverage. In her nationally syndicated column, Eleanor Roosevelt observed that her readers would be interested in the pamphlet "because laundries are so closely connected to [their] homes."[56] A New Jersey newspaper also reviewed the pamphlet, praising it for bringing attention to a dangerous industry that too often went overlooked. In Saint Louis, hometown of pamphlet author Jane Filley, a local newspaper praised her investigative approach, detailed several of the workers' stories and complaints, and gave information on a local LWS event that Filley was hosting. As far away as Alberta, Canada, reporters lauded Filley and Mitchell's thorough research—which had included interviews with 102 workers at fifty-four laundries—as well as their conclusion that union membership offered the best solution to the workers' many grievances.⁵⁷

The LWS's Washington, DC, chapter also investigated the ongoing dispute at the twelve laundries in their city and found low wages, long and uneven hours, inadequate ventilation, and poor sanitation—including the disgusting and unhygienic use of a single shared dipper and barrel for water breaks. After distributing a special bulletin, reminding members, "the League cannot take a summer vacation," the LWS donated relief funds, loaned cars to collect and deliver food, and attended union meetings in support of the laundry workers.⁵⁸

In November 1937, just months after the LWS published "Consider the Laundry Workers," laundry owners in Chicago signed a union contract impacting more than twenty-two thousand workers. Meanwhile, a strike by nearly two thousand laundry workers in Cincinnati compelled the payment of thousands of dollars in back wages owed under Ohio minimum wage laws. Offered a compromise to end the strike the next month, the workers rejected the proposal because it did not guarantee a closed, union shop.⁵⁹

Jenny Carson notes that attempts to organize New York laundry workers in the early decades of the twentieth century had been unsuccessful in part due to divisions among workers along lines of gender, race, and ethnicity. In the 1930s, however, with backing from the WTUL, efforts by Black and communist laundry workers began winning piecemeal concessions through "spontaneous work stoppages, impromptu walkouts," putting "'stink bombs' under the doors of strikebreakers," and, in one case, chaining themselves to a hotel that was using a laundry where workers were on strike.⁶⁰

In 1937, amid the national laundry workers' push, the Amalgamated Clothing Workers of America (ACWA) hired thirty young organizers. By 1941, the union had secured contracts for most of New York's thirty thousand laundry workers, nearly doubling their wages and establishing paid holidays, daily breaks, and overtime pay. The campaign was spearheaded by the workers and ACWA organizers, but the LWS's role—elevating workers' voices and involving consumers—demonstrates both the collaborative nature of organizing during the period and an awareness of businesses' multiple pressure points.⁶¹

In occupations that primarily employed women of color, workers were typically denied even the illusion of decent labor standards. Without minimum wages, overtime pay, Social Security, or workers' compensation insurance for injuries, domestic workers—who made up about one-fifth of all wage-earning women and about half of whom were Black or Latina—may as well have been living in a different century than many of their counterparts. Employers, usually white women, were customers, and they wanted to pay as little as possible for these services. Domestics were also expected to work beyond their scheduled hours if their assigned tasks were not completed. Katie Geneva Cannon, who worked as a domestic in the home of southern textile mill workers, recalled:

> They would pay you two dollars for two hours' worth of work, but you had a list of things, and if it took you longer than that, that was your business. All the work they wanted you to do, you could never do in two hours. You had to wash the clothes, hang them on the line and iron them, wash the floors, do the things like clean the refrigerator or clean out the cabinets, and all these things you did to prove that you were worthy of the job. You never just did what you were asked. You always did a little extra.[62]

Cannon was also expected to care for her employer's four children, leaving her little time with her own family. That her employers were themselves workers in another highly exploitive industry says much about the race, class, and gender politics of the period. Without daycares, having a domestic worker for childcare was a necessity for many working-class white families, who relied on at least two paychecks. But after paying their other bills, very little was left to pay even the most meager of wages to the Black women who took care of their children and their homes.[63]

Like the turn-of-the-century sweatshops that operated out of workers' own tenement homes, domestic workers were isolated in individual residences, making traditional union organizing models ineffective. Like day laborers today, domestic workers were also precariously employed and at the mercy of potential employers, often securing temporary employment only by agreeing to work for excessively long hours and low wages. Though the language of the "sweatshop" was not commonly linked to domestic work, journalists and organizers in the 1930s did use the term "slave market" to describe the informal spaces in the Bronx where housewives would hire domestics from pools of the desperately unemployed.[64] A 1938 exposé on domestic work by *The Nation*, reprinted in mainstream newspapers across the country, documented seventy-two-hour work weeks and the lowest wage of any industry. An organizer from the Young Women's

Christian Association (YWCA) said that the relationship between "mistress and maid" was from a bygone era but still persisted, as both wealthy and middle-class women squeezed their domestics for maximum work at minimum pay. Others agreed, describing the homes where domestics worked as "miniature plantations."[65] The *Pittsburgh Courier*, a prominent Black newspaper, wrote that domestics, which accounted for at least one-third of wage-earning African Americans, lived "on the very margin of existence."[66]

In New York, much of the frontline organizing of domestic workers was spearheaded by Dora Lee Jones, executive secretary of the Domestic Workers' Union (DWU). The DWU circulated petitions in support of workplace standards, recruited progressive clergy, and invited the Black press to report on the Bronx "slave market." The union also developed cross-class alliances with groups such as the WTUL, YWCA, and LWS, making specific demands on their involvement, while ensuring that the workers' voices were at the forefront.[67]

As Jones told Vivian Morris of the Federal Writers' Project in 1939, the DWU contacted rabbis and white Protestant and Catholic clergy, asking them to encourage their congregations to "stop hiring the girls from the slave marts at starvation wages."[68] Instead, the DWU recommended that parishioners designate and supervise spaces in churches or community homes that could be used for hiring and, ideally, establishing minimum wage standards. At the same time, the union also wrote to Black ministers, asking them to encourage their own congregations not to undermine their fellow workers by going to the slave marts or accepting such low wages. By involving the community, workers, and employers, Jones hoped to eradicate the slave marts, which she called "a bane to New York humanitarianism."[69]

In 1937, at the request of the DWU, the New York chapter of the LWS formed a committee to investigate one of the corners where white women "bargain[ed] for domestic workers as they do for their vegetables."[70] Committee members went undercover, pretending to be potential employers. Their whiteness served as a passport to other white women, who spoke openly about their desire for cheap help while "shopping for domestics." LWS investigators commonly heard these "shoppers" longing for "the good days when a bargain could be struck at 25 cents an hour."[71]

The next year, the LWS announced the formation of a new Harlem Neighborhood chapter, with the explicit aim of "fighting for a minimum wage and hour law for domestic workers." Meanwhile, the education committee of the Washington, DC, chapter organized a series of lectures for its members, featuring laundry, domestic, and restaurant workers.[72]

In 1940, efforts by the LWS prompted the Women's Bureau of the US Department of Labor to request that the group investigate the working conditions of Washington, DC, domestics. After eight months of research, the LWS published its findings in a monograph, "Household Occupation in the District of Columbia: Why Is the Household Employee So Heavily Out-Weighed in the Scale of Security?" Their research showed that of the two million women employed as domestic workers from 1940 to 1941, half were African American. Unsurprisingly, the study recommended that unions would be one of the most practical solutions for combating exploitive conditions. Additionally, as a more immediate form of solidarity, the LWS compiled best practices that their members could voluntarily implement as employers, such as reasonable standards for maximum hours and minimum wages.[73]

In March 1939, Nina Collier, the chair of the National Legislation Committee of the LWS, wrote a letter to the editor of *The Washington Post* on behalf of the LWS, WTUL, National Negro Congress, and several other Popular Front groups. Collier had been trying to lobby a congressional committee to expand Social Security benefits to domestics and farmworkers and had prepared testimony to demonstrate their dire need. Denied the opportunity to introduce it, Collier protested to the committee members and to the *Post*, noting that the 2,500,000 workers in question, who accounted for 5 percent of American wage earners, faced tremendous economic insecurity. The LWS, working closely with the NCL and WTUL, similarly tried to lobby the New York legislature to extend workers' compensation to full-time domestic workers.[74]

The LWS's solidarity campaigns with laundry and domestic workers aligned them with working women across race and class lines in ways that their predecessor organizations had been unable to. As historian Landon Storrs notes, the LWS was a cornerstone group in a "left-feminist consumer movement . . . [that] challenged white supremacy," including by protesting stores that refused to hire Black women.[75]

Rather than spreading out their efforts to include the decade's many battles over steel, auto, and textile union contracts, the LWS focused its energies on occupations primarily held by women. In doing so, the group connected its members to the women who produced and sold them goods and services, and who cleaned their homes and took care of their children. The LWS's campaigns were simultaneously rooted in Popular Front labor solidarity, broadening definitions of labor feminism, and antiracism.

By highlighting many of the problems associated with industrial capitalism and white supremacy, the LWS empowered middle-class women to make changes in their own lives and to advocate for better working conditions and wages. The group stands out from other consumer groups of the era both because of its sophisticated understanding of solidarity, and its members' willingness to put their own bodies on the line—often on very short notice.

The LWS embraced a variety of tactics. Like the NCL, LWS members were scholar-activists who researched and published reports meant to sway both politicians and the shopping public. Members also regularly walked on picket lines and were willing to get arrested—in part because they knew their arrests would prompt media attention. In 1935, twenty-four members were arrested while picketing May's Department Store in Brooklyn. The next year, LWS members refused to abandon another Brooklyn picket line—despite police warnings—and used their subsequent arrests and convictions to critique the "unlimited discretion of the police."[76] Describing violence and intimidation during an Alabama labor dispute with Goodyear Tires as "labor terrorism," the LWS sent one of its members to investigate "because more and more women buy automobiles and automobile tires."[77] Using a tactic that would be adopted nearly a century later in efforts to pressure Amazon, LWS members also bought stock in the Borden Dairy Company and disrupted its shareholders' meeting during a labor dispute.[78]

The LWS's risk-taking was not mere charity, and it produced results. After the speedy settlement of a strike at a 1935 New York shoe store, the union sent a thank-you note to the group, proclaiming "the marvelous support of the League has been instrumental in securing working conditions for all Ansonio salesmen, far more favorable than prior to the strike."[79]

Solidarity with workers was both the LWS's mission and its undoing, however, as the group was targeted by former foes during the early years of the Second Red Scare. Every LWS campaign created an enemy, and many business interests sought to use their resources to discredit the group as dangerous radicals. In August 1938, J. B. Matthews gave his first testimony to the House Committee on Un-American Activities (HUAC), chaired by Congressman Martin Dies. Matthews, a former executive at Consumers' Research (CR), charged a number of prominent groups with communistic activities, including the LWS. Members believed that Matthews was seeking revenge for their support during a workers' strike at CR several years earlier—a strike that humiliated him personally and cost him a great deal financially.[80]

Matthews testified that the Communist Party had deliberately formed consumer organizations to serve as fronts. As proof, he offered his own bonafides—his "long and wide first-hand experience, which includes a personal acquaintance with almost every prominent radical in America."[81] In his prepared statement for the Dies Committee, Matthews also claimed that he had served as a consultant during the early years of the LWS, making him a whistleblower—if only in his mind. Following his testimony, however, Aline Davis Hays, national president of the LWS, sent a telegram to Dies explaining the bitter history between Matthews, CR, and the LWS—and making clear that he had never been a member, let alone an advisor. Though Hays offered to appear before the committee to give testimony refuting Matthews, the committee showed no interest.[82]

Instead, Matthews's unquestioned, one-sided testimony was quickly leaked to the media. With headlines like "Dies Investigator Says Reds Utilize Consumer Groups," corporate-owned newspapers gave Matthews's accusations legitimacy and undercut the LWS.[83] In May 1939, the *Chicago Tribune*—against whom the LWS had also supported a strike—published a scathing article condemning the group for "conducting an ingenious campaign of intimidation to restrain criticism and even coerce support" for the New Deal, particularly the Wagner Act and National Labor Relations Board, making clear that Roosevelt's prolabor legislation was the real target.[84] Several LWS chapters struggled to retain membership in the wake of this Red-baiting, and the Atlanta local disbanded in February 1940.

As a Popular Front organization, the LWS attracted not only liberals, but also leftists. For example, before joining the LWS, humorist Dorothy Parker had been arrested at a 1927 rally in support of anarchists Nicola Sacco and Bartolomeo Vanzetti, prompting the FBI to open what became a one-thousand-page file documenting her commitment to civil rights, labor, and civil liberties, as well as her Hollywood blacklisting. Lillian Hellman, LWS vice president, was also blacklisted by Hollywood after refusing to answer questions from HUAC. Gale Sondergaard, LWS member and actress, also struggled to work after pleading the 5th Amendment in front on HUAC and supporting her husband, *Salt of the Earth* director Herbert Biberman, who was one of the Hollywood Ten jailed for refusing to cooperate with HUAC.[85]

Mary Cornelia Barker, Atlanta LWS chapter vice president, was involved in the intersections of education and labor, serving as the president of the Atlanta teachers union and cofounding the Southern Summer School for Women Workers in Industry. Barker also fought against the prosecution of Angelo Herndon, an African American man who was arrested and convicted of insurrection in 1932 for attempting to organize Black workers in Atlanta.[86] Jessie Lloyd O'Connor, Chicago LWS member and general secretary, meanwhile, worked as a labor journalist for the Federated Press, initially writing from Moscow, before returning to Chicago and staying at Hull House for a time. After a Federated Press journalist was shot in the leg covering the 1931 coal miners' strike in Harlan County, Kentucky, O'Connor traveled south to replace him. Like the NCL and WTUL activists who worked both in those organizations and in suffrage groups, many LWS members were lifelong activists. O'Connor, for example, continued to participate in pacifist, labor, and feminist causes until her death in 1989.[87]

In short, many LWS members, including national and local leaders, undoubtedly had communist sympathies. However, the organization was not sponsored by the Communist Party, and its success, like that of the larger Popular Front, was rooted not in its radicalism but rather in its ability to bring together a broad-based coalition in support of workers. Undoubtedly, it was this solidarity that HUAC and its backers feared, not the beliefs of various individuals. Because whatever the political leanings of LWS activists were, Matthews and the *Chicago Tribune* had a much more concrete grievance against the group—it had supported labor campaigns that cut into their profits. Red Scare animosity toward the New Deal, for the same reason, was equally transparent.

When novelist, screenwriter, and reformed ex-radical Rena Vale testified before the Dies Committee, she condemned both the Popular Front and the New Deal, despite her active participation in each. Vale's previous employment with Works Progress Administration programs, including the Federal Writers' Project and Federal Theater Project, her membership in the Communist Party, and her involvement in various Popular Front groups made her an insider like Matthews—an ideal witness for Dies. In March 1940, she penned a sensational editorial entitled "Stalin over California," for *The American Mercury*—another publication whose striking workers the LWS had supported—which the *Los Angeles Times* then reprinted. In it, Vale fed the worst fears of American conservatives: "By 1938 the Kremlin's formidable machine in California included the American League for Peace and Democracy and the Anti-Nazi League, which were influential in moviedom, and the League of Women Shoppers, rear guard of the CIO, to say nothing of a number of forums and independent clubs which had been captured and indoctrinated by communists disguised as liberals."[88] In June, Vale told the Dies Committee that she had helped organize the Los

Angeles chapter of the League of Women Shoppers, which she said, "was fostered by the [Communist] party."⁸⁹ She later also claimed that activist and singer Paul Robeson had duped her into joining the Communist Party. For those like Vale and Matthews, who were building new careers as professional anti-communists, the depth of their participation in Popular Front organizations, real or imagined, served as credentials of expertise—and in Vale's case, allowed for equally extensive political rehabilitation. After testifying for the Dies Committee, she went on to work as an investigator for the California Senate Factfinding Subcommittee on Un-American Activities (CUAC).⁹⁰

In 1941, the LWS supported striking Disney animators during a labor dispute. After an investigation by the group's Hollywood chapter, the LWS notified Walt Disney that each chapter nationwide would be receiving a report on the details of the strike. Six years later, Disney retaliated by testifying to HUAC that the League of Women Voters—a completely different organization with a similar name—was "a Commie front organization" that aimed to destroy him. He quickly corrected his misstatement by telegram, clarifying his accusation that the League of Women Shoppers were part of a worldwide communist conspiracy to smear him. Remaining LWS members tried to explain that Disney, like J. B. Matthews, was simply seeking personal revenge against the group, but as a respected member of the American business elite, his statement was taken at face value. His testimony, careless and self-aggrandizing as it was, was one of many that helped bring about the end of the worker justice movement of the 1930s. Disney was later exposed as a secret informant for the Federal Bureau of Investigation.⁹¹

Opposition to the New Deal from industrialists—and attempts to link it to socialism and the Communist Party—had long been brewing. In 1934, anti–New Deal industrialists had founded the American Liberty League, a bipartisan conservative group on a mission to "combat radicalism, preserve property rights, [and] uphold and preserve the Constitution."⁹² In 1935, the group raised nearly $500,000 from key figures in the oil, department store, agricultural, steel, and automotive industries. The group's top supporters were the chemical tycoon Du Pont family, who provided more than $100,000. The group produced numerous anti–New Deal pamphlets, including an objection to the National Labor Relations Act, which the group argued "would do violence to the Constitution" and "stimulate labor strife."⁹³ Among their many criticisms was that collective bargaining rights would lead workers to push for a closed shop.⁹⁴

In 1937, a group of bipartisan conservative politicians wrote the "Conservative Manifesto," objecting to many of the key pieces of the New Deal, including unemployment relief, increased taxes, and support for unions. The position paper served to organize long-term opposition to the New Deal, especially among conservative southern Democrats. Indeed, one of its ten provisions directly called for a "maintenance of states' rights," a demand that would echo throughout the postwar period—and into the twenty-first century.[95]

Media magnates William Randolph Hearst and Robert McCormick, whose newspapers enjoyed a readership of more than thirty million people, also vocally opposed the New Deal. Hearst publicly condemned Roosevelt's plan to increase taxes on the wealthy and corporations, referring to him as "Stalin Delano Roosevelt."[96] McCormick, who owned the widely circulated *Chicago Tribune*, was a top donor to Roosevelt's opponent in 1936 and wrote editorials with titles such as "The Communists Want Roosevelt" and "Mr. Roosevelt Reissues the Communist Manifesto."[97]

Having such a broad, vague mandate allowed ardent New Deal opponent Dies, and later Joseph McCarthy, to set HUAC's agenda on a whim. Far-right activists and businessmen quickly made the committee itself a front group, readily offering their support, providing both testimony and widespread positive media coverage, particularly in Hearst- and McCormick-owned newspapers. Media outlets covered the Dies Committee's hearings in great detail, running stories with salacious headlines. The *Tribune*'s scathing condemnation of the LWS, for example, included five prominent members' names, occupations, and photographs—but neglected to mention the paper's own conflict of interest.[98]

In the aftermath of World War II, with Roosevelt out of the White House, the Republican-led Congress began to roll back the legislation that had helped working families during the 1930s and further leverage the Red Scare to limit the influence of the labor movement and its Popular Front allies. By 1947, HUAC and the US Justice Department had expanded their list of supposed communist organizations in the United States to more than one hundred, including a range of veterans' groups, consumer activists, civil rights and anti-lynching organizations, and labor unions. Their suspicions and accusations reached as high as First Lady Eleanor Roosevelt and Secretary of State Dean Acheson.[99]

In 1949, the LWS disbanded altogether. At that point, there were only one thousand remaining members anyway, down from a peak of nearly twenty-five thousand. The group continued to serve as a bogeyman for the American Right, however. In May 1954, the libertarian magazine *The Freeman* featured an article by Helen Woodward, an original member of the LWS, entitled "How I Joined a Red Front." Woodward, a successful copywriter and advertising executive, had also been a member of the WTUL. By the 1950s, however, Woodward had shifted her political allegiances and become president of the New Jersey chapter of Pro America, a noted "extreme right-wing organization that favor[ed] isolationism."[100]

Published alongside articles condemning labor unions and publicly owned utilities, Woodward's cautionary tale in *The Freeman* presented the LWS as a sinister organization dedicated to furthering the spread of communism. The salacious tagline read, "It all seemed so sociable and high-minded that an anti-communist was drawn into a party-line group. She soon saw danger signals."[101] Woodward wrote that she had joined the LWS to support unions but instead found a group that calculated every decision to achieve notoriety and headlines at the expense of workers and consumers. Condemning the LWS's tactics as "amateurish," she mocked the group's efforts to support organized labor, particularly the Domestic Workers' Union.

In an attempt to distance herself from her past involvement, Woodward boasted that she had actually worked to undermine the LWS board's radical plans from within but felt some shame at having been tricked into supporting a communist front. She also offered tips on how to identify a front group and ultimately concluded, "no group of consumers can be of any help to a labor union."[102] Published seventeen years after her involvement with the LWS, and five years after the group's demise, Woodward's cautionary tale speaks to American capital's obsessive opposition to New Deal policies and with the labor activism of the Great Depression.

For the Right, the LWS's crime of mainstreaming the concerns of workers and empowering consumers was unforgivable. The group had helped make labor solidarity sexy—a demonstration of feminism, political and social awareness, and cultural cachet. By contrast, the second Red Scare promoted a different culture, one that was reactionary, conformist, and unquestioning of government, capital, and conservative gender norms—and that maintained the profits of those at the top.

Within the broader context of the Popular Front, the LWS recruited American women to show their solidarity with workers and to fight for economic justice in their communities. In 1939, Lillian Hellman, LWS national vice president, spoke to the Pittsburgh chapter about women's responsibility for "social and economic problems." She argued that a housewife or professional woman who could "remain indifferent to public problems not related to her own little domain belongs to . . . a bygone age."[103] The LWS believed that middle-class women had an obligation to use their privilege for the greater good, and its members viewed their role as bridging the gap between democracy and capitalism.

The LWS offered its members a variety of options, in part because its membership was not monolithic. It included thousands of women, not just famous actresses, labor leftists, or the First Lady. While some members had inherited wealth, and the organization clearly recruited from the "comfortable class," many others were wage earners themselves, from a variety of backgrounds. San Francisco chapter president Rikee Elsesser, for example, had hitchhiked from New York to California, where she became a hospital administrator and joined a number of Popular Front organizations. Leane Zugsmith, a proletarian novelist and seasoned Popular Front activist, meanwhile, used her skills to research and write about labor disputes for *The Woman Shopper*.[104]

Other members included middle-class women whose family income was vulnerable due to the economic turmoil of the 1930s, such as Alice Lesser Shepard. While Shepard earned excellent grades in high school, her family never considered sending her to college—an expanding, but still rare, prospect for women in the 1920s. Though she helped her husband with the bookkeeping for his store, attended lectures at Columbia, and worked part time for a Broadway agent, she said she still felt "uneducated, inferior in many ways" before joining the New York chapter of the LWS in 1940.[105] Because many members were not exempt from concerns over their own working conditions, there was generally little distance, and thus little paternalism, in the relationships between LWS activists and the workers they supported.

In addition to walking on picket lines and boycotting goods made under exploitative conditions, the LWS also fought exploitation in their own pantries, by choosing goods with a union label and paying domestic workers a living wage. Activists believed in standards that improved working and living conditions, trying to enforce those standards when they were laws, and working to create them for those neglected by New Deal protections. The LWS provided consumers with concrete guidelines so they could "use [their] buying power for justice."[106]

But rather than portraying members of the LWS as women who desired modest reforms to industrial capitalism to end exploitation and sweatshops, HUAC depicted them as communist-infiltrated radicals intent on harming American business interests. The LWS's objective was to encourage consumers to be active in their choices and to demand that workers be respected and treated fairly. The group highlighted many of the problems associated with the Depression-era economy and gave middle-class women the tools necessary to be useful allies for workers. To the ownership class, this was un-American, an affront to their liberty.

The Popular Front's victories—including labor laws, union recognition, and subverting white supremacy—brought millions of Americans into the middle class. It was a generational, if limited, sea change. Over the ensuing decades, additional victories by waves of civil rights, women's rights, antipoverty, and labor struggles created what historian Jefferson Cowie refers to an "extended detour" from business as usual.[107] Some of this activism clearly echoed the LWS and the broader Popular Front, particularly with its emphasis on coalitions and political theater, such as giving balloons to children or wearing bath towels in support of striking workers. In the 1960s and 1970s—long after the Popular Front's demise—solidarity campaigns by students, left-wing clergy, and progressive Democrats notably emerged to offer support for farmworkers, who, like domestic workers, had been deliberately left out of the New Deal.

Capital, meanwhile, looked to overcome its losses, exploit cracks, and seek new opportunities for cheap labor.

3

"SETTLE THE CASE, OR WE'LL BE IN YOUR FACE"

THE WORLDVIEW OF THE GLOBAL JUSTICE MOVEMENT

In 1998, the Smithsonian's National Museum of American History opened an exhibit entitled, *Between a Rock and a Hard Place: A Dialogue on American Sweatshops, 1820 to Present*. Its images and artifacts reflected the nation's early industrial era, recalling the horrors of the 1911 Triangle Fire, as well as the activism of well-known anti-sweatshop figures, such as Eleanor Roosevelt. The exhibit also included a re-creation of a more recent garment factory, which had been raided by federal authorities in 1995. Surrounded by razor wire and patrolled by armed guards, the SK Fashions Factory in the suburban Los Angeles town of El Monte had imprisoned dozens of young, immigrant women from Thailand. Threatened with rape and beatings, they had worked up to eighteen hours a day for as little as seventy cents an hour, while sewing clothes for popular US retailers such as Sears, Macy's, and Niemen Marcus.[1]

The Smithsonian exhibit called into question whether the problem of the American sweatshop had been solved, and even before it opened, it was engulfed in controversy. While Congressman George Miller, a Democrat from California who had launched hearings on the El Monte factory, rallied support for it, Texas Representative Sam Johnson, a Republican and Smithsonian regent, argued that the exhibit was illegitimate because it portrayed sweatshops in a bad light. As Johnson noted without irony, "One of the reasons Newt [Gingrich] appointed me was to keep the historical revisionism under control."[2] Representatives of the apparel industry voiced similar complaints, with one offering, "It is very difficult to put on a sweatshop exhibit that is evenhanded."[3]

By the 1990s, the regulatory regime that had outlawed child labor and created the American middle class of the 1950s and 1960s had all but collapsed. *En masse*, US corporations relocated much of their manufacturing to Latin America and Southeast Asia. At the same time, US retailers also subcontracted with a growing network of semilegal, semiunderground factories in cities like New York, Los Angeles, and San Francisco, which relied largely on the labor of desperate and often undocumented immigrant populations. Whether within or beyond US borders, the workers—typically young women—who made Americans' clothing, labored in filthy and unsafe factories, were subject to frequent sexual harassment and assault, earned far less than a living wage, had little autonomy outside of work hours, were prohibited from forming a union, and were often forced to get abortions if they became pregnant. As early as 1983, the *New York Times* was publishing lengthy pieces declaring that the sweatshop was "back."[4] After a series of high-profile scandals, the Smithsonian could not deny the parallels with earlier moments in the history of US capitalism. Even acknowledging what was increasingly becoming the new normal, however, was viewed by industry's cheerleaders as antibusiness activism. When they could no longer dismiss sweatshops as unfortunate anomalies, they switched gears, countering that sweatshops were good, actually. Their arguments, like the abysmal working conditions, echoed those of earlier eras.[5]

While mirroring the business dominance of a century prior, the "New Gilded Age" of the late twentieth century presented new challenges, as well. Assembly lines stretched around the world, and industry was more mobile than ever. Decisions were made by unaccountable, extragovernmental bodies. A probusiness—and anti-immigrant—political culture undermined organized labor and attempted to rewrite US history. A new anti-sweatshop movement also emerged, however, attempting to pressure manufacturers and retailers and to use what remained of US labor law. As part of the growing Global Justice Movement of the 1990s, anti-sweatshop activism once again became mainstream.

───

In the decades following World War II, US workers made significant gains. Many began to enjoy forty-hour workweeks, living wages, workplace safety inspections, and overtime pay. By the early 1950s, one-third of the American labor force belonged to a union, and the merging of the AFL and CIO in 1955 gave organized labor unprecedented political power. Combined with postwar economic growth and access to the G.I. Bill and other government social programs, millions of working- and middle-class Americans could afford their own homes and even college tuition for their children. High employment and low interest rates also allowed them to participate in the booming consumer culture of the period, adding appliances to their homes and cars to their garages.[6]

The privileges of this new middle class were largely reserved for white Americans, however. As jobs, neighborhoods, and schools remained racially segregated into the late 1960s, both the US super economy and massive government assistance for new homes and college tuition left many Americans behind. Specific industries, such as agriculture, which relied heavily on African American and immigrant labor, were exempted from New Deal reforms, and for decades, workers' attempts at organizing were met with violence. Though less common than in earlier periods, traditional garment sweatshops also continued to operate in major US cities, employing primarily Asian and Latina immigrants throughout the 1950s and 1960s. The AFL and CIO supported the US government's Red Scare agenda, purging suspected communists from their own ranks and helping to undercut the more radical elements of consumer and labor organizations, both in the United States and abroad. At the highest levels, powerful union executives worked closely with the CIA and the State Department and wed themselves to the political establishment. By the 1970s, the postwar boom had ended, and the heyday for American workers, limited as it was, began to unravel—just as its benefits were beginning to apply to many women and workers of color.[7]

The Women's Liberation Movement of the 1960s and 1970s had achieved numerous gains, including the right to birth control, abortion, no-fault divorce, and equal education funding. Students all over the country began to organize protests against sexual assault on their college campuses, and in 1975, the first rally against sexual harassment was held at Cornell University. The next year, a survey of nine thousand American women by the popular magazine *Redbook* revealed that 80 percent had experienced sexual harassment on the job. Two years later, Congress passed legislation prohibiting discrimination due to pregnancy. In 1980, the iconic film *9 to 5* was released, featuring three working women who face sexism at work, kidnap their boss, and implement feminist programs in the office—such as a daycare, flexible

3.1 International Ladies' Garment Workers' Union label campaign, c. 1970s. Library of Congress.

hours, and a work-from-home program. The film, though aspirational, was based on an organization of the same name, whose "Raises, Rights, and Respect" campaign began in 1973. In the 1980s, the Equal Employment Opportunity Commission (EEOC) established guidelines addressing sexual harassment in the workplace, and the US Supreme Court ruled that sexual harassment could be considered a form of sex discrimination. These gains in women's rights, like those of the early twentieth century, were often applied unevenly, and they came in an equally turbulent moment.[8]

Rising inflation and unemployment, a flood of imported goods, and an economic recession in the mid-1970s provided fertile ground for an organized, well-funded backlash to the gains of racial and ethnic minorities, women, and organized labor. As US corporations laid off millions of union workers and moved their factories overseas, President Ronald Reagan, elected in 1980, set out to redefine the relationships between government, employers, and workers by weakening and reversing the standards of the New Deal era. In 1981, Reagan fired thirteen thousand striking air traffic controllers, broadcasting to employers that the federal government would side with them over their workers—a return to an earlier era. He also appointed corporate lawyer Donald Dotson to chair the National Labor Relations Board (NLRB). Dotson believed that "unionized labor relations [had] been the major contributors to the decline and failure of once-healthy industries" and had caused the "destruction of individual freedom."[9] Under Dotson's leadership, the NLRB settled about half as many complaints as the board under the previous administration, and it averaged approximately three years to make each ruling. Reagan also closed one-third of the Occupational Safety and Health Administration's (OSHA) field offices, instead seeking voluntary compliance from employers on safety matters. To head OSHA, he appointed construction company executive Thorne Auchter, who notably burned the agency's booklets on brown lung disease because he found them "anti-business."[10] Under Auchter, injuries and illnesses in the meatpacking, steel, and textile industries increased while OSHA offered little protection.[11]

In 1982, Reagan's secretary of Labor, Raymond Donovan, proposed weakening child labor protections by advocating that young workers be paid less than the minimum wage, reducing the list of occupations too hazardous for children, and extending the number of hours per day and week that children could work. As one policymaker argued unambiguously, "Unreasonable and artificial impediments to the employment of all age groups should be eliminated."[12] Just as in the days before child labor bans, employers' desire for a cheap, unregulated workforce was sold to working people—and their school-age children—as the very definition of their freedoms.[13]

After gaining momentum through the Reagan and Bush administrations, this political agenda—an abandonment of workers' rights—became bipartisan consensus under Bill Clinton. As economist Michael Meeropol argues, "The Reagan Revolution had succeeded in shackling even a reform-minded Democratic president supposedly working with a like-minded Democratic majority in Congress."[14] During his presidential campaign, Reagan had shaped the racist, mythical narrative of the "welfare queen," an unmarried, African American woman who bred children in order to collect checks from the government that allowed her to purchase multiple Cadillacs. Despite no factual basis for the stereotype, Democrats and Republicans alike used this manufactured example to weaponize white voters' racial resentments and misogyny. As Reagan's myth became accepted common sense, as a "New Democrat," Clinton even campaigned on welfare reform, and in 1996, he signed into law the Personal Responsibility and Work Opportunity Reconciliation Act (PRWORA), destroying much of the safety net that provided assistance for poor Americans, particularly mothers and their children.[15]

Clinton also signed into law the North American Free Trade Agreement (NAFTA), eliminating trade and investment barriers between the United States, Canada, and Mexico—and accelerating deindustrialization in the United States. NAFTA and other "free trade" agreements offered promises to investors that government would not stand in the way of business interests, allowing corporations the freedom to bypass labor and environmental laws in order to maximize profits. By 1990, only half of the garments sold in the United States were produced within the country, and that percentage would shrink over the decade. Canadian and US corporations quickly shifted their production to *maquiladoras*, foreign-owned factories throughout Latin America, which overwhelmingly employed young women and paid paltry wages—and where sexual harassment and gender-based discrimination were common.[16]

The globalization of production through free trade sidestepped more than a half-century of New Deal reforms, hard-fought union wages and benefits, feminist victories, and the work of groups like the NCL, the WTUL, and the LWS. Upon signing NAFTA into law, Clinton promised that free trade would "remake the world" by establishing "an economic order . . . that will promote more growth, more equality, better preservation of the environment, and a greater possibility of world peace."[17] The "freedom" of free trade, however, was for capital to return to old models that maximized profits by re-establishing sweatshop exploitation as the norm for American consumer goods.

In search of cheaper, more pliable workers, textile mills had first moved from New England to the American South, and then on to the Global South. From 1973 to 2009, the United States lost almost two million textile and apparel industry jobs, as the US government, through the US Agency for International Development (USAID), spent millions of dollars developing "free trade zones" in Latin America. In the early 1990s, USAID even ran magazine ads actively recruiting US corporations to relocate their manufacturing. Their transparent pitches included, "Quality, industriousness and reliability is what El Salvador offers you. Rosa Martinez produced apparel for U.S. markets on her sewing machine in El Salvador. *You* can hire her for 57-cents an hour," and "Working to make your business work. 56 cents an hour is only one reason. The Dominican Republic."[18] To help ensure low wages in the free trade zones, USAID officials also worked with manufacturers to prepare a blacklist of potential union organizers. As a president of the Amalgamated Clothing and Textile Workers Union observed, "American workers, as taxpayers, are helping to pay to export their own jobs. At the same time that the government has been promoting and financing offshore production, the U.S. has lost 2.6 million manufacturing jobs."[19]

In 1965, jobs in the manufacturing sector had accounted for more than a quarter of the US workforce, but by 2006, that number was just 12 percent. Political economist Barry Bluestone estimates that as many as thirty-two million jobs were lost during 1970s and 1980s deindustrialization, contributing to increases in crime, homelessness, and drug and alcohol abuse—and decreases in social services, tax bases, and community support. As "factory towns" became ghost towns, from 1980 to 1995, the number of Americans working for "temp" agencies more than quadrupled—to more than two million people—while the number of "independent contractors" rose by 1.6 million during the same period.[20]

While the elimination of millions of union manufacturing jobs devastated the American working and middle classes, there were clear winners. Economist Paul Krugman notes that the pay for top executives ballooned from thirty-nine times what average workers earned to more than one thousand-fold. After three straight decades of steady income growth for the bottom 90 percent of American workers, the 1980s and 1990s were a triumph for those at the top. In 1978, the top .01 percent of the US population held 7 percent of the nation's wealth, but that had increased to 22 percent by 2012. While plant closings, layoffs, recessions, and the collapse of American welfare programs drove millions of Americans into poverty, they were a boon for low-wage fast food restaurants, like McDonalds, and retailers, like Walmart, which sold cheap consumer goods increasingly manufactured in foreign sweatshops.[21]

Foreign labor was not inherently cheap, however. Making the outsourcing of production profitable required sweatshop conditions: long hours, terrible pay, and rampant abuse. As author Naomi Klein notes, in Honduras, there were reports of factory managers "injecting workers with amphetamines to keep them going on forty-eight-hour" shifts.[22] In China, meanwhile, there were reports of three-day-long shifts, in which workers were "forced to sleep under their machines."[23] Factory workers routinely attempted to push back, but, as scholar-activist Ralph Armbruster-Sandoval shows in his case study of Guatemalan and Salvadoran workers' efforts in the early 1990s, companies responded with a combination of bribes, mass firings, death threats, and violence—and closed factories if workers unionized.[24]

Global shifts in manufacturing also destabilized national economies, making rich countries richer and poor countries poorer—and creating a massive global underclass of migrants. Quoting the UN Secretary-General, labor scholar Kim Moody writes that by 2013, "There were 232 million international migrants."[25] Many migrant workers, like those who were recruited by the SK Fashions Factory in El Monte, traveled to wealthy countries to do domestic, agricultural, garment, or construction work—often under-the-table, for low wages, and with few labor rights.

By the early twenty-first century, the US laundry industry employed some 150,000 workers, primarily African American women and immigrants from Latin America. The largest industrial laundry company, Cintas, reported earnings of $232 million in 2002, while paying its workers between seven and nine dollars per hour. After buying up local laundries, the company cut health insurance, pensions, bonuses, paid holidays, and sick days. Maria Colón, a laundry worker at a Connecticut plant, said that she was required to make up the hours she missed when her children were sick. "The company says we need to make up every minute of lost time, no matter what the reason—even if it means working through lunches and breaks. They say if I don't work 40 hours, I'm fired."[26]

Similarly bleak conditions also continued to plague domestic workers. By 2012, more than two million domestics were employed in the United States, primarily women of color, many of them foreign born. Recent efforts by the National Domestic Workers Alliance, an activist coalition, have established some basic worker protections in many US states, but a 2021 survey by the group revealed that more than one-third of American domestic workers still did not receive breaks and nearly one quarter did not feel safe at work. Workers also reported concerns over isolation, harassment, abuse, poverty, language barriers, and fears of deportation.[27]

In the 1980s and 1990s, while a bipartisan consensus around free trade, immigration restrictions, and the erosion of safety and environmental standards was solidifying in Washington, a new anti-sweatshop movement also emerged, making its case on basic human rights, using many of the same talking points that had built support for the New Deal and the UN, and that had been amplified in US Cold War–era propaganda.

The Global Justice Movement in many ways paralleled the Popular Front, operating as both a labor and a social movement, bringing together unions with Indigenous and environmental groups and combatting sweatshops as part of a broad mission. Organized around solidarity across national borders, the movement sought to dismantle—or at least soften—the ongoing impacts of colonialization, particularly in Latin America and Southeast Asia. Activists were particularly sensitive to the understanding that capitalism exploited women and vulnerable populations in specific ways all over the world.[28]

In 1988, Medea Benjamin, Kevin Danaher, Kristen Moller, and Kathie Klarreich formed Global Exchange, a social justice organization at the forefront of the "fair trade" movement. While "free trade" increased corporate profits by chasing lower standards for working conditions and environmental protections all over the globe, "fair trade" instead focused on the well-being of workers. Benjamin, who would later also cofound the women's anti-war group CODEPINK, had seen firsthand the impacts of globalization on developing nations while working for the UN and the free trade–focused World Trade Organization (WTO) in Latin America and Africa. Born Susan Benjamin, she took the name "Medea" as a feminist reclamation of the Greek mythological figure while studying at Tufts University. Much of her more than fifty years of activism focused on capitalism's negative front-line impacts on women. As a 2002 *San Francisco Chronicle* profile notes, "whether it's Cambodian sweatshops or California energy providers, Benjamin said they're all the fruits of wealthy corporations owning mainstream media, holding politicians in a money-girded hammerlock, and stocking university boards of regents with their top corporate officers."[29]

Global Exchange's early projects included campaigns for ethical travel and normalizing relations with Cuba, but by the mid-1990s, the group was one of the most vocal critics of the Nike athletic brand. As Benjamin later wrote in a letter to the *New York Times*, Nike CEO Phil Knight was "in the vanguard of abandoning United States workers and scouring the globe for the cheapest, most repressed labor force."[30] By the end of the decade, Nike's name would be nearly synonymous with sweatshop labor, and Global Exchange would be just one of several groups trying to make it so.[31]

In 1992, labor journalist Jeff Ballinger wrote an exposé on working conditions at Nike's factories in Indonesia. Using the paystubs of a worker named Sadisah, Ballinger showed that she would have to work more than ten hours a day, for six days a week, for two months, just to be able to afford the retail price of a pair of the Nike sneakers that she made in her factory. After hearing Ballinger speak on the radio about Sadisah and another worker named Cicih Sukaesih, Benjamin reached out. Within months, Global Exchange had organized a two-week speaking tour for Sukaesih at US universities, giving students a chance to hear about sweatshops firsthand—and planting the seeds of future student activism.[32]

Sukaesih was one of twenty-four Nike factory workers who were fired and blacklisted in 1991 after a mass walkout demanding the $1.25 minimum wage. According to Sukaesih, companies only wanted to hire very young women to work in their factories, noting, "at my age, you have to pay a bribe to a security guard just to apply for a job."[33] Many of the workers in Indonesia were also mothers, forced to leave their children behind with family members and only able to see them once a year. This disruption of family ties became a pattern for modern sweatshops, as young people from rural areas migrated to industrial hubs hundreds of miles away. Nike CEO Phil Knight, however, waved off such concerns, telling the *New York Times* that "Indonesians were lining up" to work for the company.[34]

During Sukaesih's tour, Global Exchange arranged media coverage and organized rallies outside of several Nike Town stores. Protest signs flipped Nike's famous branding on its head, with slogans such as, "Just Do It: Stomp on Workers' Rights." At a rally outside of the Nike Town store in Chicago (home of the NBA champion Bulls), protestors called on the company's most famous brand ambassador, Michael Jordan, to meet with Sukaesih, visit factories in Indonesia, and speak up for workers. After a rally outside of Portland's Nike Town, Benjamin and Sukaesih visited Nike's nearby company headquarters to try to meet with Knight. He declined, and Nike security instead called police on the two women when they offered to wait quietly in the company's lobby. To one news agency, the blunder of treating the two women like criminal trespassers threatened to "set off a public relations storm that could force the conglomerate to approve independent monitoring of its overseas subcontractors."[35]

Indeed, two weeks of negative media attention pushed Nike to soften its stance. At the company's September 1996 shareholders' meeting, in addition to celebrating record-setting profits, Knight also pledged to invite independent monitors to publicly report on their findings. More important, however, he encouraged shareholders to keep the process voluntary—and to vote down a resolution proposed by the United Methodist Church pension fund that would have made monitoring mandatory.[36]

Global Exchange and other activists continued to keep the pressure on Nike after Sukaesih's tour, including through protests of the movie *Space Jam*, which starred Michael Jordan. Knight, when speaking at Stanford University, his business school alma mater, encountered angry community activists who refused to let his stories about wonderful conditions in Nike factories go unchecked. That same month, the *Wall Street Journal* wrote in support of Nike's record, claiming that Global Exchange and its allies were merely far left anti-capitalists. However, the business-friendly publication also lamented that Nike's public relations strategy made the company look guilty and unsympathetic to consumers.[37]

In April 1997, Global Exchange activists protested the grand opening of San Francisco's Nike Town store, again demanding that Jordan shoulder any responsibility for the sweated workers who made the shoes featuring his likeness. Pulling no punches, one Chicago publication noted that American children worshipped Jordan and coveted his $140 sneakers, which were made on "backs of young Asians—mostly women—who literally work like slaves for pennies under hostile conditions to turn out Nike's products."[38] While Jordan remained quiet, Reggie White, of the NFL's Green Bay Packers, was more openly critical. Despite his endorsement deal with the company, White argued that "[Nike would] rather hire cheap labor than hire the kid in the neighborhood who is buying their shoes. There are people who need jobs here."[39] Some athletes even joined the anti-sweatshop movement directly. For example, Marion Traub-Werner, who rowed crew for the University of North Carolina, was an early member of the campus' United Students Against Sweatshops chapter. Jim Keady, a professional soccer player and college coach, later made national news by resigning his coaching position in protest of Nike and visiting Indonesia to speak to workers.[40]

Global Exchange's hounding of the company was relentless. The group coopted Nike's slogans, spoiled its grand openings, and undermined its ad campaigns. In 1997, Nike produced a series of commercials that highlighted women's empowerment through sports. In response, Global Exchange assembled a coalition of women's groups and individuals—including the National Organization for Women, the Feminist Majority, the Black Women's Agenda, and the Ms. Foundation for Women, as well as author Alice Walker and California Representative Maxine Waters—to sign an open letter to the company. In it, they pointed to the disconnect between Nike's feminist marketing campaign and the sexual harassment, forced overtime, violence, and low wages faced by the Indonesian, Vietnamese, and Chinese women working in the company's factories. The coalition openly harkened back to earlier generations of women who worked together across class lines. As Feminist Majority president Eleanor Smeal noted, "The sweatshops, which all of us thought were a thing of the past, are back again. And just like the feminists at the turn of the century fought them, it's incumbent on us to do the same."[41]

With pressure mounting, in May 1998, Nike offered additional labor concessions, pledging to raise its minimum employment age to sixteen, to use independent monitors, and to adopt US OSHA standards for air quality. The anti-sweatshop movement was not Nike's only problem, however. With shares down 16 percent, Knight admitted later that year that the company had oversaturated consumers with its brand. Indeed, Nike's research showed that 97 percent of Americans recognized the "swoosh" logo, which Knight had tattooed on his left ankle. The Nike swoosh was ubiquitous during the 1990s—ripe for use by activists such as Global Exchange, but also uncomfortably public on O. J. Simpson's favorite hat and on the feet of Heaven's Gate cult members.[42]

Earlier in the twentieth century, the League of Women Shoppers used the celebrity of its members to highlight their activism. But while the anti-sweatshop of movement of the 1990s and early 2000s sought similar platforms, activists also used brand recognition to try to shame bad actors. They tried to link companies, such as Nike, to their working conditions in the minds of the public, and thus to use their massive advertising budgets against them. Nike's many abuses made it a lightning rod for activists, but its labor practices were increasingly normal for the celebrated "free trade" economy of the period. In earlier eras, activists protested domestic sweatshops at the site of production, but the shift to a global assembly line required a new kind of solidarity—one that involved contact with workers around the world. In many cases, US activists brought workers from Asia and Latin America to the United States to speak to media, allies, and Congress. Because of the geographic gap between factories and consumers, the sites of protest also shifted to retail and advertising spaces.

In 1995, an enslaved Thai worker at the SK Fashions Factory in El Monte, California—the factory later featured in the exhibit at the Smithsonian—escaped through a ventilation shaft. Based on the worker's testimony, federal Immigration and Naturalization Service (INS) agents raided the complex and arrested those in charge.

Recruiters for manufacturers such as SK Fashions promised to pay foreign workers' travel expenses to the United States upfront. Workers expected to be provided comfortable housing and to earn $1,200 each month—enough to pay their way out of debt peonage, send money home to their families, and enjoy better lives. Instead, factory bosses took away their passports and held them captive. The El Monte compound was a literal prison, surrounded by a barbed-wire fence and armed guards to prevent workers from escaping. Wages of less than two dollars per hour made it nearly impossible to pay off their travel debts, but workers were not allowed to leave even if they fulfilled that requirement. Of the seventy-two captive workers, sixty-seven were women. Attorney Julie Su, who represented the workers in court, said, "They were forced to sew garments for up to eighteen hours a day until their fingers were raw and their vision blurred," before cramming into a room with eight to ten coworkers to get a little sleep before starting over again.[43]

Though another worker had previously escaped in 1992—and alerted police to the criminal exploitation at SK—it took three years before law enforcement raided the compound. Workers had been told by their captors that they could expect more problems if they escaped, a warning that proved prescient. Officials at INS, refusing to treat the freed workers "differently from any other illegal immigrants in custody," moved them from the El Monte Prison to a government detention center—and kept them shackled during transportation to legal meetings.[44] A coalition of unions and community organizations formed to provide legal aid, secure bail funds, and arrange lodging with private families. This group, which included Julie Su as well as fellow attorney Lora Jo Foo—a labor lawyer who had worked in a San Francisco factory at the age of eleven—became Sweatshop Watch. Though the freed workers were initially given only temporary work permits so that they could remain in the United States to testify against their former captors, after seven years, the INS finally granted them visas for permanent residency.[45]

Using public outrage over El Monte, Secretary of Labor Robert Reich, one of the few progressives in the Clinton administration, launched a "No Sweat" campaign, promoting a "Trendsetter List" of companies that were making efforts to avoid using sweated labor—just as the National Consumers' League had with its white list nearly a century earlier. As Reich reasoned, "Presumably, most consumers would rather not buy garments produced by slave labor in the United States and retailers would rather not sell them."[46] It is telling that Reich, from a high-ranking position in the US government, had resorted to a tactic that had been used by an organization that held no official power. A year earlier, Reich had also announced plans to seize goods produced in the US's domestic sweatshops. After decades of deliberate cuts to the Department of Labor (DOL), though, Reich had far too few inspectors to make good on his threat. The plan was essentially a bluff. Reich could only hope that tough talk would pressure retailers and manufacturers to police themselves. Reich's list of trendsetters also ran into trouble, when featured companies, such as Guess?, became the subjects of their own sweatshop scandals, exposing both the extent of the problem and the weakness of the watered-down regulatory apparatus.[47]

Resistant to any spotlight on their practices, however, the National Retail Federation (NRF), the industry's largest trade association, immediately fought back. As with the backlash to the New Deal in the 1930s and 1940s, big business saw even the suggestion of reform as a threat. Reich's "No Sweat" campaign was a way for industry to promote and police itself, but the NRF criticized Reich and the DOL for "wasting millions of taxpayer dollars on counterproductive media witch hunts."[48] Reich needed an even greater public scandal to get his anti-sweatshop initiative off the ground, and he soon got it.[49]

In the meantime, Sweatshop Watch went on the offensive. After securing the release of the El Monte workers from INS detention, Sweatshop Watch attorneys helped them sue both the factory operators and the contracting retailers—companies including BUM International, Fred Meyer, and Montgomery Ward—for back wages and damages. The lawsuit also included twenty-two Latinx workers who were part of same production chain. Though not physically enslaved, they too had labored under long, grueling conditions and were victims of wage theft. The choice to link slavery and human trafficking with less sensational sweatshop conditions was deliberate. Sweatshop Watch wanted the American public to see that extreme exploitation was inevitable under the demands of late twentieth-century capitalism. While denying that they knowingly contracted sweatshop labor—and after dismissively offering each worker a fifty-dollar gift card to settle the case—roughly a dozen corporations agreed to a four-million-dollar settlement after Sweatshop Watch organized letter-writing campaigns and public protests. Representing the workers, Su said of the settlement, "In the struggle for corporate accountability, garment workers can fight back and win. It's no longer sufficient for retailers and manufacturers to say, 'We didn't know so we're not responsible.'"[50] On the last day of the trial, Su brought fifty of the workers to court, and the judge validated their traumatic experiences, expressing her appreciation for their bravery. During the trial, Sweatshop Watch also launched a Retailer Accountability Campaign to hold companies such as Jessica McClintock and Liz Claiborne responsible for using sweated labor.[51]

In 1999, Sweatshop Watch joined several other nonprofit organizations and the Union of Needletrades, Industrial and Textile Employees (UNITE) in filing three class-action lawsuits on behalf of thirty thousand workers in Saipan against more than forty retailers and factories. They accused employers of conspiracy to deny workers in the Commonwealth of the Northern Mariana Islands (CNMI) their most basic human rights, alleging indentured servitude as well as other violations, such as forcing the mostly female workforce to sign away their freedom to date or get married. Activists also accused retailers of false advertising for their use of "Made in the USA" labels. Among the most well-known companies named were: The Gap, Calvin Klein, Abercrombie & Fitch, JCPenney, Polo Ralph Lauren, Oshkosh B'Gosh, Target, and Tommy Hilfiger.[52]

With the support of congressional leaders and lobbyists, the CNMI, a US territory on the eastern boundary of the Philippine Sea, had become a major hub for clothing production. Though products carried the "Made in the USA" label, factories, which primarily employed temporary workers from China, Bangladesh, and the Philippines, were not required to comply with US labor standards. While the United States had outlawed debt peonage in 1867, thousands of workers in Saipan were effectively indentured servants, desperate for the opportunity to work in supposedly American factories. In 1991, Levi Strauss and Company investigated its factories in Saipan, the largest island in the CNMI, and discovered "slavelike" conditions.[53] The company severed ties with its subcontractor Tan Holdings Corporation, which was forced to pay more than nine million dollars in restitution to its workers. According to the US Department of Labor, the Tan Corporation had routinely required ninety-hour work weeks, without overtime, at less than the island's reduced minimum wage. Tan was not an outlier, though. Such exploitation was pervasive throughout the industry. In fact, as early as 1987, the AFL-CIO had begun to pressure Congress, writing that these factories, owned by Filipino, Taiwanese, and South Korean firms, were exploiting a loophole to get around import quotas at a moment in which the US apparel industry was losing hundreds of thousands of jobs.[54]

According to the *New York Times*, by 1992, workers in Saipan were producing $279 million worth of clothing in factories that flew the American flag, while earning half of the US minimum wage. That same year, OSHA inspectors found "locked fire exits, overcrowded housing with no ventilation, exposed electrical wires, and gross lack of sanitation."[55] Other reports described raw sewage seeping into sleeping areas, four toilets to be shared by more than 150 workers, and no hot water. The tropical climate in Saipan also made the unairconditioned factories brutally hot—like "exercising with a sweat suit on in a sauna."[56] Much like the workers in the El Monte factory, the workers in Saipan went into thousands of dollars of debt to secure travel and employment. Indeed, many of the conditions were similar, as the workforce—who were mostly women—lived in crowded barracks behind barbed-wire fences that were patrolled by armed guards. One of the "Jane Does" in Sweatshop Watch's Saipan lawsuit claimed that coworkers had told her that women who became pregnant were forced to choose between abortion and deportation. From 1995 through 1999, OSHA cited the Saipan garment industry with more than one thousand violations, and the US Department of Interior reported malnourished workers, forced abortions, and contracts that required employees to waive many of their civil liberties. The powerful industry, however, had the backing of local authorities, foreign investors, retailers, and US politicians.[57]

As part of its effort to counter them, Sweatshop Watch organized a series of protest actions to highlight the exploitation in the CNMI. Along with Global Exchange, the group arranged a speaking tour for Carmencita "Chie" Abad, who had migrated to Saipan from the Philippines for factory work. After six years sewing clothes for the Gap, Ann Taylor, and apparel licensed by the University of California, Abad's work visa was not renewed, as retaliation for her attempts to organize workers. In the United States, Abad gave Sweatshop Watch's campaign a human face, showing American audiences, for example, a Gap vest that retailed for $78, while the workers, like her, who sewed it were paid just $2.15 per hour. Abad's identity as a queer Filipina woman also helped reach allies outside of organized labor. Consistently pointing out that women were at least 90 percent of the workforce at her factory, Abad effectively made the case that sweatshop labor was a women's issue. California Lutheran University invited Abad to speak on campus to mark International Women's Day. Pride at Work, whose mission is "building power for LGBTQ+ working people," invited Abad to speak at its 2001 convention. Each speaking event connected new audiences to workers in Saipan, to the lawsuit, and to the Global Justice Movement.[58]

A year into the lawsuit in January 2000, Sweatshop Watch helped organize a confrontation at the San Francisco headquarters of Gap, Incorporated, to pressure the company to meet with Abad, accept petitions with ten thousand signatures, and settle the lawsuit. When the CEO refused to meet any of their demands, activists held a sit-in in the lobby chanting, "GAP workers have been wronged, One year is way too long," and "Settle the case or we'll be in your face."[59] Police arrested fourteen people, including Sweatshop Watch's Leila Salazar, who told the press, "I am optimistic that our continued pressure on GAP Inc. will prove to be worthwhile by the end of this year."[60] That May, activists released balloons stamped with "STOP GAP SWEATSHOP" and handed out pamphlets at a shopping mall, before police arrested nineteen of them, including students and faculty from California State University, Fresno.[61]

In January 2004, the three lawsuits concluded with a twenty-million-dollar settlement with twenty-six US retailers and twenty-three Saipan factories. The deal included a code of conduct to be enforced by independent monitors, payment of withheld wages, and repatriation of workers who wanted to return to their home countries. Nikki Bas, codirector of Sweatshop Watch, called the settlement "a significant victory because it pushes the envelope on how far workers and consumers can press retailers to be responsible for the conditions under which their clothes are made."[62] These lawsuits illustrated the complex, global nature of the "free trade" economy. They held both factory owners—typically foreign investors—and American retailers responsible for the exploitation of nearly fifty thousand women, themselves migrants in Saipan.

However, the victory was not only won in court. Like the protests against Nike, direct action campaigns and other protests had repeatedly associated US companies with the working conditions that produced their goods, building public pressure and bad press. Chie Abad's speaking tour was particularly effective at naming a specific retailer, the Gap, that was popular with college students and linking its name to misery. Abad, who had been fired for trying to form a union, pointed out the inconsistencies with the working conditions and the supposed American values of democracy and civil rights that she grew up learning about. Companies such as the Gap were clearly concerned that American consumers would also take issue with those inconsistencies.

In April 1996, Charles Kernaghan, the executive director of the National Labor Committee (which will not be abbreviated, in order to avoid confusion with the National Consumers' League), testified before a congressional hearing on child labor that a Kathie Lee Gifford clothing line sold at Walmart used sweatshop labor. While inspecting factories in Honduras, Kernaghan discovered that workers were sewing garments that carried Gifford's label—and that also bore the statement, "A portion of the proceeds from the sale of this garment will be donated to various Children's Charities."[63] Gifford was a born-again Christian and cohost of *Live with Regis and Kathie Lee*, the most popular syndicated talk show in the United States. Gifford was not only a recognizable celebrity, but also one whose name itself provided the clothing line a wholesome and successful image. In its first year, the line brought in an estimated $300 million in sales.[64]

As Naomi Klein outlines in *No Logo*, US corporations in the 1980s and 1990s shifted their focus away from the production of goods and toward the creation of brand images. Deregulated trade policies allowed them to outsource manufacturing to cheap, subcontracted factories overseas. These often-short-term contracts provided retailers flexibility, plausible deniability for working conditions, and allowed them to instead focus on slick, expensive marketing campaigns for their products as lifestyles. In the public eye, highly paid celebrity ambassadors, such as Michael Jordan, Jaclyn Smith, and Gifford, became indistinguishable from the corporations they represented. Kernaghan understood the importance of celebrity to American popular culture. He saw an opportunity to expose the contradictions between Gifford's image—and her clothing line's charitable facade—with the brutality of the sweatshop. As he had hoped, his testimony set off a media firestorm.[65]

Several US television programs covered Kernaghan's testimony, in which he painted a grim picture of child labor. As Charles Bowden of *Mother Jones* magazine notes, "Charlie Kernaghan opted for a simple tactic: shaming brand-name companies. He learned that if he took the shirt off your back and showed you the blood of children in the fabric, people would snap alert."⁶⁶ Media in the United States called for a response from Gifford. Using the platform of her talk show, she tearfully claimed that she would never allow such conditions to take place—and that Kernaghan was lying. She further asserted that Walmart's inspectors had certified that the conditions at the Global Fashion Factory were in line with their code of conduct.⁶⁷

Gifford soon discovered, however, that the Walmart code did not prevent child labor or dangerous working conditions in its subcontracted factories. She quickly arranged for a friendly interview with trusted news anchor Diane Sawyer, in which Gifford pledged to hire her own inspectors to ensure that the clothing that bore her name was made under ethical conditions. Her public relations disaster was not over yet, however.⁶⁸

Three weeks later, UNITE, the union that worked with Sweatshop Watch on the Saipan lawsuit, directed national media outlets to Seo Fashions, a sweatshop subcontracted by Walmart to manufacture clothes for Gifford's line. Unlike the distant Honduran factory, Seo Fashions was located in New York City, just a few miles from the studio where *Live with Regis and Kathie Lee* taped. Workers at Seo Fashions, many of them making less than minimum wage, had not received their paychecks for weeks. In addition to the substandard pay, UNITE also emphasized the factory's unsanitary conditions. As one worker described, "Everything is dirty, the trash isn't picked up, and the two bathrooms aren't fit for pigs to use. There's never any soap or toilet paper, and the plumbing doesn't always work. So imagine the smell."⁶⁹

The intense media glare accomplished what Kernaghan had hoped, and the scandal escalated. Gifford and her husband, ABC sportscaster and former football player Frank Gifford, worked hard to salvage her reputation, including by visiting the Seo Fashions Factory—and offering each worker three hundred dollars in cash. The National Labor Committee, meanwhile, organized a speaking tour for a fifteen-year-old Salvadoran sweatshop worker named Wendy Diaz, who sewed clothes for Gifford's line. When speaking to the media and testifying to Congress, Diaz described working conditions that included the standard low pay and seventy-hour workweeks, physical abuse at the hand of supervisors, tremendous heat, abuse of pregnant women, and locked bathrooms. Diaz, an orphan who began working in sweatshops at the age of thirteen, hoped to speak to Gifford personally to ask for her help guaranteeing better conditions. As with activists' previous attempts to meet with Phil Knight and Michael Jordan, this demand made clear that specific powerful people were culpable for these working conditions.⁷⁰

Like the speaking tours by Nike factory worker Cicih Sukaesih and Gap factory worker Chie Abad, Wendy Diaz's public appearances confronted American consumers with the horrors that their purchases supported. In Diaz, they were given a face that linked child labor and sweatshops to the Kathie Lee and Walmart brands. When Gifford publicly apologized and agreed to independent monitoring of factories producing apparel for her line, Kernaghan applauded her actions in the fashion industry trade journal *Women's Wear Daily*, noting, "The action she's taking isn't going to be lost on other companies. This is going to be a real wake-up call for other apparel endorsers."[71] California Congressman George Miller organized a news conference with Diaz, Kernaghan, and clergy to urge American shoppers to hold corporations accountable for working conditions. In a press release announcing the event, Miller echoed Labor Secretary Reich, writing, "The problem goes beyond Kathie Lee Gifford and Wal-Mart. Everyday American consumers unknowingly purchase products made with child and exploited labor. If consumers had more information, they may change their purchasing habits."[72]

But while Kernaghan had used Gifford's celebrity—and hypocrisy—to shine a light on sweatshop labor, the apparel industry, with the help of the Clinton administration, quickly tried to turn the tables. Kathie Lee Gifford appeared at President Clinton's side to announce the formation of an industry-led White House taskforce. Mainstream media covered Gifford's testimony before a congressional hearing on child labor and a subsequent Fashion Industry Forum in July 1996, which was attended by major figures in fashion and retail, as well as celebrities, such as fitness icon Richard Simmons. Also present was Nancy Penaloza, a sewing machine operator at a sweatshop in New York, who described fifty-six to sixty-six-hour workweeks, extreme cold and heat, rats and mice crawling across her feet, and a boss who frequently punched her in the head. Cicih Sukaesih, accompanied by Global Exchange's Medea Benjamin and labor journalist Jeff Ballinger, attempted to join the forum, but was turned away at the door.[73]

Industry representatives, in a nod to the growing PR problem, promised a new era of labor standards in foreign factories—but rejected independent monitoring. Ultimately, the forum allowed brand leaders an opportunity to speak out against sweatshops, but it did little to combat the ills of global capital. The effort also allowed the Clinton administration to appease labor and human rights activists during an election year, while separating the issue of sweatshops from its own policy initiatives, such as NAFTA and welfare reform, which fed them. The taskforce, the Apparel Industry Partnership (AIP), subsequently evolved into the Fair Labor Association (FLA), which adopted a set of codes and agreements—and was similarly criticized as industry self-policing.[74]

The Gifford scandal and its aftermath were the pinnacle of a decade and half of work by Kernaghan's National Labor Committee. The organization was formed in 1981 with the backing of US labor leaders in order to support proworker activists in Central America, who were routinely tortured or murdered by right-wing paramilitary forces and authoritarian regimes—many of whom were supported by the US government. Operating with a bare-bones budget and workforce of only two (Kernaghan and Barbara Briggs), the National Labor Committee expanded its focus to sweatshops, conducting undercover investigations, and releasing its reports, such as "Free Trade's Hidden Secrets," "The U.S. in Haiti," "Liz Claiborne / Sweatshop Production in El Salvador," "Wal-Mart's Shirts of Misery," and "Kathie Lee Sweatshop in El Salvador." In September 1996, Global Exchange hosted Kernaghan for a lecture and film screening about Disney's billion-dollar offshore toy and clothing division, which paid Haitian workers around thirty cents per hour.[75]

Like the investigations by the NCL and the LWS—but with a global focus—Kernaghan and Briggs's reports documented the unsavory details of working and living conditions, for example, that young women who sewed clothes for Walmart in Bangladesh were paid between nine and twenty cents per hour. In November 1999, South Carolina Senator Fritz Hollings read into the official *Congressional Record* a portion of a National Labor Committee report on the working conditions for Kathie Lee Gifford's Walmart line. Amid death threats, intimidation, forced pregnancy tests, locked bathrooms, unsanitary water, searches on their way in and out of the factories, and the confiscation of food and water, Salvadoran workers had been paid the appallingly low wage of fifteen cents per article of clothing. The cost of the mandatory pregnancy tests, two days' wages, was deducted from women's pay, and they were immediately fired if they tested positive.[76]

The National Labor Committee's strategy was to target US corporations by packaging sweatshop exploitation for the celebrity and brand-obsessed tabloid news, thus putting the brands and their logos on trial. In addition to the Kathie Lee Gifford scandal, for example, the group picketed outside of the high-profile National Basketball Association (NBA) store in New York, accusing Reebok of charging seventy-five dollars for jerseys, while only paying Honduran workers nineteen cents. The concrete policy impacts of the Kathie Lee scandal are debatable, but the response by the industry and its political allies certainly reflects the pressure they felt under public scrutiny. The affair also shifted the consciousness of the American public. In 2000, the *Chicago Tribune* noted the National Labor Committee's impact, writing, "If you've ever checked the tag on a polo shirt, wondering where it was made, and whether workers there are treated fairly, Charles Kernaghan has touched your life."[77] More important, Honduran sweatshop worker Lydda Gonzalez said of the group, "We could never have dreamed that we would find such warmth, interest, and solidarity in the United States."[78]

As the anti-sweatshop movement grew, it also gained celebrity supporters. In December 1997, Rage Against the Machine guitarist Tom Morello was one of thirty-three people arrested while protesting against Guess? at a California mall. Earlier that year, the company had announced that it would be moving 40 percent of its production to Mexico, as NAFTA allowed apparel to be produced in Mexico at a tenth of the cost. Like the society women arrested on picket lines a century earlier, Morello's fame guaranteed that the event would be widely covered—including by MTV, which reached a key Guess? target demographic. Groups like the National Labor Committee, Sweatshop Watch, Global Exchange, UNITE, and others understood that the global assembly line was changing. But while it might be difficult or impossible to picket outside of a far-off foreign factory, the brands were still vulnerable locally. The Gap, Guess?, and Russell—and their shareholders—could be pressured if they were publicly linked with exploitation, sexual harassment, and sweatshops.[79]

Amid the various sweatshop scandals of the 1990s—El Monte, Saipan, Kathie Lee Gifford, the Smithsonian—American college students also began organizing on their campuses and protesting the conditions under which university apparel was being made. The most prominent student organization, United Students Against Sweatshops (USAS), was founded in 1998 by a group of students during a summer internship with UNITE. While the National Labor Committee and Sweatshop Watch used the courts and public shaming campaigns, USAS targeted another corporate vulnerability—ties to colleges and universities. Like their movement counterparts, USAS activists knew that they had little power to confront companies like Nike, Adidas, or Reebok directly—or to reach their distant factories. They could, however, pressure their own school administrators and leverage the multimillion-dollar apparel contracts that branded their universities and their sports teams. As in the 1910s and 1930s, students in the 1990s played a significant role in the fight for worker justice, using their time, resources, and privileges to denounce exploitation. In a global economy with a global assembly line, USAS helped extend a global picket line onto college campuses.[80]

In 1999, massive protests by environmental activists, organized labor, Indigenous rights activists, and students—including USAS members—shut down the Seattle meeting of the World Trade Organization (WTO). Formed in 1995, the WTO is an international economic institution that works to limit or eliminate trade restrictions, such as quotas and tariffs. Essentially, it has applied NAFTA's policies globally, by facilitating trade agreements rooted in free-market principles and, according to legal scholar Jem Spectar, "vigorously resist[ing] linkage between trade and core international labor rights."[81] In short, the WTO helps create and maintain sweatshop-friendly conditions. The 1999 protests—dismissively dubbed "The Battle in Seattle" in some media accounts—combined mass marches with nonviolent blockades of several downtown intersections. They ultimately forced the WTO to cancel many of its sessions and brought the organization to the attention of many Americans for the first time.[82]

Like the Popular Front and the many overlapping movements of the 1960s, the Global Justice Movement viewed its issues as interrelated. As Global Exchange organizer Juliette Beck wrote in 2000, "Many young people are awakening to the reality that the widespread social, ecological, and spiritual crises we've inherited are caused by living in a capitalist society that teaches us to buy without thinking and consume without caring."[83] The many movements and groups that came together in Seattle were ideologically diverse and mostly nonpartisan, but they had a common opponent in unrestrained "free trade" capital. Recognizing bipartisan support for this route to globalization, in the months after the Seattle protest, organizers also planned mass demonstrations at both the Republican and Democratic national conventions in the leadup to the 2000 election.[84]

Meanwhile, Global Exchange hired Chie Abad, the former Gap factory worker, as an educator and spokesperson, and her US college speaking tour proved an effective recruitment tool for USAS. As one activist explained before Abad spoke at the University of Dayton, "For her to tell in her own words what she's seen and witnessed has more power than someone else doing it."[85] Making clothes for the Gap and other American retailers, Abad had often worked fourteen-hour shifts, though, as she told students at Cornell University, her longest workday had been a staggering forty hours. Abad's appearances typically started with footage from a 1998 episode of the television program 20/20, for which she had worn a hidden camera into the Korean-owned Sako Factory in Saipan. After screening the footage at the University of Nebraska, Abad told students, "We need to lead the struggle to end sweatshops. We are on the right side of the history."[86]

By 2001, USAS had more than two hundred chapters on college campuses. Like its early twentieth-century predecessors, USAS had a decentralized structure that gave each chapter the freedom to adapt tactics based on what they thought would be most effective. Some USAS organizers engaged in direct action, such as sit-ins, while others worked through the university bureaucracy by joining their student government and pushing for policy changes.[87]

Students at Duke University, for example, sought to work with administrators to adopt a code of conduct for its apparel contractors. Denied even a meeting, USAS activists organized an email petition, signed by hundreds of students. Hoping to get ahead of any bad publicity, administrators conceded to meet and to adopt a code of conduct, making Duke the first university to do so. With their brand name on the line, school officials took initiative—and credit—saying, "We are doing it because it's the right thing to do. We cannot tolerate having the sweat and tears of abused and exploited workers mixed with the fabric of the products which bear our marks."[88] Even with the university doing "the right thing," however, student activists had to hold it accountable. When a rumor began circulating that administrators planned to weaken the code, more than twenty members of Duke USAS staged a sit-in in the school president's office lobby in January 1999. After thirty hours, the administration relented, promising to stick to the original agreement.[89]

Many colleges and universities sought to appease their students by joining the FLA, the industry-led successor to Labor Secretary Reich's Fashion Industry Forum. Along with other labor groups, USAS criticized the organization as essentially a public relations project. For example, one of the members of the White House's apparel taskforce, UNITE, ultimately declined to sign onto the FLA charter. In addition to insisting on (often woefully inadequate) local minimum wages as their standards in foreign countries, retailers had also resisted allowing human rights organizations to monitor their factories. They instead relied on private, for-profit monitoring firms, which only spoke to workers on factory grounds, under the watchful eye of employers. As one USAS member explained the FLA's conflict of interest, "It's like McDonald's nutritionists boasting about how healthy a Big Mac is."[90]

Compromised or not, the FLA's first report, in 2003, found numerous violations of its code of conduct in about a quarter of monitors' unannounced visits, including forced overtime, workers being fired for union activity, and job applicants being forced to take pregnancy tests before being hired. While the FLA's proponents saw in the report evidence for the legitimacy of its monitoring process, its critics saw widespread abuse in companies that had supposedly committed themselves to higher standards. Bama Athreya, former director of the International Labor Rights Forum, argues that corporate social responsibility plans like the FLA are doomed to failure because they demand no structural changes to the industry's requirement for fast, cheap, last-minute production from contracted factories. Apparel corporations in the United States may find sweatshops abhorrent, but they do not want increased pay, reduced hours, or less flexible operations to impact their bottom lines. Sweatshops look similar over time because hyperexploitation remains the most direct route to maximizing production and profits. Where labor laws do not check capital's power, the pressure to boost shareholders' dividends is insurmountable.[91]

Instead of supporting the FLA, USAS worked with university administrators, unions, workers, and other organizations, including Sweatshop Watch, to form the Worker Rights Consortium (WRC), an alternative monitoring system that was completely independent of corporate influence and that actively involved workers from the Global South its formation. The WRC boasts that in the decades since, it has secured $121 million back wages for workers and reversed the firing of 1,785 workers for union organizing. At the time of its founding, the WRC had the support of forty-four universities. Others would soon join, following student pressure campaigns.[92]

In February 1999, seven student activists at the University of Wisconsin entered their chancellor's office to demand that the university withdraw from the FLA and instead join the WRC. When additional student supporters attempted to join them, they were met with violence and pepper spray. The seven USAS activists then chained themselves together using bicycle locks and launched a four-day sit-in. They were soon joined by other students. After police broke up the demonstration, arresting fifty students during a 4 a.m. raid, thousands of students rallied in solidarity and raised more than twenty thousand dollars for bail. The student government at the University of Wisconsin-Milwaukee, a sister campus, passed a "UW Solidarity Act," and its newspaper ran a four-page report on the protests. City officials in Madison, meanwhile, showed their support by pledging "not [to] grant approval to university projects" until the charges against the students were dropped.[93] Ultimately, the university dropped all criminal charges, instead issuing each student demonstrator a fifty-dollar ordinance violation, roughly equivalent to a parking ticket.[94]

In April, more than one hundred students at the University of Arizona marched to their own president's office, also demanding a move from FLA to WRC membership. Much like the protests that would shut down the City of Seattle later that year, the march included more than carrying signs and chanting slogans. A carnival-like atmosphere, complete with skits, campus mascots, and performance artists, rolled through campus to deliver a petition signed by more than one thousand students. Sixty students then staged a sit-in outside of the president's office for the next week. Though refusing to formally withdraw from the FLA, the administration agreed to many of the students' demands. Vowing to continue the campaign, a USAS member wrote an editorial for the student paper, noting, "[It] may seem silly, absurd, even obnoxious, but if Students Against Sweatshops ever hopes to accomplish its goals, there is no other way but to continue holding rallies, sit-ins, marches, and fasts."[95]

While dozens of USAS campaigns swept college campuses, each seemingly in isolation, US apparel corporations took notice. Nike used its power to warn universities against meeting USAS's demands. For example, as WRC membership spread, the company severed an athletic equipment contract with Brown University and abandoned negotiations to renew a high-profile licensing contract with the University of Michigan. While officials at Michigan argued that the WRC represented "very moderate and prudent efforts" in line with "well-accepted standards of international human rights," Nike officials disagreed.[96] The company argued that Michigan was no longer a "compatible" partner, since its WRC membership made Nike subject to its labor code and independent monitoring.[97]

When the University of Oregon agreed to join the WRC, Nike CEO Phil Knight, an alumnus, cancelled a planned thirty-million-dollar donation. Later, when the university administration opted not to renew membership in the WRC, Knight not only reinstated his initial donation, but also added an extra twenty million dollars to it. Knight, as an individual, could wield an enormous reserve of capital to get what he wanted—in large part because his company paid its workers so poorly. Anti-sweatshop activists, however, continued to put pressure on Knight and Nike.[98]

In 1997, Jim Keady, a soccer coach at Saint John's University, had resigned rather than support the school's partnership with Nike. A theology graduate student at the Catholic university at the time, Keady rooted his protest in his understanding of social justice. He says that he asked himself, "What if I can't in good conscience as a Catholic wear and promote the equipment for a company that is oppressing and exploiting people?"[99]

After his forced resignation, Keady and another activist, Leslie Kretzu, set out to shine a light on the working and living conditions faced by Nike workers in Indonesia. Their short documentary, *Behind the Swoosh*, traces their challenges as they try to survive on the same low wages as Nike employees in the summer of 2000—and then to share those experiences with US college students. The film, which has now been viewed more than two million times on YouTube, shows workers being beaten for attempting to form unions, the burning of toxic rubber from Nike scraps and other industrial garbage as children play nearby, and the impossible choices poorly paid workers face, such as whether to purchase medicine or food. At one point in the film, Keady confronts Phil Knight in a restaurant, pleading with him, on behalf of workers, to visit Nike's factories in Indonesia. Knight ends the conversation abruptly.[100]

Behind the Swoosh refutes the arguments that were offered to Keady to dismiss his objections, namely that the wages paid to Nike's factory workers were sufficient, or even generous, due to a low cost of living. In Indonesia, Keady and Kretzu found desperate workers living together in cramped rooms, where temperatures reached 100 degrees, and that were surrounded by open sewers. Like New York tenements a century earlier, up to ten families might share a common bathroom, kitchen, and well. Countering those who would say that capitalism is the American way, Keady argues in the film that American values include "respect for democracy, for human rights, and for protection on human life."[101]

Though Nike became the most notorious sweatshop athletic brand of the period, perhaps USAS's greatest success was its 2009 campaign against Russell Athletics. When a Honduran factory that produced clothes for Russell closed after workers voted to unionize, an anti-sweatshop coalition demanded that Russell reopen it and recognize the workers' rights. When pickets at NBA playoff games garnered only minimal attention from national print and broadcast media, USAS turned to social media, such as Twitter, to attract attention and encourage a boycott of Russell products. USAS played a major role in convincing more than ninety universities to end or postpone their multimillion-dollar contracts with Russell. Under mounting pressure, the company agreed to reopen the factory, rehire the 1,200 workers, and honor their freedom of association.[102]

3.2 Nike dumping scraps in Indonesia, 2012. The company had been burning scrap shoe rubber for twenty years, giving off dangerous toxins and carcinogens. Its proximity to a river means that during the floods of the rainy season, this toxic material would wash into the river. Courtesy of Jim Keady.

While rooted in global solidarity, USAS operated at a hyperlocal level, with each chapter pressuring its own university. After several years of apparel campaigns, some chapters also became active in on-campus labor issues, for example by protesting the outsourcing of dining hall and custodial jobs. In addition to picking fights with major US corporations, USAS members exposed the fact that American universities were spaces of exploitation and conflict, as well as learning.

By the turn of the century, several decades of deindustrialization and subcontracting, as well as a drastic concentration of power in the hands of multinational corporations, had created an uncomfortable reality for US consumers. Rather than unfortunate aberrations in the US supply chain, human rights abuses had become ubiquitous. While most Americans were unfamiliar with SK Fashions, the CNMI, Global Fashion, or the WTO, global justice activists exposed that the most familiar household names were also complicit: Walmart and Macy's, Kathie Lee Gifford and Michael Jordan, Nike and Russell, and on and on. Even worse, the sweatshop conditions feeding the US economy were not some unfortunate accident. The global sweatshop economy was a deliberate project, and its architects and champions rushed to defend it.

In the mid-1990s, Congress had appeared ready to enforce US labor laws in the CNMI—in Saipan's garment factories specifically. The local government there, backed by foreign investors, hired lobbyist Jack Abramoff and his firm Preston Gates, paying them six million dollars over the next several years to help retain various exemptions from US labor and immigration standards. Abramoff routinely appeared on media outlets to praise CNMI business leaders for their diligence in preventing sweatshops. He also flew dozens of members of Congress and their aides to the CNMI on "fact-finding" trips to meet local business leaders and tour a showcase factory against the backdrop of the islands' beautiful beaches. These visitors often brought their families for all-expenses-paid trips to snorkel and golf, but they were kept away from the sweatshops, illegal abortion clinics, poverty, and crime. Abramoff touted the CNMI as a shining example of economic development without regulations to impede its success. Doug Bandow of the libertarian Cato Institute called the CNMI a "laboratory of liberty," and House Majority Leader Tom DeLay described the commonwealth as a "perfect petri dish of capitalism."[103] When accompanying Abramoff to Saipan with his family to celebrate New Year's Eve, DeLay said:

> When one of my closest and dearest friends, Jack Abramoff, your most able representative in Washington, D.C., invited me to the islands, I wanted to see firsthand the free-market success and the progress and reform you have made. . . . In the case of the CNMI, liberals in Washington and the Clinton bureaucrats are intentionally trying to kill economic freedom and return the CNMI to the days of welfare dependency. Well, I believe in the invisible hand of the marketplace, not the visible foot of the government.[104]

According to reports from the Departments of Interior and Justice, the "invisible hand" in Saipan included sex slavery, sex trafficking, and forced abortions.[105]

Beginning in 1995, a bipartisan coalition in the US Senate and the House of Representatives introduced nearly thirty bills to address wages and immigration in the CNMI. True to his word, DeLay ensured that the bills died in committee. The lawsuits by Sweatshop Watch in 1999 renewed national attention to the issue. ABC's 20/20 aired a special investigation on CNMI sweatshops, with reporter Connie Chung referring to them as a "shameful violation of human rights on American soil."[106] The story described forced prostitution, dangerous factories, and unsanitary food and water that led to food poisoning. Reporters also interviewed the governor of the CNMI, who said that he would certainly "crack down if he found any sweatshops," but he noted, without irony, that he "made a point not to visit them."[107] Implicated in the scandal, Congressman DeLay callously joked with reporters, saying, "I saw some of those factories. *They were air conditioned*. I didn't see anyone sweating."[108]

In 2006, Abramoff pled guilty to fraud and conspiracy and was sentenced to almost six years in prison, leading to an extensive and wide-reaching corruption investigation. In 2010, DeLay was sentenced to three years of prison for conspiracy and money laundering, due in part to accepting bribes to ensure that the CNMI remained a haven for sweatshops.[109]

In the aftermath of the Kathie Lee scandal, *The Free Market*, the monthly newsletter of the Auburn University–affiliated libertarian Ludwig von Mises Institute, claimed that sweatshops were "the best thing that's happened to the third world in decades."[110] Like DeLay, economist William Anderson argued that rather than exploiting children in Honduras, Gifford and Walmart were giving them the great gift of a job. Echoing the "Liberty of Contract" arguments of a century prior, Anderson described a world in which workers, including children, had the freedom and mobility to seek employment wherever they wanted and under whatever conditions they preferred. By this logic, working in a sweatshop, regardless of the conditions, was a natural expression of a worker's freedom and desire—not exploitation by the powerful, coercive forces of industry and government. Of course, in reality, that "freedom" was enforced with barbed wire and armed guards.

Defending sweatshops, and the economy that they propped up, was not just a fringe project. In the hallowed pages of the *New York Times*, well-known, center-right columnist Nicholas Kristof presented sweatshops as a stepping stone toward middle-class prosperity. He argued, in effect, that just as the working classes in the United States had magically transitioned from the brutality of early twentieth-century factories and mines to the American Dream of the 1950s, so too, would the factory workers of Honduras, Bangladesh, and Thailand. In 2000, Kristof penned an article entitled "Two Cheers for Sweatshops," claiming:

Sweatshops that seem brutal from the vantage point of an American sitting in his living room can appear tantalizing to a Thai laborer getting by on beetles. Fourteen years ago, we moved to Asia and began reporting there. Like most Westerners, we arrived in the region outraged at sweatshops. In time, though, we came to accept the view supported by most Asians: that the campaign against sweatshops risks harming the very people it is intended to help. For beneath their grime, sweatshops are a clear sign of the industrial revolution that is beginning to reshape Asia.[111]

To Kristof, anti-sweatshop activists were naïve and paternalistic, and worse, their actions actually undermined the interests of workers by destroying their opportunities. As Kristof writes, "The simplest way to help the poorest Asians would be to buy more from sweatshops, not less."[112] In a follow-up piece promoting African sweatshops six years later, Kristof doubled down, claiming that instead of fighting sweatshops, "well-meaning American university students" should "campaign in favor of sweatshops."[113] In reality, groups like Sweatshop Watch, Global Exchange, the National Labor Committee, and USAS worked directly with factory workers, and their demands were for basic labor standards and independent monitoring, not the closing of factories. This misdirection from Anderson, Kristof, and their ilk also failed to account for contemporary sweatshops in the United States itself, the existence of which undermined several of their key talking points.

Sweatshop apologists often repeated the myth that wages in foreign factories were only low by US standards, but the reality was that most sweatshops workers made somewhere between one-quarter and one-half of what they needed to afford basic nutrition, housing, heat, clothing, and transportation. Many workers also had to leave their children with family members and were rarely able to visit. Worldwide, manufacturers also locked workers inside of factories to ensure they did not take bathroom breaks or steal products—the same practice that had led to tragedy a century earlier. Kristof's rhetorical pull-quote, "What's worse than being exploited? Not being exploited," presents capital's argument—that sweatshops were the alternative to starvation and death, that those were the only two conceivable options, and that those two realities were not related.[114]

Benjamin Powell, executive director of the Free Market Institute at Texas Tech University, drew a similar conclusion, arguing that sweatshops were just part of the process of development and would raise living standards. In his defense of sweatshops, Powell claims that "what the third world so badly needs is more 'sweatshop jobs,' not fewer."[115] At the turn of the twenty-first century, though, the UN estimated that some two million workers were killed by occupational diseases and accidents every year—an average of five thousand a day. As an industry representative had complained to the Smithsonian, though, it is very difficult to describe sweatshops in a way that is "evenhanded."[116]

Meanwhile, a new rising death toll began competing for public sympathies and activists' attention. The US-led Global War on Terror caused the Global Justice Movement to shift much of its immediate focus to organizing against the occupations of Iraq and Afghanistan and the Bush administration's torture program. Global Exchange's Medea Benjamin, for example, formed the antiwar group CODEPINK, so named because of the administration's color-coded threat assessment. Students, among others, organized massive protests in opposition to the March 2003 invasion of Iraq, and criticism of the war was greeted with death threats and accusations of supporting the enemy. Like World War I, the War on Terror had a broad chilling effect on civil liberties and progressive politics, and it undercut much of the momentum of the prior decade's social movements.

The free trade initiatives of the 1990s proved to be just the latest initiative on behalf of sweatshop capital. In the early twenty-first century, sweatshops—still carefully out of sight to avoid consumers' discomfort—became more and more normalized, an assumption rather than an anomaly in the booming global economy. Though USAS, UNITE, and others continued to highlight the links between global capitalism and exploitation, incidents of child labor and even slavery barely raised eyebrows around the world.

Like the anti-sweatshop activists of the Progressive Era, the movement of the 1990s largely focused on garment production as the primary site of sweated labor, deliberately drawing historical parallels to the undeniably brutal working and living conditions the industry forced upon its workforce of mostly women and children. In the 2010s and 2020s, the focus of the next chapter, activists broadened their focus on sweatshops and hyperexploitation to include other industries, notably including fast food, retail, care, and gig work. Perhaps forecasting a new era of change, like the WTUL's Mary Anderson and NCL's Frances Perkins before them, some of the activists of the 1990s also rose to positions of greater political power, notably including Sweatshop Watch's Nikki Bas, who became president of the Oakland City Council, and Julie Su, who became acting secretary of Labor in the Biden administration.

4

"AMAZON CRIME"
THE OMNIPRESENCE OF THE NEW GLOBAL ASSEMBLY LINE

On November 26, 2021, "Black Friday," the retail industry's busiest day—thirty-one protesters were arrested for blockading roads in and out of Amazon-affiliated warehouses, depots, and other sites across the United Kingdom. Locked to barrels or suspended above street level atop bamboo structures, the protestors and their banners decried the world's largest e-commerce company for exploiting "people and the planet."[1] One demonstrator also displayed an effigy of Amazon founder Jeff Bezos and a mock "Blue Origin" rocket ship adorned with the slogans, "To Extinction and Beyond" and "Amazon Crime." The activists, members of the environmental group Extinction Rebellion, said their goal was "to draw attention to Amazon's exploitative and environmentally destructive business practices" and its "disregard for workers' rights in the name of company profits."[2] Similar protests that day targeted Amazon sites in the Netherlands, Germany, and elsewhere.[3]

A year earlier, also on Black Friday, Amazon workers in fifteen countries had organized strikes and protests demanding that the company increase pay amid the coronavirus pandemic and commit itself to a goal of zero carbon emissions by 2030. In a statement signed by unions and other groups, the protests' organizers objected to the company's massive pandemic windfall not being shared with workers, writing, "During the Covid-19 pandemic, Amazon became a trillion-dollar corporation with Bezos becoming the first person in history to amass $200 billion in personal wealth. Meanwhile, Amazon warehouse workers risked their lives as essential workers, and only briefly received a modest increase in pay."[4]

In addition to Black Friday and its e-commerce counterpart "Cyber Monday," Amazon workers and their allies have also repurposed the company's exclusive "Prime Day," which offers special deals for members and employees, as a day to protest working conditions and urge boycotts. In 2018, for example, Amazon workers in Europe walked off the job on Prime Day. In the lead-up to Prime Day in 2020, activists demonstrated outside one of Bezos' many houses, demanding that workers receive hazard pay and protective equipment. In 2021, the watchdog group Public Citizen posted to social media an "Amazon Prime Day reminder that Amazon raised prices on essential products by up to 1,000% during the throes of the pandemic."[5]

Activists have also tried to target the big money that drives the company. In spring 2021, for example, on the eve of an annual shareholder meeting, protesters rallied outside of the offices of five of Amazon's major investors, including Blackrock, T. Rowe Price, and Fidelity. Marching through Blackrock's lobby wearing protective masks, activists carried signs reading "Amazon Hurts Working People" and "Eyes on Amazon" while chanting, "Bezos, Bezos, you can't hide, we can see your greedy side!"[6] Their demands included improved working conditions, reduction of the company's carbon footprint, and an end to its cooperation with police and immigration authorities. The next year, Amazon shareholders heard—and rejected—fifteen proposals on workers' rights and the environment, including a motion by the investor-activist group Tulipshare. On its march to global dominance, Amazon has taken over retail markets, warehouse space, roads, and even calendars. Its critics, however, have tried to use all of those places—and dates—to publicize their grievances.[7]

The overlap in their demands—for better working conditions, human rights, and environmental policy—speaks to shifting alliances among social movements, which for decades had been played against one another by big business in a zero-sum game for either jobs or a livable planet. The many protest actions against Amazon in recent years also speak to a particular historical moment, in which capital, the internet, climate change—and a pandemic—are all global. They impact, and link together, people all over the world.

In many ways, the movements of the twenty-first century have extended the Global Justice Movement—which brought together labor, environmental, Indigenous rights, and student groups—while adding elements of Occupy Wall Street (OWS) and Black Lives Matter (BLM). In the decades since the Seattle WTO protests, labor organizers—notably including young people and people of color—developed relevant, savvy campaigns, such as

"Fight for $15," centered on fast food and retail workers earning minimum wage. In the aftermath of the Great Recession, ows's chant, "We are the 99%," resonated with millions of Americans who were laid off and lost their retirement savings, only to see their government bail out the financial institutions that had caused the crisis in the first place. Responding to the public executions of African Americans by police, millions of Americans also joined multiple waves of BLM protests, including perhaps the most widespread protests in US history in 2020. Meanwhile, constant climate disasters—and little movement on reducing CO_2 emissions—drove activists to try to hold wealthy nations and the fossil fuel industry accountable through mass protest and civil disobedience against oil and gas pipelines.[8]

As hubs for profit and labor exploitation, mass energy consumption, misinformation, and political manipulation, the corporate behemoths of the twenty-first century—Amazon, Apple, Google, Facebook (now Meta), and others—have become emblematic of all these issues.

From Michael Jordan and Nike to Kathie Lee Gifford and Walmart, the American consumer economy of the 1990s used brand names and celebrity icons to conceal sweatshop labor subcontracted in factories overseas, hidden in plain sight in big US cities, and relocated behind US prison walls. In these factories, terrible working conditions—and resulting tragedies—harkened back to a century prior, calling into question whether there actually is a dividing line between the present and the distant past, or if there is simply a through-line of hyperexploitation, only periodically acknowledged. In 1993, a fire in Thailand's Kader Factory killed nearly two hundred workers, who had made toys for companies like Fisher-Price, Hasbro, and Toys "R" Us. Much like the victims of the 1911 Triangle Factory Fire, the Kader workers were mostly young women. Also like the Triangle tragedy, the Thai workers had been locked inside their factory.[9]

Twenty years later, in April 2013, the collapse of the Rana Plaza Building in Dhaka, Bangladesh, killed more than a thousand workers and injured thousands more—many of whom had to have arms and legs amputated in order to escape the rubble. A fire at another Bangladesh factory just months earlier had killed 112 workers; yet another fire, two weeks after the Rana Plaza tragedy, killed an additional eight workers. The victims, all employed in the country's massive twenty-billion-dollar garment industry, made clothes for Walmart, Sears, and Children's Place, among other retailers.[10]

4.1 Thousands of garment workers and their unions rallied throughout Bangladesh on the one-year anniversary of the Rana Plaza collapse that killed more than a thousand garment workers in April 2013. Courtesy of Solidarity Center.

Obscuring these devastating continuities with the past, the "new" global economy of the twenty-first century has also promised to offer something different: the arrival of the "future," a world partially imagined in science-fiction a half-century earlier. For consumers, this future brought slick, cutting-edge technology—iPhones, iPods, and iPads. These devices provided access to a world of instant, dot-com consumption: tailor-made advertising on social media and targeted search engines, one-click streaming entertainment, and one-stop online shopping via mass retailers such as eBay, Etsy, and Amazon. Behind this futuristic convenience, however, is the reality that these devices first pass through the hands of brutalized workers. Human rights researcher Siddharth Kara wrote in 2018, for example, that as many as thirty-five thousand children—some as young as six years old—were among the hundreds of thousands toiling in the cobalt mines of the Democratic Republic of the Congo (DRC) to provide a key component of the rechargeable batteries in smartphones, computers, tablets, and electric vehicles. Another investigation of the DRC, which produces some 60 percent of the world's cobalt, noted that "children who work in the

112 CHAPTER FOUR

mines are often drugged, in order to suppress hunger."¹¹ Among the notable companies that have been linked to Congolese child labor are Apple, Google, Dell, Microsoft, and Tesla.¹²

For growing swaths of workers in the United States and beyond, the future has also arrived as the "gig economy," purportedly flexible, temporary, and voluntary employment with hip start-ups like Uber, Lyft, Door-Dash, Instacart, and others—often tied to apps on smartphones. Just as Nicholas Kristof and others had praised foreign sweatshops as wonderful opportunities for struggling workers, the gig economy, in which workers often piece together multiple "gigs" without benefits or job security, has also had its cheerleaders. For example, Steve Strauss, responding to a miserable freelance worker in *USA Today*, offered that despite the lack of benefits—and the difficulty of finding any work at all—gig workers ("a new breed of entrepreneurs, freelancers, and the self-employed who work for themselves") enjoyed unparalleled "flexibility and freedom" and represented "the future of work."¹³ Yue Zheng, writing for the *Independent*, similarly praised the "growing world of flexible employment" in China.¹⁴ Gig work has specifically been championed as an "incredible opportunity" for women, who, amid disappearing social services, are often expected to find employment while also providing care for children and other relatives.¹⁵

Despite the rhetoric of freedom and flexibility, the futuristic present that arrived was dystopian: brutal sweatshop factory labor around the globe, corporate and state surveillance documenting internet and phone activity (and using it to create algorithms of advertising and misinformation), growing corporate monopolies, and an unstable, precarious economy that increasingly monetized and transformed "free" time into longer work hours for minimal pay. Just as apparel retailers had claimed no responsibility for workers in their subcontracted factories in the 1990s, companies like Uber argued that their workers were independent contractors—not employees—thus allowing them to sidestep legal mandates around benefits, wages, and liability. While often billed as an opportunity for workers to become "their own boss," the independence in many of these gigs was comparable to that afforded to the domestic workers who sold their services at the Bronx "slave market" during the Great Depression. Their freedom was essentially the "Liberty of Contract" offered a century prior—the freedom to be independently at the complete mercy of employers and to work for poverty wages. In short, the precarity and hyperexploitation of the deregulated twenty-first-century economy was presaged by one in which those regulations had rarely materialized, an economy that thrived on the brutalization of marginalized and vulnerable groups—women, people of color, migrants, foreign workers, queer workers, and others—for more than a century. Perhaps unsurprisingly, miserable, struggling workers and those observing their industries have routinely used the term "sweatshop" to describe Apple factories, Amazon warehouses, and Uber vehicles—the latter labeled a "sweatshop on wheels."[16]

Like the sweatshop economy a century earlier, which spanned from garment factories to department stores, the sweatshops of the twenty-first century have not been limited to sites of production. Brutal labor conditions span from mines and fields that extract raw materials, such as those in the DRC, to factories where they are made into consumer products, to storage warehouses, to retailers—and throughout transportation networks that connect them all. But despite the many parallels with earlier moments, this sweatshop economy is on a scale unseen in human history. The environmental destruction in its wake is similarly unprecedented.[17]

Perhaps most sobering, considering the worsening climate catastrophe, is the fact that the bulk of global CO_2 emissions have been emitted just in recent decades, since the dawn of the "free trade" era in the previous chapter. As the Institute for European Environmental Policy noted in 2020, more than half of the world's CO_2 emissions since 1751 has been produced just in the past thirty years. As of 2019, China was the worst offender, emitting nearly a third of the world's greenhouse gases—more than "the entire developed world combined"—and more than double the United States, the second largest emitter.[18] The full, global picture is more complicated, however, as China's per capita emissions are about half that of the United States—and China's contribution includes manufacturing for US corporations and US customers. In 2020, for example, the United States imported $434.7 billion in goods from China—roughly a quarter of that electronics. As the UN Environment Programme outlined in its urgent 2022 report, the distribution of CO_2 emissions tells a radically different story when measured by consumers rather than national borders, as wealthy consumer populations—such as those of the United States and the European Union—far outpace net-exporter nations, such as China and India.[19]

Though the fossil fuel industry rightly gets much of the attention surrounding the climate catastrophe, Amazon, which devotes significant resources to maintaining a well-refined, environmentally conscious corporate image, offers a lens into the relationship between consumption and pollution. In 2019, Jeff Bezos announced that the company would reach net-zero carbon emissions by 2040, but the company's emissions have instead grown steadily. According to one estimate, Amazon's annual output is roughly equivalent to that of 180 gas-fired power plants. Further, the company's own estimates of its carbon footprint may leave out the production of about 60 percent of the items it sells, by counting only those that are Amazon-branded.[20]

To its customers, the company's global environmental footprint may seem abstract or distant, but there are many local impacts, as well. In the United Kingdom, for example, a 2021 undercover investigation into waste at just one of Amazon's hundreds of warehouses found that workers there were required to destroy roughly 130,000 unsold or returned items each week, including electronics, books, medical masks, and household goods—many of them unopened and in their original packaging. In Southern California, where Amazon delivers a billion packages a year, corporate warehouses, including Amazon's, are often located in areas where residents are disproportionately low-income people of color. The constant truck traffic in and out of the hundreds of warehouses has been linked to high rates of asthma, cancer, and cardiovascular disease among residents. Meanwhile, plastic from Amazon packaging winds up in waterways all over the world. In 2020, a conservation organization estimated that Amazon produced some five hundred million pounds of plastic packaging each year—enough to "circle the Earth 500 times."[21] Amazon officials countered that the actual number was closer to one-quarter of that, which is still stunning.[22]

As omnipresent as Amazon is, however, the company is not alone. It is merely a trendsetter. In 2019, the global economy produced an estimated 53.6 million metric tons of "e-waste"—smart phones, tablets, video game consoles, large appliances, and other electronics—a number growing steadily each year. Less than 20 percent of that waste was disposed of in any environmentally conscious way. Paralleling CO2 emissions, the largest producers of global electronic waste were in Asia, but the highest waste per capita belonged to wealthy consumer regions, such as the United States and Europe.[23]

The brutal working conditions in twenty-first-century sweatshops echo those of earlier historical periods. Like a century ago, massive wealth is being accrued by consistently pushing workers to the limits of their physical and mental health, whether they are sewing clothes, making children's toys, or building iPhones. The threat that twenty-first-century sweatshops represent to future life on Earth, however, puts them in their own historical epoch.

Central to the global sweatshop economy is China. The country's rapid economic growth since opening to foreign investment in the late 1970s, and especially after joining the WTO in 2001, has been so tremendous that some have dubbed it the "China Miracle" or the "China Dream."[24] One of the key reforms was the establishment of special economic zones (SEZ), where global capitalism could thrive unrestrained within the otherwise communist country. Offering tax and trade incentives, minimal regulations, and local autonomy, the SEZs drew billions of dollars in foreign investment into China from Hong Kong, Singapore, Japan, the United States, and Western Europe. Primarily located on the coast for easy port access, the zones also drew millions of rural migrants and were viewed by officials as "social and economic laboratories in which new, controversial approaches to the challenges of modernization may be tried out."[25]

Inside these investor-friendly SEZ "laboratories," workers regularly labored for twelve-hour days before returning to sleep in company dormitories. In what is closer to a "China Nightmare," work absences were strongly discouraged, and workers were pressured to report to the assembly line through illnesses and injuries. In November 1993, just months after the Kader Toy Factory fire in Thailand that killed two hundred workers, a fire broke out at a Hong Kong–owned toy factory in Shenzhen, the first SEZ in China. Eighty-seven workers were killed and fifty-one sustained severe burn injuries. The windows of the factory had been barred and only one door of the three-story building was unlocked. Officials had been too worried about losing foreign investment to insist on the legally required safety precautions. Like the Kader workers, and the Triangle factory workers, most of the Shenzhen factory's four hundred employees were young women between sixteen and twenty-five-years old—migrants from rural parts of China.[26]

In Hong Kong, labor leaders said that workers there had experienced similar abuses in the 1950s and 1960s and expressed horror that such poor conditions had followed investments into China's SEZ. Activist Chan Ka Wai organized a Christmas boycott of toys linked to the Shenzhen factory, hoping to shine a light on the plight of Chinese workers. Even the Chinese Communist Party's official newspaper, *People's Daily*, had harsh words for management and local authorities when a chemical factory in Shenzhen exploded, killing fifteen and injuring more than eight hundred workers. Nevertheless, dangerous and exploitive conditions continued to characterize factories in the SEZs.[27]

Among the most infamous operators in China's SEZs is Foxconn, which has become nearly synonymous with the twenty-first-century sweatshop, in part because of the global spotlight on suicide among its workers—fourteen deaths in 2010 alone. The company, founded by billionaire Terry Gou in the 1970s, initially operated out of Taiwan, before opening its first overseas factory in the Shenzhen SEZ in 1988. Employing 150 migrant workers, two-thirds of whom were women, Foxconn's six-story building included dormitories and a cafeteria—much like the first textile mills of England and the United States, which had kept young women onsite and under the watchful eyes of their employers during the early 1800s. Foxconn then underwent rapid expansion in the early 2000s, growing from a workforce of 9,000 in 1996 to 1,300,000 in 2012. By then, its factory-dorm compounds were massive.[28]

As scholars Pun Ngai and Jenny Chan outline, by manufacturing component parts in-house and contracting with nearby mines, Foxconn effectively "integrates production into a chain extending from raw material extraction to final assembly to reduce market uncertainties and to enhance cost- and time-effectiveness."[29] This vertical monopoly has in turn allowed Foxconn to acquire massive contracts with many of the world's largest technology companies, including Apple, Amazon, Dell, Sony, Nintendo, Google, Microsoft, and Toshiba. By 2021, the company's annual revenue topped $200 billion.[30]

A combination of the tightly controlled Chinese state media and the United States's own propaganda interests has made accurate labor reporting in China difficult. Foxconn, for example, offered journalists only strictly curated access to factories—much like officials in Saipan had in the 1990s. Whistleblowers and investigators have also faced retribution. The picture painted by the precious few sources available is a grim one. During busy periods, twelve-to-fifteen-hour shifts six or seven days a week were not uncommon. Whistles guided the workday, and eating, laughing, and talking were all forbidden in the factories. Workers were not permitted to bring any electronic devices into work, and they were not allowed to wear any metal, even on their clothes. Workers did, however, breathe in aluminum dust from the polishing machines, and the tiny shards cut their eyes and hands. To appease monitors, the company provided masks and cotton gloves, but they were too flimsy to offer any real protection. Foxconn complexes housed tens of thousands of workers, and the strict rules from the workplace extended into dormitories. Up to ten people shared each sex-segregated room, and workers were sometimes required to share beds due to shortages. Each dorm floor housed about three hundred workers and contained one public shower and restroom. Workers reported standing in long lines to use filthy restrooms covered in excrement.[31]

To boost morale following the wave of worker suicides in 2010, the company relaxed some of its rules against talking on the shop floor, inadvertently opening women workers to a barrage of crude jokes, unwanted advances, and other sexual harassment. When women complained to supervisors, however, their concerns were dismissed as the inability to take a joke from "boys being boys." As a #MeToo movement swept China in 2018, similar complaints were made public by an anonymous Foxconn assembly-line worker in an essay entitled, "I Am a Woman Worker at Foxconn and I Demand a System That Opposes Sexual Harassment." According to the worker, the "rampant" abuse included "loud dirty jokes, ridiculing female colleagues about their looks and figures, [and] using the excuse of 'giving direction' to make unnecessary body contact."[32]

Among the most egregious labor practices at Foxconn has been its reliance on child interns. Vocational colleges were required by the Chinese government to send students to work in factories. As interns, the students were supposed to be protected by labor law that prevented them from working more than eight hours a day. Instead, they regularly worked their scheduled eight hours, plus two hours of overtime every weekday, and a full ten-to-twelve-hour shift on Saturdays. These children did not have the legal status as employees, and they also did not receive the technical training that Foxconn promised. Rather, they were assigned to work on one spot of the assembly line for hours on end. Their teachers, meanwhile, were required to supervise—and manage—them.[33]

As one seventeen-year-old intern explained to *The Guardian*, "I tried telling the manager of my line that I didn't want to work overtime. But the manager notified my teacher and the teacher said if I didn't work overtime, I could not intern at Foxconn and that would affect my graduation and scholarship applications at the school. I had no choice, I could only endure this."[34] When stories like this one have publicized Foxconn's illegal employment practices, company officials have blamed local management and pledged to fix the problem. However, the thousands of schoolchildren at its disposal made possible Foxconn's cheap and quick assembly of a wide range of products, such as the Amazon Alexa devices that the distraught seventeen-year-old helped build. These labor practices were–and are—the norm, not the exception, in the assembly line that produces much of the clothing, technology, and other consumer goods in American homes.[35]

In 2017, Foxconn signed a deal with Amazon to make the Echo, Echo Dot, and Kindle, creating fifteen thousand new jobs. In addition to the child interns, this labor force also included "dispatch workers," hyperprecarious temp workers recruited by employment agencies. In 2014, Chinese labor laws had been updated to require that dispatch workers could not comprise more than 10 percent of a workforce. However, four years later, factories were found to be exceeding those limits by as much as fourfold. At Foxconn, dispatch workers often put in sixty-hour weeks, accruing up to eighty hours in monthly overtime, far more than the thirty-six hours allowed.[36]

After the horrific and well-publicized suicides in 2010, Foxconn went on a public relations blitz. The company set up a "Care and Love" hotline that workers could call if they needed emotional support and organized an anti-suicide rally and some recreational activities. Foxconn installed mesh nets outside of the worker dormitories and stationed patrols along the roofs, though as one worker told *The Guardian*, "The nets are pointless. If somebody wants to commit suicide, they will do it."[37] But while careful to appear responsive, the company also took steps to distance its brutal working and living conditions from its employees' deaths, framing the suicides as the result of preexisting personal problems. For example, it began requiring new applicants to answer a thirty-six-question psychological test, ostensibly to weed out those with mental illnesses.[38]

Workers, however, repudiated the company's explanation. Even amid severe hopelessness and desperation, they attempted to use this apparent public relations weakness to their advantage. In January 2012, for example, 150 workers at a Foxconn factory in Wuhan that manufactured Xboxes for Microsoft climbed to the top of their six-story dormitory, threatened mass suicide, and demanded severance pay. Microsoft and Wuhan officials took the threats seriously, and the company negotiated with the workers, who had endured freezing temperatures for eight hours.[39]

The bleak protest was part of a growing movement of disgruntled Foxconn workers. In June 2012, more than one hundred workers at a Foxconn factory in Chengdu allegedly rioted. Foxconn and local officials adamantly denied that protests were over wages or poor working conditions, and instead pointed to alcohol, disruptive new hires, and misunderstandings. A few months later, some two thousand workers also rebelled at a Foxconn factory in Taiyuan, which made iPhones, prompting officials to send five thousand police to quell the situation. While Foxconn dismissed the altercation as the result of a personal disagreement, workers said that it was in response to a brutal beating by security guards. There is little transparency on these topics, but what is clear, even without more specific details, is that workers were miserable and that they periodically pushed back.[40]

While schemes to contract and subcontract with foreign manufacturers have generally allowed US retailers to claim ignorance of—and distance from—the working conditions that produce their goods, the suicides at Foxconn were egregious enough to compel a response from Apple. Speaking publicly to celebrate the success of the company's iPad, CEO Steve Jobs called the deaths at Foxconn "troubling" and "a difficult situation," but, he said with pride, the company's factory was "not a sweatshop."[41] Nonetheless, Apple moved a few of its iPad and iPhone orders to other factories as a warning to Foxconn to handle the crisis—or at least manage the fall-out. In January 2012, Apple also joined the FLA—the group lambasted by USAS as a PR stunt—to demonstrate its commitment to human rights. The FLA subsequently investigated Foxconn and released its findings that August, heaping praise on Apple and Foxconn for improvements. However, independent organizations, such as the Economic Policy Institute, were quick to point out that Apple itself financed the FLA, and that major issues, such as wage theft and violations of Chinese overtime laws, had gone unaddressed.[42]

As evidence of its commitment to improve working conditions, in 2013, Apple made public an internal report that found 106 cases of child labor in its manufacturing, as well as "a catalogue of other offences, ranging from mandatory pregnancy tests, to bonded workers whose wages are confiscated to pay off debts imposed by recruitment agencies."[43] Admitting that there was a problem seemed to be the first step toward fixing it. In 2020, however, an investigation found that Apple had continued to contract with a Chinese manufacturer for three years, even after it had caught that company, repeatedly, employing children as young as fourteen. Insiders noted that the situation was not uncommon among Apple's suppliers.[44]

Self-regulation through corporate codes of conduct and industry-led monitors like the FLA, protected companies by deflecting public criticism, but—as activists had warned—they failed to protect workers. When workers, activists, and journalists could point to violations of labor laws, such as those limiting the hours of student interns and dispatch workers, neither management nor local officials—let alone US retailers—chose to intervene. This effective collusion between employers and government has increasingly led to the reemergence of the solidarity model at the turn of the last century—essentially cooperation between workers and sympathetic (and generally more privileged) outsider allies, often rooted in independent investigations.

One group that launched its own investigations of Foxconn was the Hong Kong–based Students and Scholars Against Corporate Misbehaviour (SACOM), which was created by professors and students from eight different universities in 2005. Hoping to learn more about about the impacts of global capitalism on Chinese workers, the group's members read about the US-based efforts of USAS and its WRC, and they gradually developed relationships with activists and scholars in the United States and in Europe, notably including American labor historians and sociologists. SACOM was the first organization to publicize Foxconn's reliance on child workers and illegal overtime, as well as its workers' suicides. The group quickly became a widely respected source on working conditions in Chinese factories.[45]

Jenny Chan, then a sociology student in Hong Kong, says that through their studies, the students began to understand that Chinese labor laws and regulations—though "beautiful" on paper—were not being implemented and that even large, modern factories could be sweatshops. Chan says that US and European companies were cutting costs by violating labor and environmental laws, while government officials looked the other way to attract and retain them. To pressure global corporations, the students of SACOM traveled to mainland China to interview workers and collect photographs, labor contracts, and other documents. "What we found," Chan says, were "broken arms and the loss of young lives. It was shocking."[46] Though their pressure campaigns involved public press conferences, the research phase was "undercover." Chan says, for example, that group members approached workers while distributing flyers touting Chinese labor laws, both highlighting violations and providing a pro-government cover story in case they were questioned.[47]

SACOM's first campaign, in 2005, was strategically timed around the opening of Hong Kong Disneyland and highlighted the disconnect between the "magic" of Disney and the sweatshop conditions for workers producing the company's toys and gifts. Sweatshop Watch activist Karin Mak traveled from California to China to coproduce an eleven-minute investigative video, which SACOM then sent to Charles Kernaghan's National Labor Committee. Kernaghan screened the video at a press conference, allowing US media to hear from workers about the forced overtime in hot factories using machines without even basic safeguards—and to see their injured hands. Chan says that the opening of Hong Kong Disneyland provided a unique opportunity to investigate the hidden human costs in the supply chain that produced Mickey Mouse and Winnie the Pooh toys and books ("Everyone loves Mickey Mouse and Winnie the Pooh," she says).[48] While

4.2 A six-meter-long banner titled "No More iSlave" when SACOM protested at a large shopping mall in Hong Kong in 2011. This was planned to protest the 2010 suicides at Foxconn and coincided with Apple opening its first store in Hong Kong. Courtesy of Jenny Chan.

government officials and media excitedly touted new jobs and economic growth, SACOM capitalized on global interest in the park's opening to highlight the working conditions behind the scenes. Three years later, SACOM followed up on the company's lack of transparency and progress, writing:

> Disney has denied social responsibility for Chinese migrant workers, predominately young girls, who produce their merchandise. There is no fairytale ending for overworked Disney toy workers, who often work up to seven days a week and sixteen hours a day making toys based on characters from Pirates of the Caribbean during peak production seasons.[49]

Like the apparel tags in the Kathie Lee Gifford scandal of the 1990s, the National Labor Committee and SACOM understood the value of a smoking gun—in this case a sweatshop worker holding up a Mickey Mouse book in the video—and the need for international pressure to force companies to act. In addition to the forced overtime and poor pay, SACOM put a spotlight on the dangerous conditions in Chinese factories. In its 2008 Disney report, SACOM documented hundreds of workers' fingers cut off by machines used to make Disney-branded books for children.[50]

SACOM also publicized the chemical poisoning taking place at Wintek, a contractor making touch screens for Apple devices. The chemical, hexyl hydride, evaporated more quickly than alcohol, which proved to be a compelling justification for Wintek and Apple management. Wintek did not improve ventilation when making the switch, nor did the company assess the possible risk of the chemical, which was well known in industry. Workers suffered nerve and eye damage, as well as swelling and pain in their feet, and fatigue. More than sixty workers were hospitalized, and an occupational disease hospital eventually linked hexyl hydride to the injuries. The poisoning, and the cancelation of an annual bonus, prompted a protest by two thousand workers. In response, the company reinstated the bonus and discontinued the use of hexyl hydride. Apple refused to comment on the poisoning, instead hiding behind its corporate code of conduct.[51]

Drawing on USAS's relationship to universities, Chan says that rather than appealing to individual consumers, the most successful corporate pressure campaigns leverage the collective buying power of institutions—churches, colleges, and government offices—to bargain with companies like Dell, Samsung, and Apple. Because they negotiate such large contracts, institutions can demand protections for workers and the environment as a requirement for doing business. These agreements can alter the power dynamic even more by pushing for independent monitors.[52]

SACOM's initial successes attracted funding for an office and professional staff. In addition to building capacity and stability, the group's members—many of them college students—were able to study abroad or move for work opportunities without fear that their campaigns would collapse. By 2015, however, the relative freedoms that had allowed activists to operate in Hong Kong began to erode amid a clampdown by the Chinese government. Chan, now a professor, says that her classes are recorded, and that there are topics she cannot discuss openly. "Several professors in Hong Kong who advocated for democracy were put in jail," she says. "No one knows if they will get out ever again, because the severest penalty is lifetime imprisonment."[53] In 2021, SACOM was forced to shut down entirely, cutting off one of the main sources of information on Chinese labor abuses.[54]

In the United States, the New York–based China Labor Watch (CLW), formed by Chinese activist and political refugee Li Qiang in 2000, has also worked to investigate working conditions in China and amplify workers' struggles—albeit from afar. For nearly a decade, Qiang volunteered with Charles Kernaghan's National Labor Committee, working together to coordinate factory investigations in China. By 2008, CLW had offices both in the United States and in China, and its reputation drew worker-activists to share their stories. However, maintaining the organization's funding has been a long-term challenge. As Qiang notes, CLW seeks to critique, not cooperate with, transnational corporations. As a result, the organization is at odds not only with industry, but also with private foundations, which often have corporate ties, and with the US government, which generally seeks to bolster, not undermine, American business interests.[55]

CLW's many projects have included working with undercover investigators in China, connecting Chinese whistleblowers to international media outlets, and boosting existing media coverage of Chinese labor conditions. In doing so, the organization has exposed illegal activity in the supply chains of numerous major corporations, notably including Apple and Amazon. In 2015, CLW published a report on Chinese toy manufacturers, producers of an estimated 75 percent of the world's toys. Drawing on news reports and US government documents, CLW focused on five major factories, which together employed some twenty thousand workers and supplied companies such as Hasbro, Mattel, Walmart, and Disney. In addition to documenting long hours, child labor violations, and workers' exposure to toxic chemicals, the CLW report also outlined some of the workers' efforts to push back against their employers. At one company, one hundred workers went on strike, demanding severance pay before the factory's impending relocation. When another factory, a Disney toy supplier in Shenzhen, also denied workers their severance, some traveled to Hong Kong to protest at Disneyland—where they were attacked and bloodied by riot police and K-9 units.[56]

In 2017, CLW published a three-month undercover investigation into factories that produced shoes for Guess?, Amazon, Ann Taylor, Kendall and Kylie, and the Ivanka Trump brand. After speaking with workers and entering the factories to take photos, investigators reported fifteen-hour workdays with just two days off per month. During busy times, workers were expected to labor eighteen-hour days—off at 1:30 a.m. and back to work at 7:10 a.m. The investigators also discovered illegal use of student interns, forced overtime, forging of pay stubs to show higher wages than were actually paid, physical and verbal abuse of workers, and greater fines being levied against women workers than against men. CLW published the report and sent letters to the brands that sourced from the factories, hoping to apply public pressure using Ivanka Trump's connection to the White House. CLW received no responses. However, the three investigators—Su Heng, Li Zhao, and Hua Haifeng—were subsequently discovered and arrested, and CLW's efforts in China were then forced underground.[57]

Another CLW contact, Tang Mingfang, was tortured and sentenced to two years in prison for "infringement of commercial secrets" after whistleblowing about illegal labor practices in Foxconn's Hengyang Factory.[58] A quality control engineer for Amazon's Kindle and Echo Smart speakers and displays, Mingfang had contacted CLW to report the factory's illegal use of student labor and was then connected with *The Guardian*. Though Amazon responded to the report with an investigation of the factory—and overtures about its commitment to ethical working conditions—the company did not use its position to shield the whistleblower. After his two-year prison term, Mingfang wrote an open letter to Jeff Bezos, which CLW published. In it, he described his arrest and forced confession, noting that police officers "battered [him] multiple times" and "repeatedly slapped and hit" him in the face and head. He also described being handcuffed into a "semi-crouching position" throughout the night, "unable to stand or sit down." Mingfang wrote that his "entire body shivered and shook" as he reluctantly signed a confession.[59]

Li Qiang describes factories in China as having "slave-like" working conditions, with few labor protections.[60] He says that when he asks workers about human rights, they dismiss the concept as fake—as American propaganda. What is tangible to them is daily oppression at the hands of US companies, like Apple, in "sweatshops funded by America."[61] Qiang says that women working in these factories, in addition to facing sexual harassment and assault, often must leave their children in their hometowns to be cared for by relatives, seeing them perhaps twenty days per year. This arrangement, while deeply scarring to multiple generations in China, is used by the Chinese government to attract foreign investment.[62]

Despite Steve Jobs's assurances to the contrary, Chinese factories—Foxconn and many others—were, and are, clearly sweatshops, with dangerous and miserable working conditions, brutally long hours, child labor abuses, and violent repression of labor activism. Though tight control over media access has limited the information that reaches consumers in the United States and Europe, corporations such as Apple and Amazon are fully aware of the conditions in their contracted factories.

In the case of Amazon, sweatshop conditions are also pervasive throughout its massive distribution networks in the United States, Europe, and beyond. And while not as repressive as China, information is controlled in the United States, as well. Amazon, for example, requires its warehouse workers to sign nondisclosure agreements (NDAs), and even its temporary workers must sign noncompetition agreements. Though it is unclear how restrictive these contracts are, the threat of legal action almost certainly has a chilling effect on current and former Amazon employees. Even an incomplete picture of Amazon working conditions in China, the United States, and elsewhere, though, makes clear that Amazon's supply chain, from the cobalt mines in the DRC, to the factories in China, to the warehouses worldwide, to the delivery trucks that drop smiling packages on Americans' doorsteps, relies on sweated labor.[63]

Located on the outskirts of cities throughout North America, Western Europe, India, Japan and elsewhere, Amazon's fulfillment warehouses—where products await purchase and shipping—have promised high wages and great benefits to attract Amazon employees. Inside, however, workers have struggled to meet management's expectations of extreme efficiency, describing the environment as a "pressure cooker."[64] Angel Rajal, an Amazon warehouse worker in Las Vegas, says that while handling returns, he was expected to process forty to sixty items per hour, or else risk being written up or fired. During his four years, Rajal was written up twice for dropping below the required quota—once when he was tending to a bloody nose and once for leaving early because of a family emergency. Karen Salasky, a former Amazon warehouse worker in Allentown, Pennsylvania, says the job made her cry herself to sleep. After essentially collapsing from the pace and the warehouse's extreme heat, Salasky was fired. She laments, "I don't know how they can treat people this way. I think the faster you work, the bigger raise they get, and they're just benefiting themselves and not caring about people."[65]

Amazon's warehouses are massive—the size of seventeen football fields—leading workers to walk up to thirty miles during each ten-hour shift, often in extremely hot temperatures. While other warehouses prop doors open in the summer months, Amazon has refused to do so, citing concerns about theft. In June 2011, an emergency room physician joined workers in reporting these unsafe conditions—including temperatures above 100 degrees—to federal regulators. In response, Amazon arranged for on-site medical staff during summer months and encouraged workers to constantly hydrate. Salasky says that previously she had "never worked for an employer that had paramedics waiting outside for people to drop."[66] In addition to the extreme heat, the wide range of consumer goods in Amazon's warehouse have also led to a variety of injuries. In December 2018, for example, a machine ruptured a can of bear repellent spray, sending twenty-four workers in a New Jersey warehouse to the hospital.[67]

In July 2022, a warehouse worker in New Jersey died of an apparent heart attack during the company's extra busy Prime Day. Amazon officials denied that the worker's death was caused by the job, but coworkers said they had repeatedly complained about the heat in the unairconditioned warehouse and had requested fans just hours before their colleague collapsed. Three years earlier, a warehouse worker in Etna, Ohio, also suffered a heart attack and died on the job—and was not found for twenty minutes. A year before that, a worker in the same warehouse had also died of a heart attack. In just the first three months of that year, twenty-eight 911 calls were made from the Etna warehouse, including five for injuries and five for concerns about self-harm. For consumers, Prime Day represents an opportunity for bargains and early holiday shopping, but for workers, it means additional stress and misery—and in some cases, death.[68]

In the seventeen US states that collect this type of data, emergency workers were called to Amazon warehouses at least 189 times for mental health crises, including suicide attempts, between 2013 to 2018. The fulfillment centers were dangerous in other ways, as well, and injuries there have doubled the national industry average. In Minnesota, for example, according to Amazon's own figures, between 2018 and 2020, one in every nine Amazon warehouse workers suffered an injury. In May 2018, a UK report revealed that ambulances had been called to Amazon's warehouses there six hundred times in a three-year span.[69]

Like Foxconn, Amazon has responded to the mental health crisis caused by its sweatshop working conditions not by changing those conditions—say, by reducing quotas or offering breaks long enough to reach break rooms—but, instead, by launching a public relations campaign. While Foxconn deemed suicide nets and a care hotline sufficient, Amazon focused on a much more elaborate—and expensive—program that included hourly reminders to stretch, more nutritious food in break rooms, and other "wellness" initiatives, with names such as "WorkingWell," "EatWell," and "AmaZen." The program's most dystopian component involved the installation of "Zenbooth" pods, where an exhausted worker could briefly meditate, cool off in front of a fan, and enjoy blue-tinted light—before returning to their grueling schedule.[70]

Much of Amazon's success has come from "Prime" membership. For an annual fee, Amazon Prime entitles members to free, two-day shipping on many of the items sold on the website. This quick turnaround has forced high quotas at every stage, from the factories, to the warehouses, to the delivery vans. The 2020 Covid-19 pandemic, which boosted Amazon sales when consumers avoided in-person shopping, only intensified the pressure on delivery drivers to fulfill the companies' promises. In the United Kingdom, Amazon became the largest private delivery service, accounting for about 15 percent of the almost 5.5 billion packages sent in 2021. Angel Rajal, the Amazon worker in Las Vegas, switched to delivery driving after four years in the fulfillment warehouse, hoping for more freedom and less isolation. During his ten-hour shifts, he was expected to deliver four hundred packages. He was allotted thirty seconds for each. Amazon also installed surveillance cameras in its delivery vans, and drivers received notification "dings" if they took a drink of water or changed the radio station. As dings added up, drivers were then punished by having their hours docked or by being fired. If any packages remained at the end of a shift, drivers have said that they were not allowed to work (or get paid for) the next day. Like domestic workers in an earlier chapter, drivers continued their work off the clock, delivering packages even beyond their nine and ten-hour shifts in order to keep their jobs. The drivers, classified as independent contractors rather than company employees, have complained that the number of stops and packages increased so much that they were not able to put on seatbelts in between deliveries, break for lunch, or stop to use the bathroom—let alone have a moment for "AmaZen" relaxation.[71]

In 2021, when rumors began to circulate that delivery quotas in the United States prompted workers to urinate in bottles, Amazon representatives attempted to get ahead of the story, patronizingly posting on Twitter (now X), "You don't really believe the peeing in bottles thing, do you? If that were true, nobody would work for us."[72] Within twelve hours, Amazon's statement had gone viral. The blunder was quote-tweeted more than nine thousand times, drew media attention, and focused public scrutiny on an indignity that was not previously well-known. In a gross, but incredibly effective form of social media protest, drivers then posted pictures of bottles, cups, and bags of urine in Amazon delivery vans. One worker noted that he specifically stopped for coffee every morning before clocking in so that he would have a cup to urinate in during his shift. A journalist also produced pictures of an employee manual, with rules about cleaning vans at the end of shifts, which specifically pointed to bottles of urine. When covering the story, *The Guardian* closed an article by noting the number of bathrooms in Jeff Bezos's own home—a whopping twenty-five. Amazon walked back its denial but deflected responsibility, saying it was an industry-wide problem, worsened by public restrooms being closed because of the pandemic. The drivers, however, pointed to delivery quotas, which made breaks effectively impossible even when restrooms were available. Meanwhile, Amazon's model of free, two-day shipping set the pace for other e-commerce businesses and delivery services, prompting them to adopt similar practices in order to be competitive.[73]

Amid the "pee bottle" uproar, some Amazon delivery drivers walked off the job in protest, while others posted photos to social media of packages that they had deliberately delivered upside down, transforming the company's smiling logo into a frown. However, coordinating effective protest proved difficult, as the drivers, like domestic workers, were isolated, operated independently over long hours, and were contracted by different employers.[74]

As sensational as the pee bottle story was, the accessibility of bathrooms was only one of the many hazards for the growing network of independent contractors who deliver Amazon's packages at such high speeds. A 2022 study found that Amazon delivery drivers suffered injuries—trips, falls, dog bites, and vehicle accidents—at 2.5 times the industry average. In 2021, one in five of the company's delivery drivers had been injured, and one in seven had been injured so severely that they could not do their jobs. In August 2022, a twenty-five-year-old driver was killed when his truck went off an embankment in Washington. The next month, a seven-year-old in North Carolina was hospitalized after being hit by an Amazon delivery truck while walking home from school. A month after that, a woman in California was killed in a collision with an Amazon delivery truck, and an Amazon delivery driver in Missouri was killed after being attacked by dogs. The accidents and injuries are ubiquitous—just some of the costs of doing business for Amazon's own "sweatshops on wheels."[75]

Amazon is perhaps not unique, and the business practices of other industry leaders, whether Apple, Walmart, or Nike, are similarly emblematic of the modern sweatshop economy. Amazon is a trendsetter, however, establishing standards for delivery drivers and warehouse workers that competitors can only hope to emulate. In the United States, the company's promise of cheap, easy consumption, as well as employment, comes on the heels of decades of deindustrialization, inflation, and cuts to public services. In the twenty-first-century United States, there are dwindling economic opportunities for working-class people, and American cities and workers are both desperate.

In March 2020, Amazon opened a new warehouse in Bessemer, Alabama, just outside of Birmingham. The 855,000-square-foot building boasted 1,500 employees, twenty-two miles of conveyer belts, and the capacity to ship one hundred thousand items daily. City boosters were eager for the jobs, and famous athlete Bo Jackson returned to his hometown to tour the site while it was still under construction. "It's impressive," Jackson said. "Bessemer needs it."[76] He was not wrong that Bessemer residents needed good jobs. According to the recent census data, the majority Black city of twenty-six thousand has a median household income of just $30,000 and a poverty rate of more than 25 percent. The city had been a major steel industry hub throughout most of the twentieth century, but by the 1980s, it was in crisis, as industry disappeared and left poverty, crime, and misery in its wake. To Bessemer, news of the Amazon warehouse and its promise of jobs with full benefits, educational incentives, and an average hourly wage of $14.65, was cause for celebration. Welcoming the company, Bessemer Mayor Ken Gulley said, "Words cannot truly express the excitement this announcement has brought to our city."[77]

The opening of the Bessemer warehouse coincided with the onset of the Covid-19 pandemic and widespread shifts in the United States to remote learning, working, and shopping—a boon for Amazon. During the first fifteen months of the pandemic, Amazon shares increased in value by 87 percent and Jeff Bezos's personal net worth jumped an astonishing $86 billion. Following the lead of numerous US companies, Amazon offered its warehouse workers hazard pay bumps of an additional two dollars per hour in recognition of their increased risks and exposure. However, Amazon had cut even this paltry bonus, which only added up to an additional eighty dollars a week for full-time employees, by early June 2020. By then, at least eight Amazon workers had died, and more than one hundred of the company's warehouses had confirmed Covid-19 cases. Rescinding the bonus, however, was not a denial of the virus' dangers—it was a comment on the disposability of warehouse workers. After all, the company's corporate employees in Seattle were allowed to work remotely for another year and a half. The warehouse workers, by contrast, received regular messages about infections and outbreaks among their coworkers, and by October 2021, more than twenty thousand Amazon workers had contracted the virus.[78]

In addition to the dangers of the pandemic, the Bessemer workers experienced constant worry that they were not moving fast enough. Workers were fired for minor infractions—even technological glitches—without warning or additional training. They were forced to take unscheduled breaks, based on production needs, and then were not able to take their regular breaks when they needed and expected them. One warehouse worker recounted, "I went out to break one day, and I was stopped by security to do a random security check. When they made me take my shoes off and empty my pockets, and I asked if I would get that time back for my break. They said no."[79] Additionally, Amazon scheduled its biggest sale of the year, Prime Day, for October 2020, further extending the peak holiday season for already exhausted workers. Another Prime Day was planned for June 2021, during the heat of the summer. While the Bessemer warehouse did have some air conditioning, the warehouse's size made it largely ineffective. According to workers, the loading dock was especially miserable with the sticky humidity and heat of the Alabama summer.[80]

Sara Marie Thrasher worked at the Bessemer warehouse in 2020. "They work you to death," she says. "I had my watch on, which said I walked 12 miles and 50 flights of stairs."[81] Byron Tollison, who also worked at the warehouse, says it was "like a sweatshop."[82] Indeed, for all its technocratic innovations, Amazon's obsession with maximizing workers' production regardless of the impacts is nothing new. Jeff Bezos's sweatshops are just some of the most recent in a long history.

Many of the Bessemer workers said that the conditions were of much more concern than their wages. One warehouse worker, Jennifer Bates, testified in front of the US Senate that the shifts were long, the pace was extremely fast, and the company's surveillance made her feel like Amazon considered warehouse workers to be no more than machines. While there were elevators in the facility, they were not for employees. The few breaks that workers were legally entitled to were whittled down to almost nothing after climbing four flights of stairs and walking through the massive warehouse. Bates, whose first job was picking okra as a thirteen-year-old, was among the Bessemer workers who contacted the Retail, Wholesale and Department Store Union (RWDSU) about organizing at Amazon. Already a leader in her church, she wanted to improve conditions, especially after hearing so many coworkers complain that they were sore and injured from the job, but they could not afford to quit. Another worker, Darryl Richardson, told *The Guardian* he had expected safety and opportunities for growth to be bigger priorities when working for one of the richest men in the world. As a warehouse "picker," Richardson's quota required transferring 315 items each hour from different containers to bags on a conveyor belt. A video monitor kept him updated and on-task, every minute of his shift. Like their counterparts in delivery trucks, bathroom and water breaks would prevent warehouse workers from meeting those quotas.[83]

In this context, Bessemer workers began organizing to join the RWDSU. Richardson searched Google for "Amazon Union," and the RWDSU's name popped up. Richardson and other Amazon workers began meeting in secret with RWDSU organizers, primarily in parking lots to maintain pandemic "social distancing" safety, and talking with coworkers and handing out union cards at the warehouse gates. When Amazon discovered the campaign, the company changed the timing of the traffic light at the gate, so that workers would not be able to stop their cars to get cards. As in China, where officials refused to enforce labor laws out of deference to corporate interests, Amazon's influence was so great that the company even had the power to intervene in Bessemer's traffic signals—a fact confirmed by a Jefferson County spokesperson.[84]

In the United States, when workers want to form a union, either the employer can choose to recognize it voluntarily, or, much more commonly, workers must gather the signatures of 30 percent of the workforce showing their interest in a union, which then prompts the National Labor Relations Board (NLRB) to hold an election. Under the Obama administration, the NLRB had allowed for "micro-units" of workers, like those at an Amazon warehouse, to be considered a single bargaining unit. For union organizers, this meant a more manageable task. President Donald Trump's NLRB, however, overturned the decision, allowing companies to challenge the size of bargaining units more easily. So, when the RWDSU proposed that Bessemer's 1,500 full and part-time warehouse workers make up one unit, Amazon countered that more than five thousand workers—including seasonal workers, truck drivers, and robotics workers—should be in the unit. Trump's NLRB agreed. Union organizers nonetheless collected more than three thousand signatures on authorization cards—far more than were required. The campaign received international press coverage and even prompted President Joe Biden to film a video supporting collective bargaining rights and criticizing Amazon. The intense media scrutiny focused global attention on workers' rights and union-busting. Voices of workers like Darryl Richardson and Jennifer Bates were elevated and offered American consumers a rare glimpse at the source of their Amazon packages. As Bates told US senators:

> It's frustrating that all we want is to make Amazon a better place to work. Yet Amazon is acting like they are under attack. Maybe if they spent less time—and money—trying to stop the union, they would hear what we are saying. And maybe they would create a company that's as good for workers and our community as it is for shareholders and executives.[85]

Amid the health and economic crises of the Covid-19 pandemic—and as Amazon posted record profits, and Bezos boastfully pursued his childhood fantasy of space travel—Bates's testimony was compelling.[86]

The Bessemer union campaign also linked social struggles at an important historical moment. The warehouse workers were about 85 percent African American, and majority women—demographic groups disproportionately likely to support organized labor. In the South, struggles for civil and labor rights also had a long, overlapping history, and the RWDSU boasted an especially strong record on civil rights. The Bessemer warehouse had also opened just a few months before George Floyd's murder at the hands of a Minneapolis police officer in May 2020, which set off months of protests around police brutality and more expansive issues of racial injustice. During the Bessemer union drive in March 2021, Black Lives Matter (BLM) organizers led a caravan of civil rights activists through Bessemer to show solidarity with the workers. As BLM Director Patrisse Cullors said, "Black workers have historically been the backbone of this country, its institutions, and innovations. Therefore, it is fully within our rights and dignity that we be treated and compensated fairly. Just as we have the right to live, we also have the right to work. This fight in Alabama is simply part of the larger movement for collective liberation."[87] Workers saw the struggle to form a union as a fight not only over wages, time off, benefits, and health, but also for their community and their dignity. Even with the vocal support of a sitting president, however, the odds were stacked against them.[88]

Amazon's powers extended far beyond stop lights, and the company used its considerable resources to fight the Bessemer union drive. According to the RWDSU, Amazon created "an atmosphere of confusion, coercion and/or fear of reprisals and thus interfered with the employees' freedom of choice."[89] The company posted anti-union banners throughout the warehouse and anti-union flyers in the bathrooms, and it mailed out anti-union pamphlets with threatening messages that jobs would be at risk if the warehouse unionized. Management also required employees to attend meetings where they disparaged the union and described union officials' supposedly luxurious lifestyles—a tremendous irony, given Jeff Bezos's extravagant wealth. While Amazon requested in-person voting only, the union, fearing intimidation of workers, requested a mail-in vote.

Citing the ongoing pandemic, the NLRB rejected Amazon's request. In response, the weekend before voting began, Amazon had an official mailbox installed where workers enter and exit the warehouse and sent out a text message to workers saying, "Voting has begun! The US Postal Service has installed a secure mailbox just outside the BHM1 main entrance, making mailing your ballot easy, safe, and convenient. Vote now! BE DONE BY 3/1!"[90] Workers had until March 29, 2021, to cast their vote, and many felt intimidated knowing that the company had cameras aimed at the mailbox outside the warehouse. The company later acknowledged that it had 1,100 security cameras throughout the facility, including in the parking lot.

4.3 A union election sign outside the entrance to Amazon's warehouse in Bessemer, Alabama, on March 10, 2020. Courtesy of Luis Feliz Leon.

According to RWDSU Communications Director Chelsea Connor, the mailbox also was not a typical large blue box that workers would recognize as official, but rather something similar to what might be found in an apartment building. Placed under a tent in the parking lot and covered in pro-Amazon messages, it was never clear to workers or the RWDSU who had access to the box.[91]

Ultimately, Amazon's underhanded tactics triggered a second election from the NLRB. By then, the RWDSU estimated that only half of the 6,100 workers who had voted in 2021 still worked at the Bessemer warehouse, pointing to the extreme dissatisfaction among Amazon workers. This time, the sides switched positions, with the union requesting in-person voting, while Amazon wanted it done by mail. Because the highly contagious Omicron variant of Covid-19 was tearing through the South, the NLRB ruled that voting would again be done by mail, and the infamous mailbox would remain. According to Connor, workers saw the mailbox as a "monument to Amazon's power" and believed that it would "continue to emit undue influence in this [second] election."[92]

Many of the workers who voted against forming a union in the first election complained to organizers that Amazon had not delivered on its promises, and workers' lives had not improved in a year. By the time the new vote started in February 2022, the Covid-19 vaccine was widely available, and workers and organizers from the RWDSU and other unions were able to conduct a more traditional—and exciting—campaign, with face-to-face meetings, rallies, yard signs, and passing out flyers. Amazon again claimed victory, and the RWDSU again accused the company of unfair labor practices, including threats to close the warehouse if the union won and retaliation against workers wearing union buttons.[93]

Meanwhile, other frustrated workers began to organize new unions all over the United States at companies such as Starbucks, Chipotle, and REI. Connor, from the RWDSU, says, "Workers are constantly saying that [the Bessemer organizing campaign] was the spark that inspired them. 'This tiny town in the middle of nowhere is taking on Amazon. Well, I can take on my local coffee shop. I can take on my local retail store.' This campaign made unionism a dinner table conversation."[94] While the Bessemer union drive influenced workers far and wide, Amazon's outsized power left workers there spinning their wheels, once again waiting to hear if unfair labor practices would prompt another vote.[95]

In April 2022, a thousand miles from Bessemer, Amazon workers at the Staten Island Warehouse in New York voted and made history, forming

4.4 Demonstrations were planned in more than fifty US cities on March 20, 2021, to support the Alabama Amazon union. This Philadelphia rally included a ten-foot-tall Bezos puppet and a Bezos piñata, which was broken in front of the Whole Foods store. Courtesy of Joe Piette.

the Amazon Labor Union (ALU). Two years earlier, in the first weeks of the Covid-19 pandemic, workers at the warehouse, known as JFK8, were exposed to the virus and some had tested positive. Christian Smalls, who had worked for Amazon for five years at that point, demanded that JFK8 managers shut down the warehouse to properly clean and sanitize it and promised not to give up "until Amazon provides real protections for our health and safety."[96]

The company refused, and Smalls organized a walkout that led to his termination. He then began organizing protests outside of Jeff Bezos's homes—the first outside of Bezos's $16 million 5th Avenue apartment in August 2020—demanding reinstatement of hazard pay, paid sick days, personal protection equipment, and greater transparency around workers' exposure to Covid-19. In October 2020, Smalls and others also marched to Bezos's $165 million Beverly Hills mansion. As one protestor told the *Los Angeles Times*, "When a multibillion-dollar company is subjecting its employees to substandard working and safety conditions during a global pandemic and, as a result, transmitting Covid-19 to 20,000 employees—it goes beyond negligence. . . . They have the resources to keep their employees

AMAZON CRIME **137**

safe and healthy, and actively choose not to."[97] The protest, like those that would pop up around the world on Black Friday the next month, reflected workers' frustrations that they were risking their lives every day to line the pockets of a man more interested in space travel than his employees' health and safety.[98]

Many viewed Bezos not only as the face of Amazon, but of capital, as well, and held him responsible for an economy willing to kill workers in order to maximize profits. Paralleling tragedies like the Triangle Fire and industrial disasters of an earlier era, at least five hundred thousand American workers had died from COVID-19 by the end of 2022. Many were infected at their workplaces. While perhaps less sensational because these deaths happened incrementally rather than all at once, they certainly speak to the greed, misery, and death that have been the hallmarks of the sweatshop economy for more than a century.[99]

Activists who had seen Smalls on the news joined the protests at Bezos's mansions, and some even sought jobs at Amazon in order to organize from within. Ultimately, organizers collected the required 30 percent of union authorization cards at JFK8 and at a second Staten Island warehouse, LDJ5. Though the LDJ5 campaign failed, at JFK8, the union won by five hundred votes, and the ALU was formed. The next month, Smalls and other labor organizers went to the White House to meet with President Joe Biden, Vice President Kamala Harris, and Secretary of Labor Marty Walsh. President Biden greeted Smalls, who was wearing a jacket that read "Eat the Rich," with a hug, saying, "You're trouble, man. I like you, you're my kind of trouble."[100]

Like anti-sweatshop activists in each of the previous three chapters, Smalls represented a direct line from workers to the White House. Aside from a few off-the-cuff—and accurate—comments about sweatshop conditions, however, the Bessemer and Staten Island campaigns were examples of labor organizing, not the broader solidarity movements of previous periods. Groups like SACOM and CLW paralleled the early twentieth-century work of the NCL, but even though Chinese workers, too, were working for Amazon, there does not seem to have been a tangible connection between warehouse workers, drivers, and factory workers thousands of miles away—at least not yet. The Biden administration's public meeting with Christian Smalls, however, may reveal an awareness of US labor's growing power—and perhaps the potential for something bigger.

Amazon's business model preys on and profits from desperate workers, struggling cities, and impatient shoppers—from the SEZs in China to Bessemer, Alabama. As stated earlier, the ability of companies like Amazon to squeeze workers, governments, and other businesses can be traced throughout entire supply chains—in Amazon's case, from mines to factories to customers' mailboxes. From another perspective, Amazon is a powerful empire—a giant octopus with tentacles that extend to factories, warehouses, and delivery trucks throughout the world. In this analogy, the imperial capital—the head of the octopus—is Seattle, Washington.

Famously started in a garage in nearby Bellevue in 1994, by 2018, Amazon was Seattle's largest employer with roughly forty-five thousand corporate workers, who earned more than thirty-five billion dollars between 2010 and 2018. For companies such as Amazon, Microsoft, and Starbucks, Seattle provided a socially progressive and naturally beautiful backdrop, in addition to major perks for those at the top. As activist-scholar Katie Wilson notes in *The Cost of Free Shipping*, Washington's tax system is incredibly regressive. There is no state income tax, and the "poorest quintile pay nearly 18 percent of their income in state and local taxes, while the wealthiest 1 percent pay less than 3 percent."[101] Jeff Bezos has been active in keeping it that way.

As Seattle has grown considerably in recent decades, many have pointed to the impacts of those companies and their corporate employees on rising housing costs and increased homelessness. Seattle City Council Member Kshama Sawant sees Amazon as one of the "most important players among the capitalist class who have disproportionate clout" in both local and national politics. The high cost of living in Seattle has led to an exodus of poor and working-class residents, and according to Sawant, "it has become a playground for the wealthy."[102] By 2018, as Amazon began looking to expand into other cities with its new headquarters, HQ2, Seattle had the country's third highest rate of homelessness, after New York and Los Angeles.

In 2010, in the aftermath of the Great Recession, community and labor organizations sponsored a state referendum to increase taxes on high-income households in order to fund public education and health services. Though it initially enjoyed public support, an opposition campaign funded by Bezos, Microsoft CEO Steve Ballmer, and others quickly turned the tide against it.[103]

In 2017, a Seattle activist group called Housing for All, along with labor activists and homeless service providers, began pushing for a citywide tax on large businesses to provide funding for housing and social services.

AMAZON CRIME **139**

After a series of protests, the city council rejected the proposal, but it did form a task force of various stakeholders. The group's conclusion was that the city needed to increase social spending by $150 million, half of which could come from a tax on big businesses. After a series of negotiations between city council members, the mayor, and corporate representatives—negotiations in which Amazon representatives talked the city down to about half the original proposal—the Seattle City Council unanimously passed a corporate tax to raise about fifty million annually. Seattle businesses with more than twenty million in annual gross revenue were to be taxed $275 per employee.[104]

Within days, Amazon, Microsoft, Starbucks, and investment firm Vulcan launched the "No Tax on Jobs" campaign to kill the law before it could take effect—and to reinforce the narrative that big businesses' responsibilities to their communities were strictly as "job creators." Just as Nike CEO Phil Knight had rescinded a major donation in retaliation for the University of Oregon's anti-sweatshop policy in 2000, Amazon effectively held the city of Seattle hostage. The company announced that it would halt construction on a new building and hinted that it might move to a different city altogether. The corporate campaign spent half a million dollars in a month. Despite Seattle's low unemployment rate, the mayor and seven of its nine city council members took the threat seriously. They quickly repealed the tax and released the statement, "We heard you." Even after getting exactly what it wanted, however, Amazon went on the offensive to ensure an even more obedient city council. The company gave $1.4 million to a Super PAC managed by the city's chamber of commerce, which then spent nearly three million dollars to try to elect a new slate of pro-business city council members. The 2019 effort also specifically targeted socialist council member Kshama Sawant, who had refused to vote to repeal the tax. Despite millions of dollars in corporate backing, only two of the Super PAC's seven candidates were elected, and Sawant was reelected. The amount of money spent in this local election was unusual—in 2015, Amazon had only spent twenty-five thousand dollars—and pointed to escalating tensions in the city.[105]

Emboldened, in 2020, Sawant relaunched the effort to tax Seattle's biggest companies under the banner "Tax Amazon," noting that big business had "shown us over and over and over again that they are not on our side."[106] Within months, Sawant was facing an expensive recall campaign that had nationwide right-wing backing. A year and a half later, however, she won—again. Sawant argues that large corporations pursue profits by capturing government, from city halls to Congress. Proud of her campaigns, Sawant says, "we have disrupted that normal process and enabled actual class struggle."[107]

A century ago, business interests throughout the United States ran "company towns," housing coal, lumber, and textile workers in company-owned homes and on-site dorms, much like Foxconn's. These companies controlled not only where their workers worked and lived, but also their access to mail, stores, utilities, and social services. Today, megacorporations like Amazon and Foxconn wield a similar ability to bend city policies to their will, from Seattle and Bessemer to Shenzhen and Zhengzhou. Amazon also engages in a version of the industrial paternalism that was popular at the turn of the last century. In 2022, Amazon gave ninety-six million dollars to Seattle-area projects focused on affordable housing, education, and STEM. These types of donations and sponsorships generate goodwill and loyalty in the community, and—unlike the taxes that the company paid to defeat—they are voluntary, at the complete discretion of the company, not the public. As powerful as Amazon and other twenty-first-century sweatshop companies are, however, they are not invincible, as Sawant's campaigns demonstrate. Broad, if sporadic, opposition has been building over the last decade. Like Nike's ubiquitous "swoosh," Amazon's ever-present tentacles have also created countless sites of protest, from China, to Seattle, and beyond.[108]

Bessemer and Seattle are not the only US cities to have complicated relationships with Amazon. When the company announced that it was seeking a location for a second headquarters in 2017, it accepted proposals from more than two hundred cities throughout North America, each offering a massive incentive package. Amazon had promised that HQ2 would come with fifty thousand high-paying jobs and five billion dollars in construction for the lucky, winning city. In addition to the standard offers of corporate welfare through tax cuts, fee reductions, and other perks, city leaders also demonstrated the lengths that they were willing to go to win. New York City Mayor Bill de Blasio lit up city landmarks with Amazon's signature color, orange. The City of Tucson, Arizona, tried to have a twenty-one-foot cactus delivered to the company's Seattle headquarters. A city in Georgia offered 345 acres of land—and to rename itself Amazon, Georgia—in exchange for the HQ2 contract. In hopes of bringing HQ2 to Canada, Calgary's boosters hung banners in Seattle that read, "Hey Amazon, not saying we'd fight a bear for you . . . but we totally would."[109]

Ultimately, Amazon announced the New York and Washington, DC, metropolitan areas as the cowinners of its sweepstakes—promising twenty-five thousand white-collar jobs to each—and promised an additional operations hub to Nashville, Tennessee. As details emerged about the two billion dollars in tax breaks and incentives offered by government officials, activists began organizing protests. They argued that HQ2 would have a negative impact on residents of the cities, pointing to a likely increase in homelessness, skyrocketing rents (in cities already famous for high costs of living), inadequate infrastructure—notably public transit—and a negative impact on local businesses. The New York location was also criticized for Long Island's flood risks amid climate change and rising sea levels.

Like the National Consumers' League had a century prior, some activists used the proximity to Christmas to their advantage, criticizing the New York mayor by singing "DeBlasio the Neoliberal Mayor" to the tune of "Rudolph the Red-Nosed Reindeer." New York activists were also lucky to have a physical space to protest—the Amazon Bookstore on 34th Street. As part of a "Cyber Monday" day of action organized by two dozen community groups in November 2018, activists occupied the bookstore for about thirty minutes. They handed out signs and boxes with Amazon's trademark smile turned upside down, and then continued the protest on the sidewalk, chanting, "G-T-F-O, Amazon has got to go."[110] The next month, activists rallied on the steps of City Hall, again outlining their many grievances with the company and relaying firsthand accounts from Amazon workers. According to a news report, "On the way to City Hall, there were 'Amazon Crime' stickers on nearly every lamppost."[111]

More important, some local elected officials joined protests of the HQ2 plans, in part because they believed that the community had been left out of negotiations, which had all occurred at the state level. Then Representative-elect Alexandria Ocasio-Cortez tweeted, "Amazon is a billion-dollar company. The idea that it will receive hundreds of millions of dollars in tax breaks at a time when our subway is crumbling and our communities need MORE investment, not less, is extremely concerning to residents here."[112] In a dig at Amazon's efforts to conceal its activities, New York state Senator Michael Gianaris, who represented Long Island, said that he planned to introduce legislation to forbid companies, such as Amazon, from requiring NDAs. In its negotiations with government officials, Amazon had often insisted on keeping terms secret. In many cases, even the company's identity was withheld from the public by going through third-party development firms.[113]

The following February, Amazon shockingly reversed its decision, announcing that it would only move forward with the Virginia location of HQ2. De Blasio and the company blamed each other, but one community activist proudly took credit on behalf of New Yorkers, proclaiming, "This announcement marks a landmark victory for our communities and shows the power of the people, even when taking on the world's richest man."[114] Clearly frustrated, even de Blasio—the man who lit up the New York skyline in orange—began adopting similar rhetoric, criticizing the corporate consolidation of power in an op-ed for the *New York Times*.[115]

The HQ2 sweepstakes had allowed Amazon to dominate news cycles and demand the focused attention of hundreds of government officials throughout the United States and beyond. However, that spotlight also created an opening for Amazon workers and other activists to publicize their protests. In Seattle, drag queens and pilots demonstrated outside of the company's annual shareholders' meeting—the former encouraging the company to choose a queer-friendly state for HQ2; the latter protesting working conditions on the company's cargo jets. In the United Kingdom, workers went on strike on Black Friday, a "holiday" almost single-handedly transplanted to Europe by Amazon in recent decades. In December 2018, warehouse workers from New Jersey, Brooklyn, and Queens demonstrated outside of the New York City Amazon Bookstore on 34th Street to demand a living wage, predictable hours, health care, paid sick days, and the right to form a union. Their signs read, "Santa and Warehouse Workers Deliver Gifts During the Holidays" and "Warehouse Workers Make the Holidays Happen."[116] Supporting the workers' campaign and articulating the reality for many struggling cities, Newark Mayor Ras Baraka noted, "We want to make sure that our residents have jobs, but we want to make sure they have decent jobs, not . . . part-time jobs with no healthcare in bad conditions."[117] In response to the protest, Amazon said that its warehouse workers—one hundred thousand full-time and thousands more part-time and contract employees—already enjoyed a "safe and positive workplace."[118]

That same month, Somali American warehouse workers rallied outside of the Shakopee Amazon Fulfillment Center near Minneapolis, Minnesota, chanting, "Hear our voice."[119] A far cry from Amazon's "safe and positive" description, the warehouse had the highest average injury rate among all industries in the state. As in New York, local leaders also joined the protest. Then Representative-elect Ilhan Omar, the first Somali American elected to Congress, congratulated workers for standing up to Amazon, saying that consumers needed to know that the people responsible for packaging their holiday gifts were not all happy with their working conditions. The next summer, workers in Shakopee also participated in a six-hour strike during Amazon's Prime Day. The workers described having nightmares from their unreasonably high quotas.[120]

Amazon, too, kept busy. While the HQ2 debacle captured the headlines, the company was actually in a constant state of planning expansions, scouting and purchasing land for new warehouses, and listening to proposals from various local governments around the globe—often anonymously. One of the company's many secret missions was "Project Olive," a plan for what would have been one of the largest warehouses on Earth. Amazon's choice for the warehouse's location was Grand Island, a thirty-three-square mile freshwater island on the New York side of the US-Canada border. In addition to being a fragile ecosystem on an important migratory path for birds, the island's access points were limited to just two bridges. Residents were surprised that developers would propose building a warehouse there at all, let alone one so large. Despite the ecological threat that it represented, though, the development's name evoked green, natural imagery—much like "Amazon" itself, though area residents did not know yet who was behind the project.[121]

Dave Reilly, a political science professor and activist with the Coalition for Responsible Economic Development for Grand Island (CRED4GI), says that neither the town's board nor its code offices were prepared for a project of Olive's scale. The immediate impacts would be extensive, and the long-term effects even more so. Local activists, however, had built a small network through previous campaigns on the island. But while Amazon could employ lawyers, a development firm, and a PR firm to push its agenda full-time, CRED4GI was limited to a handful of volunteer community members, such as Reilly. The group's many difficult tasks included rallying public support and sifting through a deliberately overwhelming amount of data about the project, which had presented to them in massive computer files. As Reilly says, "It's unfortunate, but we're stuck in a system that from the very start disadvantages those of us who take an interest in our community. The bulk of the responsibility [for representing the public interest] falls on citizens with limited time and limited resources, whereas [representing businesses' interests] is the business of the developer and the town."[122]

Amazon made a compelling case that the warehouse could bring good jobs to an area devastated by decades of deindustrialization. But as desperate as the western New York Rust Belt was for economic opportunities, as a warning, CRED4GI pointed to a recent deal down the road in Buffalo, where city leaders had given Tesla almost one billion dollars in tax incentives and kickbacks to build a factory to employ 1,500 workers—but the company had not delivered on its promises of community investment.[123]

As more details about Project Olive became public, CRED4GI found that many of the island's residents were already concerned about its size and scope, how it would affect their daily lives, and its impact on the environment. Around-the-clock truck traffic, for example, threatened to clog the island's bridges and damage already crumbling infrastructure. Because the warehouse was to be so massive, residents' homes also would have literally backed up to it. As CRED4GI later boasted:

> When we asked the people of Grand Island how much money we would take in exchange for our way of life, the resounding answer was that no amount of money was worth that cost. And that's when we knew we had won. Once we demonstrated to each other that we are united in our commitment to our community together, it was only a matter of time before Amazon walked away.[124]

According to Reilly, CRED4GI distributed more than seven hundred "No Amazon Warehouse!" yard signs, researched and wrote talking points, collected signatures for petitions, and conducted outreach to neighbors. The group also showed up to town meetings to show their opposition—often on very little notice—and their rallies drew some area residents to their first-ever protests. Ultimately, Grand Island residents won. Amazon abandoned the project, at least temporarily.[125]

Reflecting on the campaign, which concluded in 2020, Reilly notes that the victory sometimes feels small. Not only could Amazon renew its efforts in Grand Island later, but the company could also just take many of the same problems to a slightly different location. He says, "It feels like these projects are never done, and they always come back. It's incredibly frustrating, because you want to be able to say, 'We're done. We can move on to other things in our lives.' And you really can't." But, Reilly says, small victories matter. "It does feel like you're being pushed back and, in many ways, it feels like a losing battle. But those moments are precious and worth fighting for. Those struggles and that community-building . . . those are the moments that really make life worth living."[126]

It is difficult to overstate the power and resources at Bezos's and Amazon's disposal, as they blaze a global trail of sweatshops, homelessness, and environmental destruction. Just by dangling the hypothetical jobs of HQ2, the company had the mayor of the country's largest city practically eating from its corporate hand—and he was not alone. By proposing to open a new warehouse, the company was greeted as a potential savior in countless US cities devastated by deindustrialization—Bessemer and many others. Even in a notably progressive, West Coast city like Seattle, the company could bring much of the city government to its knees almost overnight.

But Amazon's power is not absolute. In Grand Island, residents prevented Amazon from building its massive warehouse. In Staten Island, warehouse workers won a union. In Seattle, while the campaign to recall Kshama Sawant raised nearly one million dollars, the campaign to support her essentially matched it—and with about twice as many donors. In the twenty-first century, corporations have enjoyed Gilded Age levels of concentrated wealth, legal advantages, and government connections. Their extreme mobility, meanwhile, provides an advantage that the factory owners who relocated production to the US South in the 1920s, and later the Global South in the 1980s, clearly laid the groundwork for—but could not have fully imagined. Now, as then, however, that corporate power is constantly being challenged.[127]

In 2023, three Amazon warehouses were sanctioned by the Department of Labor for health and safety violations. As OSHA Assistant Secretary of Labor Doug Park, announced bluntly, "Each of these inspections found work processes that were designed for speed but not safety, and they resulted in serious worker injuries."[128]

Amazon and its contemporaries are not just sweatshop employers. They have built a global sweatshop economy—designed for speed and profit but not safety—that depends upon brutal labor exploitation at nearly every step of the supply chain. For these companies, sweatshops are the rule, not the exception. Congolese workers—some of them children—breathe toxic cobalt dust while monitored by armed guards, as they dig in crowded open-air pits and hope that tunnels do not collapse onto them. Factory workers in China, many of them separated from their families in company dorms, suffer injuries, exhaustion, and sexual harassment on the job—and are driven to suicide. Their teenage coworkers, too, are required to work shockingly long—and illegal—hours as "interns," in order to graduate. Warehouse workers in Ohio are literally worked to death, subjected to immense physical and mental stress—and heart attacks. Delivery truck drivers on streets in every US city and town are compelled to urinate in bottles and sprint down sidewalks, or risk losing their jobs. These are not the unusual occurrences of busy, peak seasons. They are the typical conditions that workers can expect when clocking in each day. These are not merely unhappy workers or the result of a few "bad apples" in management. Rather, this is sweated labor, with conditions deliberately designed to maximize corporate profit, efficiency, and flexibility.[129]

Meanwhile, technology and internet-based companies, such as Amazon, Google, Facebook (now Meta), Twitter (now X), Tesla, Uber, and many others, have carefully curated their images as young, cool, multicultural organizations, often deriving liberal credibility from their start-up locations of San Francisco, Seattle, and Portland. However, they have had antagonistic relationships to unions and regulation that are essentially identical to those of the far less hip coal and oil industries in conservative "Right to Work" states. And tech companies have been more than willing to relocate—or threaten to relocate—to those "Red" states. Elon Musk, for example, shortlisted cities in Texas, Tennessee, and Oklahoma for a new Tesla factory and headquarters, ultimately settling on Austin. When Musk announced that he himself would be moving to Texas in 2020, the *Wall Street Journal*, citing his billions of dollars in Tesla stock options, noted, "Taking up residence in Texas comes with personal benefits for Mr. Musk: The state doesn't collect state income or capital-gains tax for individuals."[130] Both Musk and Bezos also chose to launch their privatized space programs in Texas, a state that would allow them to hide any negative environmental impacts, avoid taxes, and quietly displace already marginalized residents.

Perhaps it is fitting that the robber barons of the New Gilded Age are so committed to using the world's concentrated wealth on vanity projects that re-create what was already accomplished a half-century ago. Similarly, their collective economic contributions seem mostly to be a reproduction of the sweatshop economy of the early twentieth century—long hours, dangerous conditions, poor pay, indifferent management, and a vulnerable workforce—with the dystopian addition of computers beeping at workers to keep them running to meet quotas. But, as much as the working conditions in modern sweatshops resemble those of a century ago, increasing corporate monopoly power and the ubiquitous reliance on smart phones and other high-tech products has made consumer-side resistance difficult. Capital's advances have far outpaced the tactics of "white lists" and early shopping flyers. In the case of Amazon, its few remaining competitors, such as Walmart, do not offer much of an alternative in terms of labor or environmental policies.

Linking the activists and organizations in this chapter and building a cohesive movement is an urgent, ongoing project. It seems likely that the solutions to the many problems of our time will not be found in rocket ships but rather in university classrooms in Hong Kong, parking lots in Bessemer, and community meetings in Grand Island. The lives of workers, the survival of cities and towns, and the fate of the planet depend on it.

CONCLUSION

For nearly two hundred years, the bosses of industrial capitalism—the owners, the corporations, the rich—have built fortunes by squeezing sweatshop workers. The garment industry whose cruelty earned it the "sweatshop" moniker in the 1800s looks, today, remarkably similar to its distant predecessors. Its principles and practices, meanwhile, are widespread, used to compel maximum production from laundry and domestic workers, workers in electronics factories, farmworkers, delivery drivers, and many others.

At the turn of the last century, employers touted the laissez-faire argument that American workers' freedoms and rights were protected best through "Liberty of Contract," the absence of labor unions—or of any regulation of hours, wages, or conditions, for that matter. Capital's free market cheerleaders in state legislatures, in media, and on the US Supreme Court made the case, and enshrined it into law, that workers were most free when bosses were given near-absolute freedom and control of the workplace.

That supposedly "free" economy annually killed at least thirty-five thousand American workers and injured another million or so. Children working in textile mills, garment factories, and mines had to have their hands and arms amputated. Bosses locked workers inside factories, offering them no escape from fires and explosions. American workers, exhausted by workweeks of up to one hundred hours, filled hospitals while suffering from rheumatism and pneumonia. When workers tried to push for even minor changes, their bosses hired private security forces—and called on state and federal troops—to violently put down strikes. During the Uprising of 20,000, when workers hoped to achieve a fifty-two-hour workweek, police and company thugs assaulted women picketers, breaking their ribs and cracking their skulls. And, when even the most basic regulatory laws passed, businesses had the mobility to simply relocate to the US South and cash in on its promise of a cheap and pliable labor force.

During the Great Depression of the 1930s, New Deal legislation—one of the most significant shifts in labor rights in US history—slowly began charting a middle-class destiny for millions of American workers. Minimum wage laws, Social Security, government jobs programs, child labor bans, and union rights became federal law, but many workers, especially people of color and women, were deliberately left out. Domestic workers—isolated, precarious, and especially vulnerable to wage theft, sexual assault, and harassment—regularly worked seventy-hour weeks under conditions that civil rights activists condemned as "miniature plantations."[1] A quarter of a million Americans, mostly women, worked in the laundry industry and regularly experienced horrific burns from the heat, steam, and chemicals. Even business-friendly publications criticized factories in which thirsty workers could only drink toilet water from shared cups. The economy of the next several decades would represent unparalleled prosperity for the mostly white middle class, but it also continued to rely on the exploitation of a large underclass working in agricultural fields, homes, and other sweatshops.

By the 1990s, two decades of neoliberal laissez-faire policies had gutted labor laws—and the power of unions—and actively helped companies move their manufacturing to the Global South and into immigrant neighborhoods in New York and Los Angeles. Both major political parties supported "free trade," which, like Liberty of Contract, promised to benefit workers—this time, worldwide—by allowing corporations the freedom to bypass a half-century of labor and environmental protections.

While profits soared, Thai immigrants in California were held captive behind razor wire fences, paid half of the US minimum wage, and forced to work for up to eighteen hours a day. On the other side of the globe—though still on US soil—workers in Saipan were also paid less than half of the US minimum wage while working in unairconditioned factories and sleeping in sewage-strewn quarters. Pregnant workers were given the option of abortions or immediate deportations, while corporate lobbyists and US politicians golfed and vacationed nearby. In New York, workers subcontracted by Walmart reported backed-up toilets, a lack of soap and toilet paper, and weeks of wage theft, as they sewed clothes for Kathie Lee Gifford's line. Meanwhile, Nike workers in Indonesia were beaten for trying to form unions, and entire communities were subjected to toxic fumes from the burning of shoe scraps.[2]

In the twenty-first century, the global economy has become ever more global and more high tech. Following decades of deindustrialization and cuts to social services—and shifts from retail to internet shopping—US cities and states now compete awkwardly with their counterparts all over the world, offering massive taxpayer-provided subsidies and other incentives to global corporations in hopes of attracting jobs. Even when they are successful, however, they do not return the middle-class, union jobs lost by the millions in the late twentieth century—and some of the projects never materialize at all. In Wisconsin, for example, despite massive public investment and the displacement of residents, the American Foxconn factory—which President Donald Trump hailed as the "Eighth Wonder of the World"—has yet to deliver on its promise of job creation and manufacturing revival.[3]

In a glimpse of the wonder being recruited by Wisconsin's boosters, at the Foxconn campus in Shenzhen, China, more than a dozen workers jumped from buildings to their deaths. When an Amazon whistleblower leaked information about illegal child labor, he was arrested, tortured, and imprisoned. In the Democratic Republic of Congo, enslaved children mine cobalt for Tesla and Apple. In Bangladesh, more than a thousand garment workers, producing apparel for JCPenney and the Children's Place, were killed when their shoddy factory collapsed. A decade later, striking Bangladeshi garment workers, who sew apparel for the likes of Tommy Hilfiger and Calvin Klein, were beaten and killed by police—while factory owners withheld their paychecks.[4]

Meanwhile, in the United States, Amazon opted to keep ambulances on-call rather than lower warehouse productivity quotas, while compelling delivery drivers to use their vans as bathrooms. On behalf of companies including McDonald's and Disney, politicians in several US states have rolled back child labor laws, just as the US Department of Labor reported an almost 300 percent increase in violations in recent years. In 2022, meanwhile, workers at some 80 percent of Southern California garment factories—producing clothing for Dillard's, Nordstrom, and Von Maur, among others—reported violations of the 1938 Fair Labor Standards Act. Some cited pay as low as $1.58 per hour. In Texas, new legislation undermined existing city ordinances that had required water breaks for construction workers in the record-breaking summer heat. Today, as ever, the hyperexploitation of workers is common and incredibly profitable.[5]

This is sweatshop capital. This is the history of a US, and global, economy that has, for more than a century, bolstered its profits through the hyperexploitation of desperate workers. The collective priorities of employers are reflected in the working conditions that they dictated whenever they had the liberty to do so—long hours and low wages, maximum production for maximum profit.

There is nothing natural or accidental about these conditions. At every turn, employers—"sweaters"—have actively pursued and maintained them. When they could, business owners used private and state violence to attack and coerce their workers, whether striking New York garment workers or Chinese whistleblowers. When regulations passed, bosses challenged them in business-friendly courts. New York bakery owner Joseph Lochner fought, and overturned, the state's sixty-hour workweek. Oregon laundry owner Curt Muller opposed the state's law limiting women to ten-hour workdays—and lost only because the court sought to protect women as future mothers. New York laundry owner Joseph Tipaldo, arrested for refusing to follow the state's minimum wage law for women and children, fought and overturned the law, and—like Muller—had his legal fees covered by industry organizations. More recently, Nike CEO Phil Knight used his vast wealth to coerce the University of Oregon to abandon student anti-sweatshop initiatives, while Amazon spent millions of dollars fighting Seattle's tax to support housing and services for poor and working-class residents. To maintain nonunion workforces, Amazon, SpaceX, and Trader Joe's, among others, have launched efforts to outlaw the National Labor Relations Board, established in 1935, altogether. And, when industry has not gotten exactly what it wanted, the bosses simply moved their production—to the US South, to Saipan, to El Salvador, to Indonesia, to Bangladesh, to China—to places where friendly regimes would let them run their sweatshops.[6]

This model has created fortunes for CEOs, investors, factory owners, and others in the United States and beyond for generations. It has also created an unimaginably large mountain of consumer goods and waste. However, for those at the bottom of this economic hierarchy—the people in so many of the factories, the mines, and the fields—there was no "Great Exception" during the mid-twentieth century. For those working in sweatshops, they did not disappear with the New Deal or reappear in the 1990s.

―――

When I began this project, I was looking for examples of anti-sweatshop activism, in hopes of making sense of the many parallels between the sweatshops of the 1910s and the 1990s. I had hoped that perhaps the answers to stamping them out could be also found in those earlier periods. But while I do think that this history has important lessons for the present, in researching this book, I found that the conditions themselves were essentially a constant—but also that workers had continually pushed back against them. In the early 1900s, garment workers by the thousands went on strike in Chicago, New York, and elsewhere. Other workers attended labor colleges to refine their organizing skills. In the 1930s, striking laundry workers shut down ten dry cleaning plants in Washington, DC, while others chained themselves to a hotel that was using scab labor. Domestic workers recruited allies from the Black press and the clergy, inviting them to witness the misery of the "slave market." In the 1990s, women like Cicih Sukaesih, Wendy Diaz, and Chie Abad traveled across the world to share their stories of sweated labor. In 2012, workers at multiple Foxconn factories in China protested or rioted. More recently, warehouse workers in Bessemer, Alabama, and Staten Island launched union drives against one of the world's most profitable retailers.

The historical ebb and flow—the change between these various historical moments—was largely limited to how well the language of "sweatshops" and labor exploitation resonated with a mainstream audience and could be translated into mass mobilization to check the power of businesses and pressure elected officials. The National Consumers' League and the Women's Trade Union League both emerged during the Progressive Era at a moment of new possibilities for political activism for women. In the context of a broad movement for change, they supported working-class women's efforts to form unions and oppose sweatshops. A few decades later, as part of the Popular Front, the innocuously named League of Women Shoppers also supported workers' actions. Joining picket lines, disrupting shareholders' meetings, and conducting intensive research into sweatshop industries, the LWS made so many enemies that it was ultimately red-baited and forced to disband.

In the 1990s, Sweatshop Watch, Global Exchange, UNITE, and other groups filed a class-action lawsuit over the sweatshop conditions in Saipan factories contracted by US retailers. The National Labor Committee and United Students Against Sweatshops organized campaigns to put corporations and universities, respectively, in the hot seat. Together, the many activists of the Global Justice Movement made sweatshops mainstream news—and used the attention to push for change. In the twenty-first century, an anti-sweatshop movement has yet to coalesce, but the activists of China Labor Watch and Students and Scholars Against Corporate Misbehaviour have risked arrest to investigate factories in China and to share workers' stories. Elected officials in the United States, including Kshama Sawant, Alexandria Ocasio-Cortez, Michael Gianaris, Ras Baraka, and

Ilhan Omar have all criticized Amazon's negative impact on communities and workers. A handful of concerned residents in a small New York community distributed seven hundred "No Amazon Warehouse!" yard signs and encouraged their neighbors to begin seeing themselves as activists who could stand up together.

The sweatshop economy has been a constant, but these movements of workers and activists have achieved many tangible victories. In the aftermath of the Triangle Fire, survivors, activists, and clergy pushed for the creation of citywide Bureau of Fire Prevention, and they continued to push for statewide reforms, as well, establishing the Factory Investigation Commission, which hired former sweatshop workers and WTUL and NCL activists. Despite its mixed legacy, the protective legislation established during the Progressive Era was a major victory for working-class women, particularly in highlighting the "second shift" that women labored upon returning home from the mill, factory, or laundry plant. The Popular Front lent its support to many of the thousands of labor strikes during the 1930s. Workers at a New York shoe store believed that the League of Women Shoppers' participation specifically was the difference that helped them win their strike. By the end of that decade, tens of thousands of laundry workers had union contracts, a cause that was helped by the LWS's pamphlet "Consider the Laundry Workers." Sweatshop Watch secured visas and back wages for the Thai workers who had been enslaved and imprisoned in El Monte. Student activists all over the United States pressured university administrations to join the Worker Rights Consortium for independent monitoring of overseas factories manufacturing licensed apparel. CRED4GI prevented Amazon from building a massive warehouse on its thirty-three square mile island, while Amazon's JFK8 warehouse workers successfully organized a union. On paper, each of these victories was unlikely—a win for marginalized workers against incredibly powerful employers.

In *Unraveling the Garment Industry*—which, like this book, examines alliances between workers and more privileged allies—scholar Ethel Brooks warns that transnational activism focused on sweatshops can favor "consciousness-raising [among consumers] over strikes or other tactics of shop-floor-level organizing."[7] Brooks cautions that granting consumers "the right to act as political agents through the fact of their purchasing power" risks reproducing the inequalities that make sweatshops possible to begin with.

In many of the examples in this book, however, privileged activists were deliberate about centering workers and acting out of solidarity, not charity. Though Anne Morgan abandoning the WTUL and undermining workers' demands during the Uprising of 20,000 is often—and rightly— used to demonstrate the limits of some wealthy activists' dedication to the cause, the reality was more complicated. As easy as it is to point out the shortcomings of Progressive Era activism, the WTUL—to its credit— structured its executive board to give working-class women most of its seats. The group's leadership included numerous former garment workers, including Leonora O'Reilly, Rose Schneiderman, and Agnes Nestor. In the 1930s and 1940s, the LWS likewise centered workers, responding to their requests for assistance, joining their pickets, and organizing speaking appearances by laundry, domestic, and restaurant workers. In the 1990s, Global Exchange and the National Labor Committee similarly organized US tours, to allow workers to speak about their own experiences. Cross-class alliances, particularly when picking fights with incredibly powerful forces, are challenging and messy. There are many positive examples in these pages.

I would also add an addendum to Brooks's critique of purchasing power as privilege. While limiting political action to consumption alone (which even the National Consumers' League was not doing) is neither effective nor empowering, fighting against sweatshops is not just the privilege of consumers in wealthy, Western nations—it is their responsibility. The sweatshops in this book, whether in New York, El Monte, or China are *our* sweatshops. They exist to make *our* consumer goods, whether we order them through Amazon or buy them at Walmart or JCPenney.

When I spoke to Li Qiang of China Labor Watch, I asked him what he believed would have to happen to create a future where Chinese workers had real rights and decent working conditions—beyond the changes that public pressure campaigns and whistleblowers could achieve. He suggested that wealthy Western countries, whose companies use sweatshop labor, could pass legislation to allow workers to sue those companies. In short, laws could provide global accountability for free trade's global exploitation. These types of reforms, of course, would have to be the work of activists in wealthy countries, mobilizing to pressure their governments.[8]

Whatever the solution, I am convinced that it will take a mass movement. Kshama Sawant, the city council member from Seattle, believes this movement is already building. As she told me, "When the working class gathers enough collective power to make it an actual David versus Goliath fight, we can defeat them. . . . The smartest capitalists, they understand that any victory by the working class is a threat, because it provides an example. It raises people's confidence, because they feel, 'Well, if they can do that there, then why can't we do it here?'"⁹

Sawant's call for unity echoes a similar message by garment worker and WTUL leader Rose Schneiderman, who more than a century earlier said, "Each boss does the best he can for himself with no thought of the other bosses, and that compels each to gouge and squeeze his hands to the last penny in order to make a profit. So we must stand together to resist, for we will get what we can take, just that and no more."¹⁰ In short, the power of those at the top is their incredible wealth and the connections that it can buy. The power of those at the bottom, meanwhile, is their strength in numbers, which is useful only when they act together.

Every chapter in this book represents a David versus Goliath story—a ragtag group of workers and activists picking a fight with incredibly powerful business owners who, in addition to immense wealth, boasted political influence and legal advantages. And yet, in every example, these workers' movements found ways to extend their reach to the highest levels of the US government. In addition to Eleanor Roosevelt's work with the LWS in the 1930s, two decades earlier, first daughter Helen Taft had been involved with the NCL. Both the NCL's Frances Perkins and Sweatshop Watch's Julie Su went on to head the US Department of Labor. Mary Anderson and Frieda Miller of the WTUL led the Women's Bureau. Amazon Labor Union organizer Christian Smalls met with President Joe Biden at the White House. There is a lesson here about how powerful people's movements can be, even with the deck stacked against them.

A disproportionate number of the activists and workers in this fight have been women, largely because industry deliberately sought out workers whom they thought they could get away with mistreating—poor women, children, immigrants, and people of color. In each chapter, college students also played major roles, pressuring their institutions, organizing their classmates, and joining picket lines. In every case, activists chose to reject the individualism of consumer culture, or "Liberty of Contract," and instead build common cause with others and wield collective power.

What the next decade will look like is truly an open question. It remains unclear whether shoppers in the United States, Europe, and elsewhere will continue to buy the fruits of misery from Apple, Amazon, Walmart, and essentially everyone else while the planet burns and workers suffer horrific traumas, or if, instead, a movement of workers, consumers, and other activists will force something different.

What is clear, at least to me, is that if such a movement is going to succeed, it will require the bravery of Clara Lemlich, who was beaten mercilessly on picket lines during the 1909 Uprising but remained defiant, and of Tang Mingfang, the Chinese whistleblower who faced torture and imprisonment in order to speak truth to power. Such a movement will require the persistence of investigators and truth tellers, like the NCL, the LWS, and SACOM. It will also require the creativity of the NCL and Amazon protesters who repurposed popular holiday songs and shopping days—and built bamboo barricades. It will require the resourcefulness of the workers who released mice in their store, who enlisted a picketing donkey, and who made protest balloons to distribute to children.

NOTES

INTRODUCTION

1. Esbenshade, *Monitoring Sweatshops*, 126–27; Joe Murphy, "Pipe Dreams," *Pacific Daily News*, October 28, 1987.
2. Kingsley, *Cheap Clothes and Nasty*; Frager, *Sweatshop Strife*; Collins, *Threads*.
3. Great Britain. Parliament. House of Lords. *Fifth Report of the Select Committee on the Sweating System* (April 1890), cxxxiv–cxxxv.
4. Beaudry and Mrozowski, "Archeology of Work and Home Life in Lowell, Massachusetts," 6; Dublin, "Women, Work, and Protest in the Early Lowell Mills," 99–116; "Observations of Lowell by an Associationist, 1846"; Green, *The Company Town*, 3–7.
5. Mary, "Factory Thoughts," *Voice of Industry*, June 12, 1846.
6. Dublin, "Women, Work, and Protest in the Early Lowell Mills"; "Observations of Lowell by an Associationist, 1846."
7. Ngai and Chan, "Global Capital, the State, and Chinese Workers," 403; Dublin, "Women, Work, and Protest in the Early Lowell Mills"; "Inside 'iPhone City': The Massive Chinese Factory Town Where Half of the World's iPhones Are Produced," *Business Insider India*, May 7, 2018.
8. "The Poetry and Brief Life of a Foxconn Worker: Xu Lizhi (1990–2014)," translated by friends of the Nao project and published to libcom.org, https://libcom.org/article/poetry-and-brief-life-foxconn-worker-xu-lizhi-1990-2014
9. Chan, Selden, and Ngai, *Dying for an iPhone*, 188–92.
10. Hapke, *Sweatshop*, 1.
11. Bender, *Sweated Work, Weak Bodies*; Cudd and Holmstrom, *Capitalism, For and Against*; Brooks, *Unraveling the Garment Industry*; "A Trip to the iFactory: 'Nightline' Gets an Unprecedented Glimpse Inside Apple's Chinese Core," ABC News, February 20, 2012; "Suicides at Foxconn," *The Economist*, May 27, 2010; Charles Duhigg and David Barboza, "Human Costs Are Built Into an iPad," *New York Times*, January 25, 2012; David Barboza, "Foxconn Plans to Lift Pay Sharply at Factories in China," *New York Times*,

February 18, 2012; Nicholas Kristof and Sheryl Wudunn, "Two Cheers for Sweatshops," *New York Times*, September 24, 2000; Nicholas Kristof, "In Praise of the Maligned Sweatshop," *New York Times*, June 6, 2006; Nicholas Kristof, "Where Sweatshops Are a Dream," *New York Times*, January 15, 2009; Powell, *Out of Poverty*, 48–63; Miklós, "Exploiting Injustice in Mutually Beneficial Market Exchange," 59–69.

12   United States General Accounting Office, Efforts to Address the Prevalence and Conditions of Sweatshops: Report to the Chairman, Subcommittee on Commerce, Consumer and Monetary Affairs, Committee on Government Operations, House of Representatives, November 1994.

13   Courtenay Brown, Testimony before the Senate Finance Subcommittee on Fiscal Responsibility and Economic Growth Public, Hearing on Promoting Competition and Economic Growth in the Technology Sector (December 2021). For example, Steve Strunsky, "More Janitors Sue Wal-Mart for Violations of Civil Rights," *Record*, February 3, 2004; Jane Von Bergen, "High Court Won't Hear Wal-Mart Appeal," *Philadelphia Inquirer*, April 5, 2016; Kate Perez, "Child Labor Laws Violated at McDonald's Locations in Texas, Louisiana, Department of Labor Finds," *USA Today*, July 25, 2023; Noam Scheiber, "Judge Finds Amazon Broke Labor Law in Anti-Union Effort," *New York Times*, January 31, 2023; Michael Sainato, "'I Have Not Seen One Cent': Billions Stolen in Wage Theft from US Workers," *Guardian*, June 15, 2023.

14   Stein, *Out of the Sweatshop*, xv.

15   Milkman, *The Cost of Free Shipping*, xii.

16   Taylor, *Sweatshops in the Sun*; Fink, *Sweatshops at Sea*; Gordon, *Suburban Sweatshops*; Garson, *The Electronic Sweatshop*; Fraser, *White-Collar Sweatshop*.

17   Among others: Kessler-Harris, *Out to Work*; Sklar, *Florence Kelley and the Nation's Work*; Boris and Orleck, "Feminism and the Labor Movement," 33–41; Storrs, "Left-Feminism, the Consumer Movement, and Red Scare Politics in the United States," 40–67; Storrs, *The Second Red Scare and the Unmaking of the New Deal Left*; Orleck, *Common Sense and a Little Fire*.

18   Notably, Cowie, *The Great Exception*.

19   Marymount University Center for Ethical Concerns. The Consumers and Sweatshops (November 1999), https://marymount.edu/academics/services-resources/center-for-ethical-concerns/history/surveys/.

20   Storrs, *Civilizing Capitalism*; Glickman, *Buying Power*; Cohen, *A Consumers' Republic*.

21   "Court Scolds Pickets," *New York Times*, February 12, 1937.

22   The president of the Chicago League of Women Shoppers used this term to describe the group's members. League of Women Shoppers, "League of Women Shoppers Pamphlet," 1937, JLOP.

1. "THE STRUGGLE HAS BUT BEGUN"

1. "Consumers' League Meets," *New York Times*, January 27, 1909; "Christmas Shopping Easier This Year," *New York Times*, December 5, 1909.
2. Consumers' League of Buffalo, "To Christmas Shoppers," reel 113, NCLR; Consumers' League of Columbus, Christmas card, reel 13, NCLR.
3. Margaret Chanler Aldrich, "The Week Before Christmas" (1912), reel 13, NCLR.
4. Mary Theiss, "The Consumers' League," *Good Housekeeping* 47 (July 1908), 656–58; "Christmas Shopping and the Consumers' League," *Vassar Miscellany* 37 (1908): 165; Julia Blanshard, "Consumers' League Works to Protect Children: Past Conditions Changed Greatly by Organization," *Miami News*, November 18, 1929.
5. Bulletin of the United States Bureau of Labor Statistics, no. 78, 1908, issue 78, 423.
6. Chang, *Ghosts of Gold Mountain*, 229–30; Adamson, "Punishment After Slavery," 555–69.
7. Nestor, "I Became a Striker," 176–82; Fraser, *The Age of Acquiescence*, 66.
8. See, for example, Brecher, *Strike!*
9. Patten, *The Consumption of Wealth*, vi.
10. Remus, *A Shoppers' Paradise*, 12–20; Leach, *Land of Desire*, 6; Finnegan, *Selling Suffrage*, 2
11. Cobble, "Labor Feminists and President Kennedy's Commission on Women," 145.
12. Benson, *Counter Cultures*, 128–38; Leach, *Land of Desire*, 6.
13. "Suffrage Marching On," *Sun*, January 3, 1909; Orleck, "The Needle Trades and the Uprising of Women Workers," 84–95; Vapnek, *Breadwinners*, 131–33.
14. Henry, *Trade Union Woman*; National Consumers' League, "The Consumer's Control of Production"; Vapnek, *Breadwinners*, 70–83.
15. "What Has the National Consumers' League Done for Saleswomen?," *New York Times*, August 25, 1901.
16. Sanville et al., "The Consumer's Control of Production," 5; "Inception and Growth of Consumers' League in Wisconsin," *Oshkosh Northwestern*, January 26, 1901.
17. National Consumers' League, "WRECKS," date unknown.
18. Florence Kelley, "The Story of a Salesgirl's 'Merry Christmas': A Reason for 'Do Your Shopping Early," *Day Book*, December 4, 1911.
19. "White Label Goods: Local Store Makes Stand with Consumers' League on Cleanly Factory Conditions," *Milwaukee Journal*, August 11, 1902.
20. Sanville et al., "The Consumer's Control of Production," 28.
21. Frederic Haskin, "National Consumers' League," *Evening Star*, November 10, 1912; "Consumers' League Plans to Improve Quality of Wares," *Washington Times*, January 2, 1912.

22. Helen Taft had acted as an official hostess at the White House while her mother recovered from a stroke in 1909, lending even greater prestige to her activism, "Anti-Sweatshop Fight Is Started," *Washington Herald*, March 12, 1912; "Consumers' League Plans to Improve Quality of Wares," *Washington Times*, January 2, 1912.
23. Opdycke, *Jane Addams and Her Vision*, 159.
24. Kessler-Harris, *Out to Work*, 166; Sklar, *Florence Kelley and the Nation's Work*, 309; Vapnek, *Breadwinners*, 123–25; Dreier, "Florence Kelley," 70–76.
25. Arnesen, "Women's Trade Union League," 1514.
26. Flexner and Fitzpatrick, *Century of Struggle*, 237.
27. See Dye, *As Equals and as Sisters*; Jacoby, "The Women's Trade Union League and American Feminism," 126–40.
28. "Novel Method Is Found to Spread Union Gospel," *Atlanta Semi Weekly Journal*, July 14, 1911.
29. "Women as Strikers," *Will Maupin's Weekly*, April 28, 1911.
30. Glickman, *Buying Power*, 177.
31. Boris and Orleck, "Feminism and the Labor Movement," 34.
32. Lasch-Quinn, *Black Neighbors*, 10.
33. Lasch-Quinn, *Black Neighbors*, 10–15.
34. Schofield, "The Uprising of the 20,000," 170.
35. Orleck, *Common Sense and a Little Fire*, 27–32; Hyman, "Immigrant Women and Consumer Protest," 91–105; "Shaw Takes a Hand in Waist Strike," *New York Times*, January 6, 1910; Von Drehle, *Triangle*, 62; Hyman, "Immigrant Women and Consumer Protest," 91–105.
36. "Employers Answer Dr. Wise: His Support of the Strikers Based on Misinformation, They Say," *New York Times*, December 14, 1909.
37. "Employers Answer Dr. Wise," *New York Times*.
38. "Employers Answer Dr. Wise," *New York Times*.
39. "Clothiers Declare for the Open Shop: National Association Stands for Right to Sell and Hire Labor," *New York Times*, April 13, 1904.
40. Mrs. C. P. Huntington, wife of a railroad magnate, gave one thousand dollars, and Mrs. John J. Emery, wife of a real estate developer, gave two hundred dollars. "Standing By Union," *New York Tribune*, December 14, 1909; Von Drehle, *Triangle*, 59–60.
41. Von Drehle, *Triangle*, 75; Norwood, *Strikebreaking and Intimidation Mercenaries and Masculinity in Twentieth-Century America*, 79–81; Katz, *All Together Different*, 54–55.
42. Henry, *Trade Union Woman*, 62.
43. Henry, *Trade Union Woman*, 62.
44. "Miss Morgan Aids Girl Waiststrikers," *New York Times*, December 14, 1909.
45. "Police Break Up Strikers' Meeting: Raid Union Members to Arrest Eight Accused of Attacking Shirtwaist Workers: Pickets Parade in Autos Miss Morgan and Mrs. Belmont Lend Their Machines—Miss Mulholland Drives Her Own," *New York Times*, December 22, 1909.

46. "Puts Up Her Mansion: Mrs. Belmont Goes Security for the Striking Shirt Waist Makers," *New York Citizen*, December 20, 1909, reel 11, no. 971, PWTUL.
47. "Women to Rescue," *New York Tribune*, December 20, 1909.
48. Norwood, *Strikebreaking and Intimidation*, 28.
49. *Wellesley College News*, January 26, 1910, Wellesley College Archives, Margaret Clapp Library, Wellesley College, Wellesley, MA.
50. National Consumers' League, 1910 Annual Meeting Minutes, reel 4, NCLR.
51. "Exhibit a Lesson to Women Shoppers: Fine Garments They Wear Made by Tenement Workers at Starvation Wages," *New York Times*, January 12, 1910.
52. "Exhibit a Lesson to Women Shoppers," *New York Times*, January 12, 1910.
53. Miriam Finn Scott, "What the Women Strikers Won," *Outlook*, July 2, 1910, 480.
54. "Women Learning to Stand Together," *Allentown Democrat*, February 2, 1910.
55. Schofield, "The Uprising of the 20,000," 172; Von Drehle, *Triangle*, 172.
56. Kate Aronoff, "4 Women's Strikes That Were Anything but a Privilege," *In These Times*, March 8, 2017, www.inthesetimes.com.
57. As quoted in Donald Robinson, "Labor Leader's Wife Helped Form Amalgamated Clothing Workers 30 Years Ago," [unidentified Chicago newspaper, 1945], Amalgamated Clothing Workers of America Papers, box 120, folder 4, Kheel Center, Cornell University; WTUL of Chicago, "Official Report of the Strike Committee," 4–5, PWTUL.
58. Women's Trade Union League of Chicago, "Official Report of the Strike Committee: Chicago Garment Workers' Strike, October 29, 1910–February 18, 1911," 25; Weiler, "The Uprising in Chicago," 125.
59. WTUL of Chicago, "Official Report of the Strike Committee," 3.
60. Weiler, "The Uprising in Chicago," 124–25.
61. Pastorello, *A Power Among Them*, 27–32.
62. Katharine Coman, "A Sweated Industry," *Life and Labor* (January 1911), 15.
63. Weiler, "The Uprising in Chicago," 122, 127–29; "Use College Girls as Garment Strike Pickets," *Newark Evening Star*, October 28, 1910.
64. "Social Lights Lead Strikers," *Cairo Bulletin*, November 2, 1910.
65. "Society Women Act as Pickets," *New York Evening Journal*, October 31, 1910; "Chicago Bruisers Found They Were Rough Handling Society Women Instead of Working Girls," *Ocala Evening Star*, November 3, 1910.
66. Weiler, "The Uprising in Chicago," 126.
67. Caroline A. Lowe, "Solidarity Among Women as Shown by the Garment Workers' Strike in Chicago," *Progressive Woman* (August 1911).
68. "Society Women Act as Pickets," *New York Evening Journal*, October 31, 1910.
69. Raymond Robins to Mary Dreier, February 4, 1911, folder 51, box, 2, Margaret Dreier Papers, Special Collections Library, University of Florida, Gainesville, FL.
70. Weiler, "The Uprising in Chicago," 132.

71 WTUL of Chicago, "Official Report of the Strike Committee," 37–38.
72 WTUL of Chicago, "Official Report of the Strike Committee," 33–35.
73 Mary Domsky-Abrams, interview by Leon Stein, date unknown, www.trianglefire.ilr.cornell.edu; Greenwald, "The Burning Building at 23 Washington Place," 58.
74 Von Drehle, *Triangle*, 116–38.
75 Eraclio Montanaro, interview by Leon Stein, February 3, 1958, https://trianglefire.ilr.cornell.edu/primary/survivorInterviews/EraclioMontanaro.html, accessed March 5, 2025.
76 Mary Domsky-Abrams, interview by Leon Stein, date unknown, https://trianglefire.ilr.cornell.edu/primary/survivorInterviews/MaryDomskyAbrams.html, accessed March 5, 2025
77 Max Hochfield, interview by Leon Stein, January 20, 1957, https://trianglefire.ilr.cornell.edu/primary/survivorInterviews/MaxHochfield.html, accessed March 5, 2025.
78 "Tell of Many Firetraps: Women Trade Unions Move to Protect Working Girls," *New York Tribune*, December 8, 1910.
79 Greenwald, "The Burning Building at 23 Washington Place," 81–82.
80 Quoted in Greenwald, "The Burning Building at 23 Washington Place," 60–61.
81 "Women Appeal to Public to Aid Fire Sufferers," *Evening World*, March 27, 1911.
82 Quoted in Greenwald, "The Burning Building at 23 Washington Place," 61.
83 Von Drehle, *Triangle*, 86, 176.
84 Mailly, "The Triangle Trade Union Relief," 544–47.
85 Stein, *Out of the Sweatshop*, 135.
86 Mailly, "The Triangle Trade Union Relief."
87 Report of the Joint Relief Committee, Ladies Waist and Dressmakers Union, Local 25 on the Triangle Fire Disaster, January 15, 1913, New York, box 1, Cornell University, Kheel Center for Labor-Management Documentation and Archives, Ithaca, NY.
88 The "unidentified" were identified in 2011, approximately one hundred years after the fire. Amateur genealogist and historian Michael Hirsch spent four years researching the identities of the six unknowns. See Joseph Berger, "100 Years Later, the Roll of the Dead in a Factory Fire Is Complete," *New York Times*, February 20, 2011.
89 "Plan Big Memorial Parade," *Sun*, April 4, 1911.
90 Bruere, "What Is to Be Done?," 194–95.
91 "Plan Big Memorial Parade," *Sun*, April 4, 1911; Von Drehle, *Triangle*, 193.
92 "147 Dead, Nobody Guilty," *Literary Digest*, January 6, 1912, 6.
93 Stein, *Out of the Sweatshop*, 143.
94 Rose Schneiderman, "We Have Found You Wanting," April 2, 1911, www.trianglefire.ilr.cornell.edu.

95 Greenwald, "The Burning Building at 23 Washington Place," 74–75.
96 Greenwald, "The Burning Building at 23 Washington Place," 82–86.
97 "Triangle Waist Fire: Parade of Relatives and Friends of Victims as a Protest Against Conditions," *Sun*, November 14, 1911.
98 Mary Domsky-Abrams, interview by Leon Stein, date unknown, www.trianglefire.ilr.cornell.edu.
99 Storrs, *Civilizing Capitalism*, 15; Von Drehle, *Triangle*, 194.
100 "Fire Prevention Bureau Awarded $200,000 for 1912," *Evening World*, January 4, 1912.
101 New York (State) Factory Investigating Commission, *Preliminary Report of the Factory Investigating Commission* (Argus, 1912), 2, 5–6, 14–21, 35–36, 39–40.
102 "Minutes of the Hearing of the New York State Factory Investigating Committee," October 10, 1911, www.trianglefire.ilr.cornell.edu; Boris and Orleck, "Feminism and the Labor Movement," 34–35; Von Drehle, *Triangle*, 214.
103 September 30, 1964, LFPC; Von Drehle, *Triangle*, 215; "Woman Secretary of Safety Committee," *Buffalo Evening News*, June 30, 1912; "Men and Women," *Buffalo Commercial*, June 26, 1912.
104 Florence Kelley, "Social Standards in Industry: Progress of Labor Legislation for Women" (1923), box 10, FKP; *Lochner v. New York*, 198 US (1905).
105 Florence Kelley, "Judicial Obstacles to Labor Legislation" (1924), box 9, FKP; *Muller v. Oregon*, 208 US 412 (1908).
106 Florence Kelley, "Social Standards in Industry: Progress of Labor Legislation for Women" (1923), box 10, FKP.
107 *Muller v. Oregon*.
108 Kessler-Harris, *In Pursuit of Equity*, 30–32.
109 *Revised Laws of Massachusetts*, ch. 106, $24 (1902), 66.
110 Ginsburg, "Muller v. State of Oregon," 359–70.
111 McCammon, "The Politics of Protection," 217–49; Kessler-Harris, *In Pursuit of Equity*, 32.
112 "Should There Be Labor Laws for Women? No, Says Rheta Childe Dorr; Yes, Says Mary Anderson," *Good Housekeeping* (September 1925), 156–80.
113 "Should There Be Labor Laws for Women?," 156–64.
114 "Should There Be Labor Laws for Women?," 156–64.
115 "Should There Be Labor Laws for Women?," 166–80.
116 Belmont, "Work of the Woman's Party for the First Five Years."
117 For more on the evolution of protective legislation, see Stansell, *The Feminist Promise*, 197–99; Zimmerman, "The Jurisprudence of Equality," 188–225.
118 Commercial Department of Alabama Power Company, *Alabama Power Pamphlet on Alabama Textiles* (1919), Birmingham Public Library Archives, Birmingham, AL.

119 Commercial Department of Alabama Power Company, *Alabama Power Pamphlet on Alabama Textiles*.

120 Commercial Department of Alabama Power Company, *Alabama Power Pamphlet on Alabama Textiles*.

121 Edwin S. Smith, "Press Release—November 19, 1932," folder 479, box 25, RCLM.

122 Consumers' League of Massachusetts, "Three Years of Anti-Sweatshop Work," folder 478, box 25, CL of M Records; "White Flag," Misc. Newspaper Clippings (1932), folder 479, box 25, CL of M Records; English, *A Common Thread*, 111–12, 116–17; Alabama State Archives, Montgomery; United States Women's Bureau, *Women in Alabama Industries: A Study of Hours, Wages and Working Conditions* (Washington, DC: Government Printing Office, 1924), Archive of American Minority Cultures, W. S. Hoole Special Collections Library, University of Alabama, Tuscaloosa; Blanshard, *Labor in Southern Cotton Mills*, 8; Pamphlet Collection, Wisconsin Historical Society, Madison, WI; Sweet Briar College Department of Economics, *Labor Laws of Twelve Southern States* (National Consumers' League, 1934).

123 Stevens, "The Great Open Shop Conspiracy," 6.

124 During the 1919 Seattle General Strike, the city's mayor called the AFL leaders "Reds" and accused them of an "attempted revolution." Ed Weston, interviewed by Robert Friedheim in 1946, folder 6, box 1, Robert Friedheim Seattle General Strike Collection, University of Washington Libraries, Seattle, WA; Black, "The Enemy Within Our Gates," 76; *Journal of the American Bankers Association* 14 (1922), 67–79.

125 Flink, *The Automobile Age*, 220; Saez and Zucman, "Wealth Inequality in the United States Since 1913," 521–23.

126 Moore, "Historical Interpretations of the 1920s Klan," 341–57; Baker, *Gospel According to the Klan*.

127 "Bryn Mawr School for Women Workers," *Maryland Women's News*, May 21, 1921.

128 "Girls to Study," *Saint Paul Echo*, May 1, 1926; Bryn Mawr Summer School for Women Workers in Industry Pamphlet (1929), MCBP; Hollis, *Liberating Voices*; Altenbaugh, *Education for Struggle*; Howlett, *Brookwood Labor College and the Struggle for Peace and Social Justice in America*.

129 "Unionism Story Told Bryn Mawr," *Butler County Press*, August 23, 1929; "Interviews Miss Firth," *Abbeville Press and Banner*, August 4, 1922; Carson, *A Matter of Moral Justice*, 94.

130 Heller, "The Women of Summer," 275.

131 "College Girls to Share Their University," *Casper Daily Tribune*, June 1, 1924.

132 Orleck, *Rethinking American Women's Activism*, xiii.

2. "DON'T OVERLOOK ANY CHANNEL FOR PUBLICITY"

1. Benson, *Counter Cultures*, 134.
2. "The Heart of Milwaukee," *Working Woman*, February 1935, 3.
3. Mitchell, *Consider the Woolworth Workers*, FMC, 34.
4. Opler, "Monkey Business in Union Square," 149–64.
5. The women identified themselves as Anne Miller and Anne Friedman. "Girl Striker Heckles La Guardia; Chained to Box, Foils Ejection," *New York Times*, January 21, 1935.
6. "125 Pickets Seized at Ohrbach Store," *New York Times*, February 17, 1935.
7. Harry Fisher, a member of the Young Communist League who would later fight against fascism in the Spanish Civil War, included this encounter in his memoirs. See Fisher, *Comrades*, 12.
8. Therese Mitchell, "Photograph of Ohrbach's Strike," 1935, Labor Arts Project at New York University https://www.laborarts.org/28044/?collection=&field=&keyword=league+of+women+shoppers, accessed March 4, 2025.
9. "Court Scolds Pickets," *New York Times*, February 12, 1937.
10. Rebecca Drucker, "Letter from Rebecca Drucker to Ida M. Tarbell, April 29, 1935," reel 03.1022.00, Ida M. Tarbell Collection, Special Collections Pelletier Library at Allegheny College, Meadville, PA.
11. Hargrave and Kitch, "*Life* on Campus," 170–88; "All-American College Girls," LIFE, June 24, 1940, 61.
12. Miller, *The New Deal as a Triumph of Social Work*, 128–45; Kessler-Harris, *Out to Work*, 171; May, *Unprotected Labor*, 110; Cobble, *The Other Women's Movement*, 50–54.
13. Ware, *Beyond Suffrage*, 5.
14. DuBois, *Suffrage*; Dumenil, *The Second Line of Defense*, 204–54; Blee, *Women of the Klan*; Kinville, *The Grey Eagles of Chippewa Falls*, 29–35.
15. Hancock, "Black Women and Suffrage"; Davis, *Women, Race and Class*, 70–86; Cahill, "Our Democracy and the American Indian," 41–51.
16. DuBois, *Suffrage*, 183–85.
17. Ware, *Holding Their Own*, 6, 21–24, 27; Kessler-Harris, *Out to Work*, 257; Reagan, *When Abortion Was a Crime*, 26–30.
18. Paul McCrea, "Seeking the Route to Fair Wages," *Nation's Business*, June 1933, 26–27.
19. Ware, *Holding Their Own*, 29, 38–41; Kessler-Harris, *Out to Work*, 262–63; Rader, "Delineating Agriculture and Industry."
20. Ware, *Holding Their Own*, 29, 41–44.
21. Miller, "The University of Michigan," 70.
22. See Denning, *The Cultural Front*; Naison, *Communists in Harlem During the Depression*; Cohen, *When the Old Left Was Young*; Lorence, *The Unemployed People's Movement*.

23. Beatrice Lumpkin, "Joy in the Struggle: My Life and Love," 56 (unpublished memoirs) Communist Party USA, http://www.cpusa.org/beatrice-lumpkin-offers-joy-to-cpusa-org-readers/, accessed September 12, 2012. Lumpkin was a lifelong activist and took part in the unemployed struggles, the fight to free the Scottsboro Nine and Angelo Herndon, student strikes against war and fascism, CIO organizing with laundry and steelworkers, and anti-imperialist movement.
24. League of Women Shoppers, "League of Women Shoppers Handbook," January 1940, WGRPC; "Shoppers League Picnic and Party," *Saint Louis Star-Times*, June 2, 1939.
25. Elinore Morehouse Herrick, "A Sister Organization," *Woman Shopper*, November 1935, folder 424, box 25, RCLM.
26. League of Women Shoppers, "League of Women Shoppers Handbook," January 1940, WGRPC.
27. "The Heart of Milwaukee," *Working Woman*, February 1935, 6; Atlanta League of Women Shoppers, "Special Bulletin, July 1939," MCBP.
28. League of Women Shoppers, "League of Women Shoppers Pamphlet" (1937), JLOP.
29. Chicago League of Women Shoppers, "Dear Woman Shopper," folder 1, LWSP.
30. "Objectives," Atlanta League of Women Shoppers, Raoul Family Papers, Manuscript, Archives, and Rare Book Library, Robert W. Woodruff Library, Emory University.
31. League of Women Shoppers, "League of Women Shoppers Pamphlet" (1937), JLOP.
32. Invitation to Grady Hotel meeting, Atlanta League of Women Shoppers, MCBP.
33. Atlanta League of Women Shoppers, *Woman Shopper*, September 1939, MCBP.
34. Los Angeles League of Women Shoppers, "90% of the Buying Is Done by Women," folder 11, LWSP; Chicago League of Women Shoppers, "Women Do 85% of the Buying" (1942), folder 10, LWSP; "Buyers Label Slighted: Three Women's Leagues Renew Drive for Consumer Cooperation, *New York Times*, January 23, 1938.
35. Cracker Calling Card (1939), folder 10, LWSP.
36. League of Women Shoppers, "The Question Box," *Woman Shopper* (January–February 1938), folder 11, LWSP. For more on food-related consumer activism, see Deutsch, *Building a Housewife's Paradise*.
37. The LWS Constitution states, "Local chapters shall have complete autonomy with respect to their activities subject." See "Agenda for Meeting of Constitution Committees—1/14/39," folder 1, LWSP; "Picket Decision Assailed: Women Shoppers See Ruling as Giving Police Undue Power," *New York Times*, November 19, 1936; "Court Scolds Pickets," *New York Times*, February 12, 1937; In January 1939, a court found that Randolph

Hearst had interfered with union organizing in Chicago, a violation of the Wagner Act. For more information on the contentious relationship between the LWS and Hearst magazines, see Storrs, "Left-Feminism"; LaVille, *Cold War Women*, 150–56; Atlanta League of Women Shoppers, "The Woman Shopper," September 1939, MCBP; Erwin Below, "Buyers' Strike Backed by Two Miami Groups," *Miami News*, July 11, 1946.

38   "People's House Art Show," *New York Tribune*, May 14, 1922; "Cottons: Mrs. Aline Davis Hays Resigning from Ameritex Sudanette," *Women's Wear Daily*, June 11, 1934; "Heads Women Shoppers; Mrs. Aline D. Hays Elected by National League," *New York Times*, May 22, 1938; Chelsea Dowell, "Village People: Arthur Garfield Hays," *Village Preservation Blog*, December 15, 2016 https://www.villagepreservation.org/2016/12/15/village-people-arthur-garfield-hays/.

39   Helen Kay, "Letter from Helen Kay to Ida M. Tarbell, January 7, 1936"; Rebecca Drucker, "Letter from Rebecca Drucker to Ida M. Tarbell, April 29, 1935"; Ernest L. Meyer, "Making Light of the Times," *Capital Times*, December 15, 1936.

40   Eleanor Roosevelt, "My Day," *Richmond News Leader*, December 18, 1940; Eleanor Roosevelt, *My Day*, July 9, 1937, Eleanor Roosevelt Papers Project, George Washington University, http://www.gwu.edu/~erpapers/myday/, accessed March 10, 2013.

41   "Picketing Women Wear Mink Coats," *Columbus Telegram*, November 21, 1936.

42   Susan Shepard Erlich, "A Woman Gentle and Wise: Fond Memories of My Mother, Alice Elsie Lesser Shepard," collected in 2000, folder 15, LWSP; Glickman, "The Strike in the Temple of Consumption," 99–128; "People," *Time*, February 26, 1940.

43   "52 Pickets Freed in Mercury Case," *New York Times*, July 19, 1935.

44   Lewis Cohen, "A Socialist Training School," *Student Outlook*, October 1935, http://newdeal.feri.org/students/out01.htm, accessed June 14, 2012.

45   The LWS sent postcards to the store's patrons asking them to sign and deliver an attached card that read, "I have been a customer of Ansonia. I do not feel inclined to favor your store while your employees are denied a union and a living wage." "League Forces Shoe Settlement Strike," *The Woman Shopper*, August 1935, folder 424, box 25, RCLM; New Jersey League of Women Shoppers, "Special Bulletin," December 1937, folder 11, box 118, JLOP; Atlanta League of Women Shoppers, "The Woman Shopper," September 1939, MCBP.

46   "The Heart of Milwaukee," *Working Woman*, February 1935, 6.

47   Carson, *A Matter of Moral Justice*, 29, 95; Carson, "Taking on Corporate Bullies," 453–79; Filley and Mitchell, *Consider the Laundry Workers*, 52.

48   Carson, *A Matter of Moral Justice*, 16.

49   Carson, *A Matter of Moral Justice*, 23.

50   "Exploding Boiler Kills Girl," *Topeka State Journal*, December 28, 1920.

51 "Laundry Accidents Lead," *Butler County Press*, October 12, 1923; "Girl Killed in Laundry," *Madison Daily Leader*, September 21, 1920; "Four Women Killed in Laundry Explosion," *Seward Daily Gateway*, May 14, 1928; "Women Near Panic as Chlorine Fumes Make Scores Sick," *Evening Star*, January 9, 1929.

52 "LABOR: Little Martyrs," *Time*, September 28, 1936.

53 "Laundry Workers Ordered to Strike," *Washington Times*, March 16, 1937; "Pickets Gassed in New Jersey," *United Automobile Worker*, June 5, 1937; "Cleaners' Union to Push Parley: Expect to Resume Negotiations Tomorrow—12 Plants Reported Closed," *Evening Star*, June 27, 1937.

54 Filley and Mitchell, "Consider the Laundry Workers," 48, FMC.

55 "'Consider . . .': A Review," *Commonwealth College Fortnightly*, September 1, 1937, 4.

56 Eleanor Roosevelt, "My Day," *Charlotte News*, July 10, 1937.

57 "Consumers Seek Justice," *Edmonton Bulletin*, July 3, 1937; "Laundry Workers Revealed as Modern Drudges of Service," *Morning Post*, July 7, 1937; "St. Louis Society Girl Bears Torch for Laundry Workers," *Saint Louis Star and Times*, August 3, 1937.

58 Washington League of Women Shoppers, "Special Bulletin," June 1937, folder 11, box 118, JLOP.

59 "Inside Laundry Workers Win First Union Pact in History of Chicago," *Butler County Press*, November 26, 1937; "Laundry Workers Reject Proposal," *Butler County Press*, December 17, 1937.

60 During a laundry workers' strike in 1934, Eleanor Roosevelt apparently also directed her Secret Service detail to join wealthy WTUL women on the picket lines. Carson, "Taking on Corporate Bullies."

61 Carson, "Taking on Corporate Bullies," 459–60; Cobble, *The Other Women's Movement*, 44; Carson, *A Matter of Moral Justice*, 102–6. As Carson notes, though the gains for workers are clear, the ACWA essentially destroyed the movement led by Black and communist workers, who were fiercely critical of union leadership, 146–53.

62 Byerly, *Hard Times Cotton Mill Girls*, 39.

63 Esther Gray, "Domestic Workers—Cheap," *Woman Shopper* (1937), LWSP; US Bureau of the Census, *Census of Population and Housing, 1930*, table 12; Kessler-Harris, *Out to Work*, 270.

64 Baker and Cooke, "The Slave Market," 331, 340.

65 "Domestics Should Organize," *Pittsburgh Courier*, September 11, 1937.

66 "Housewife Is Called the Worst," *Des Moines Register*, June 19, 1938; "A 'Break' for Domestic Workers," *Pittsburgh Courier*, January 6, 1934.

67 Dora Jones, interview by Vivian Morris, February 2, 1939, *American Life Histories: Manuscripts from the Federal Writers' Project, 1936–1940*, Library of Congress, Washington, DC; May, *Unprotected Labor*, 121–27, 158–59.

68 Jones, interview by Vivian Morris, February 2, 1939.

69 Jones, interview by Vivian Morris, February 2, 1939.

70. Esther Grey, "Domestic Workers—Cheap," *Woman Shopper* (1937), LWSP.
71. At the time, the DWU was calling for forty cents an hour. Grey, "Domestic Workers—Cheap," *Woman Shopper* (1937), LWSP.
72. "Harlem Neighborhood League to Meet, Wed," *New York Age*, April 30, 1938; "Shoppers Arrange Series on Labor," *Evening Star*, October 23, 1938.
73. Washington League of Women Shoppers, "Household Occupation in the District of Columbia: Why Is the Household Employee So Easily Out-Weighed in the Scale of Security?" (1941), folder 12, LWSP. See Hunter, *To 'Joy My Freedom*; Jones, *Labor of Love, Labor of Sorrow*.
74. Nina Collier, "Domestic Workers and Social Security," *Washington Post*, March 23, 1939, folder 3, League of Women Shoppers Records, Washington, DC, Schlesinger Library, Radcliffe Institute, Harvard University, Cambridge, MA; Grey, "Domestic Workers—Cheap," *Woman Shopper* (1937), LWSP; "League of Women Shoppers Protest," *Gazette and Daily*, March 18, 1939; "Act to Insure Maids Against Home Injuries," *Brooklyn Citizen*, January 26, 1942.
75. Storrs, "Left-Feminism, the Consumer Movement, and Red Scare Politics in the United States, 1935–1960," 48.
76. "Picket Decision Assailed: Women Shoppers See Ruling as Giving Police Undue Power," *New York Times*, November 19, 1936.
77. League of Women Shoppers, "Workers Terrorized: League Representative Reports on Gadsden, Ala., Charges," *Woman Shopper* (1937), folder 11, LWS. Goodyear's union-busting tactics were so extreme that both local and national media reported on the violence in Gadsden. For example, see Maxwell Stewart, "Gadsden Is Tough," *The Nation* 145 (1937), 69–70; Martin, "Southern Labor Relations in Transition," 545–68.
78. "Wives of Three Educators March in Picket Lines," *Joplin Globe*, February 10, 1937; "Business: League v. Borden," *Time*, April 1936.
79. The LWS sent postcards to the store's patrons asking them to sign and deliver an attached card that read, "I have been a customer of Ansonia. I do not feel inclined to favor your store while your employees are denied a union and a living wage." "League Forces Shoe Settlement Strike," *Woman Shopper*, August 1935, folder 424, box 25, RCLM.
80. The 1935 labor dispute at Consumers' Research (CR) was bitter, pitting antiunion board of directors members F. J. Schlink and J. B. Matthews against strikers and their allies. The LWS marched with workers on the picket line and published articles stating their support in *The Woman Shopper*. Several workers left CR to form a new organization called Consumers Union (CU). This new organization maintained a similar format of testing consumer goods and publishing their findings in *Consumer Reports*. Consumers Union also sought to implement changes to show their commitment to workers. It lowered the subscription price of the newsletter, included information about working conditions, and organized a committee to advise the board on labor issues. Consumers

Union's subscription quickly outpaced CR as liberal consumers shifted their loyalties. In January 1936, the National Labor Relations Board (NLRB) sided with the strikers. The NLRB ordered CR to offer to rehire the employees they fired and those who went on strike, recognize the union, and pay back wages. See L. B. Glickman, "The Strike in the Temple of Consumption" and "Matthews Meets Denials, Attacks," *New York Times*, December 11, 1939.

81   J. B. Matthews, "The 'United Front' Exposed: The Prepared Statement of Mr. J. B. Matthews, a 'Fellow Traveler,' Before the Congressional Committee Investigating Un-American Activities" (League for Constitutional Government, 1938), 30, Fromkin Memorial Collection, University of Wisconsin-Milwaukee Special Collections Library, Milwaukee, WI.

82   "Tead Defends College: Says Brooklyn Staff and Students Have Right to Own Views," *New York Times*, August 24, 1938; Matthew Josephson and Russell Maloney, "The Testimony of a Sinner: Profile of J. B. Matthews," *New Yorker*, April 1944, 32, folder 40, box 1, Thomas Brooks/Colston Warne Collection, Consumer Movement Archives, Kansas State University, Manhattan, KS; Colston Warne, interviewed by Sybil Shainwald, April 1971, folder 59, box 2, Thomas Brooks/Colston Warne Collection, Consumer Movement Archives, Kansas State University, Manhattan, KS.

83   "Dies Investigator Says Reds Utilize Consumer Groups," *New York Times*, December 11, 1939.

84   "Bare Campaign of Intimidation on Wagner Act," *Chicago Daily Tribune*, May 7, 1939.

85   "Women Shoppers Plan Public Forum on Friday at YWCA," *Minneapolis Star*, December 9, 1941; Julissa Trevino, "Dorothy Parker's FBI File Is Available to Public for First Time in a Decade," *Smithsonian Magazine*, May 10, 2018; Peter W. Kaplan, "Gale Sondergaard, Actress; Played Villainesses in Films," *New York Times*, August 16, 1985.

86   See "Protest Against the Indictment of Angelo Herndon," MCBP.

87   Raised by activist parents, at age eleven, O'Connor accompanied her pacifist mother on the "Peace Ship," which sailed to Europe during World War I. WTUL member, pacifist, suffragist, and labor lawyer Inez Milholland also sailed on the ship. See David Traxel, *Crusader Nation*, 206–7; Kenan Heise, "Jessie Lloyd O'Connor, 84, Activist, Author and Feminist," *Chicago Tribune*, January 8, 1989; John Dos Passos, "Harlan: Working under the Gun," *New Republic*, December 2, 1931.

88   Rena Vale, "Stalin Over California," *Los Angeles Times*, March 29, 1940.

89   "Says Reds Formed Women Shoppers," *New York Times*, June 23, 1940.

90   Vale, *Against the Red Tide*; Deutsch, "Against the Red Tide."

91   Herbert Mitgang, "Disney Link to the F. B. I. And Hoover Is Disclosed," *New York Times*, May 6, 1993; Cohen, "Toontown's Reds," 190–203.

92   "League Is Formed to Scan New Deal, 'Protect Rights,'" *New York Times*, August 23, 1934.

93 American Liberty League, "The Labor Relations Bill: An Analysis of a Measure Which Would Do Violence to the Constitution, Stimulate Industrial Strife and Give One Labor Organization a Monopoly in the Representation of Workers Without Regard to the Wishes of the Latter," April 1935.

94 American Liberty League, "The Labor Relations Bill," 3, 9; "National Affairs: League's Lenders," *Time*, January 13, 1936; "National Affairs: Mutual Friends," *Time*, April 20, 1936.

95 Moore, "Senator Josiah W. Bailey and the 'Conservative Manifesto' of 1937," 21–39.

96 Procter, *William Randolph Hearst*; Farmer, *American Conservatism*.

97 "The Communists Want Roosevelt," *Chicago Daily Tribune*, December 27, 1943; "Mr. Roosevelt Reissues the Communist Manifesto," *Chicago Daily Tribune*, September 7, 1938.

98 "Bare Campaign of Intimidation on Wagner Act," *Chicago Daily Tribune* May 7, 1939. In January 1939, a court found that Randolph Hearst had interfered with union organizing in Chicago, a violation of the Wagner Act. For more information on the contentious relationship between the LWS and Hearst Magazines, Inc., see Storrs, "Left-Feminism, the Consumer Movement, and Red Scare Politics in the United States, 1935–1960," 40–67; Storrs, *The Second Red Scare and the Unmaking of the New Deal Left*.

99 LaVille, *Cold War Women*, 150–56; "Hiss Trial Brings Out Mrs. Acheson Gave Tea to Launch Communist Front," *Knoxville Journal*, January 9, 1950; "US Officials Linked in Red Plot to Wreck Industry," *San Francisco Examiner*, December 11, 1939; "Listed Among Red Groups," *Evening Star*, March 26, 1947; "Consumers' Guide Aided Communists, Dies Report Holds," *Evening Star*, December 11, 1939.

100 "Women Shoppers Disband," *Miami News*, July 30, 1949; Ben Hanford, "Trade Unionists and the Call One Day's Wage Fund," *New York Call*, September 6, 1909; "New Jersey Republicans Split by McCarthy-Liberals Struggle," *Geneva Daily Times*, October 7, 1954.

101 Helen Woodward, "How I Joined a Red Front," *The Freeman* 4, no. 17 (1954): 594. Ludwig von Mises Institute Digital Archives, https://mises.org/freeman/freeman-may-1954-b, accessed on March 4, 2025.

102 Woodward, "How I Joined a Red Front," 596.

103 Anne Weiss, "Economic Duty Has No Limit: Playwright Tells About League Activity," *Pittsburgh Press*, February 9, 1939.

104 Barker also helped to fight against the prosecution of Angelo Herndon, an African American man who was arrested and convicted of insurrection in 1932 for attempting to organize Black workers in Atlanta. See "Protest Against the Indictment of Angelo Herndon," MCBP.

105 Even after the LWS disbanded, Shepard remained empowered to become a lifelong activist, working on issues as diverse as education for returning

World War II veterans and increasing women's participation in electoral politics. See Susan Shepard Erlich, "A Woman Gentle and Wise: Fond Memories of My Mother, Alice Elsie Lesser Shepard," collected in 2000, folder 15, LWSP.

106 League of Women Shoppers, "League of Women Shoppers Handbook," January 1940, WGRPC.

107 Cowie, *The Great Exception: The New Deal and the Limits of American Politics*, 9.

3. "SETTLE THE CASE, OR WE'LL BE IN YOUR FACE"

1 Liebhold and Rubenstein, "Bringing Sweatshops into the Museum," 57–74; Irvin Molotsky, "Furor Builds over Sweatshop Exhibition," *New York Times*, September 20, 1997; "Sweatshop: Smithsonian Plan for Exhibit Opposed," *Los Angeles Times*, September 10, 1997.

2 Molotsky, "Furor Builds over Sweatshop Exhibition"; Marie Cocco, "Sweatshop Politics," *Berkshire Eagle*, September 29, 1997.

3 Molotsky, "Furor Builds over Sweatshop Exhibition."

4 William Serrin, "After Years of Decline, Sweatshops Are Back," *New York Times*, October 12, 1983.

5 Bao, "Sweatshops in Sunset Park," 117–40.

6 Albrect, *World War II and the American Dream*; Griffith, *The Crisis of American Labor*; Rohe and Watson, *Chasing the American Dream*; Cowie, *Stayin' Alive*.

7 Several scholars have critiqued the dominant narrative of the postwar "Golden Age" as overly simplistic, arguing that the economic conditions were more complex. See Marglin, *The Golden Age of Capitalism*; Webber and Rigby, *The Golden Age Illusion*; Hill, "The History of the Smith Act and the Hatch Act," 315–46; Leberstein, "Shooting Rabid Dogs," 289–314.

8 Farley, *Sexual Shakedown*, 11–17, 30–37, 49–68; Cobble, *The Other Women's Movement*, 212–17.

9 United States Congress House Committee on Education and Labor, Subcommittee on Labor-Management Relations, "Joint Hearings Before the Subcommittee on Labor-Management Relations of the Committee on Education and Labor and the Manpower and Housing Subcommittee of the Committee on Government Operations," House of Representatives, 98th Congress, First Session, Hearings Held in Washington, DC, June 15 and 29 (1983), 46.

10 United States Congress House Committee on Education and Labor, Subcommittee on Health and Safety, "Oversight on the Proposed Transfer of the NIOSH Facilities from Rockville, Md., to Atlanta, Ga., and Cincinnati, Ohio, Hearings Before the Subcommittee on Health and Safety of the Committee on Education and Labor," House of Representatives,

97th Congress, First Session, Hearings Held in Washington, DC, July 28 and September 15, 1981, 79.

11   OSHA's staffing dropped from 2,951 in 1980 to 2,211 in 1987. See American Federation of Labor-Congress of Industrial Organizations, "Death on the Job: The Toll of Neglect: A State-by-State Profile of Worker Safety and Health in the United States," 2009.

12   US Congress, House Subcommittee on Labor Standards, Committee on Education and Labor, "Oversight Hearings—Proposed Changes in Child Labor Regulations," 97th Congress, 2nd Session, July 28 and August 3, 1982.

13   Donovan, a wealthy businessman in the construction industry, was antagonistic to organized labor, and his approach to his cabinet position was to shrink the protections, regulations, and budgets of institutions set up to protect workers. While serving as the secretary of Labor, Donovan was indicted for fraud and forced to resign. Joseph Fried, "Raymond Donovan, 90, Dies; Labor Secretary Quit Under a Cloud," *New York Times*, June 5, 2021.

14   Meeropol, *Surrender*, 236.

15   Hancock, *The Politics of Disgust*, 23–64; Hays, *Flat Broke with Children*, 3–32.

16   Lichtenstein and Stein, *A Fabulous Failure*, 224–30; Tuttle, *Mexican Women in American Factories*, 5–24, 65–89; Broughton, *Boom, Bust, Exodus*, 75–88; Farrell-Beck and Parsons, *Twentieth Century Dress in the United States*, 249; Armbruster-Sandoval, *Globalization and Cross-Border Labor Solidarity in the Americas*, 70–71.

17   President William Jefferson Clinton, "Remarks on the Signing of NAFTA," December 8, 1993.

18   *Paying to Lose Our Jobs: A Special Report*, National Labor Committee (1992).

19   Doyle McManus, "U.S. Aid Agency Helps to Move Jobs Overseas: Enterprise: Officials Say Central America Is Assisted in Luring Businesses That Might Have Gone to Asia," *Los Angeles Times*, September 28, 1992; National Labor Committee, *Paying to Lose Our Jobs: A Special Report*, National Labor Committee (1992); Whalen, "Sweatshops Here and There," 45–68; Minchin, "Shutdowns in the Sun Belt," 258–288.

20   Organization for Economic Cooperation and Development, International Trade by Commodities Database (OECD, 2006); Bluestone, *Beyond the Ruins*, ix; Moody, *On New Terrain*, 25.

21   Paul Krugman, "For Richer," *New York Times*, October 20, 2002; Saez and Zucman, "Wealth Inequality in the United States Since 1913," 519–78; Kuhn, Schularick, and Steins, "Income and Wealth Inequality in America, 1949–2016," 3469–3519.

22   Klein, *No Logo*, 215–16.

23   Klein, *No Logo*, 215–16.

24   Armbruster-Sandoval, *Globalization and Cross-Border Labor Solidarity in the Americas*, 37–39, 72–75.

25   Moody, *On New Terrain*, 1.
26   Carson, "Taking on Corporate Bullies," 453–79; David Moberg, "Hung Out to Dry," *In These Times*, August 11, 2003.
27   Malone, "Domestic Work in the United States," 65–88; National Domestic Workers Alliance, "Domestic Workers Bill of Rights Survey and Stories" (July 2021), https://www.domesticworkers.org/, accessed May 14, 2024.
28   Desai, "Transnational Solidarity," 15–32.
29   Joe Garofoli, "S. F. Woman's Relentless March for Peace," *San Francisco Chronicle*, October 26, 2002.
30   Medea Benjamin, "Nike's Workplace Abuses Violate Civil Rights," *New York Times*, April 4, 1997.
31   "Letters To the Editor," *San Francisco Examiner*, July 5, 1996.
32   Jeff Ballinger, "The New Free-Trade Heel," *Harper's*, August 1992.
33   Bob Herbert, "Trampled Dreams," *New York Times*, July 12, 1996.
34   Bob Herbert, "Trampled Dreams," *New York Times*, July 12, 1996.
35   Farhan Haq, "U.S.-Indonesia: Nike Endorses Monitoring After Labour Flap," Inter Press Service, July 25, 1996; Jim Dwyer, "These Sneakers Really Stink: 1 Woman Shames Nike and Crosses the Jordan," *New York Daily News*, July 18, 1996; "Protesters Rally for Nike Workers in Asia," *Chicago Tribune*, July 16, 1996.
36   Bob Baum, "Labor Controversy Tempers Nike's Big Day," *Columbian*, September 17, 1996; "Investors Vote Down Inspection Nike Inc. Stockholders Derailed a Request for an Independent Group to Examine Asian Plants," Associated Press, September 18, 1996.
37   Scott Russell, "Speaker: Put the Run on Reebok, 'Space Jam,'" *Madison Capital Times*, November 21, 1996; Marjie Mohtashemi, "Protests as Nike CEO Addresses Stanford Students; Knight Defends Firm's Asian Wages," *San Francisco Examiner*, May 1, 1997; Greg Rushford, "Nike Lets Critics Kick It Around," *Wall Street Journal*, May 12, 1997.
38   "Michael Jordan, Nike and the Exploitation of Slave Labor," *Midwest Today*, January 1997.
39   Todd Douglas, "Put Ethics Before Greed to End Exploitation," *The Record*, April 15, 1997.
40   Harvey Araton, "Athletes Toe the Nike Line, but Students Apply Pressure," *New York Times*, November 22, 1997; "Kickin' Up Their Heels: Nike to Send UNC Students to Asia," *Sports Business Journal*, November 11, 1997.
41   Steven Greenhouse, "Nike Supports Women in Its Ads but Not Its Factories, Groups Say," *New York Times*, October 26, 1997; "Nike's Treatment of Women Overseas Assailed; Spokesman Defends Pay," *Dallas Morning News*, November 2, 1997.
42   Patti Bond, "Nike Promises to Improve Factory Worker Conditions Change for the Better: Shoe Maker to Raise Minimum Age, Minimum Wage for Employees," *Atlanta Constitution*, May 13, 1998; Timothy Egan, "The Swoon of the Swoosh," *New York Times Magazine*, September 13, 1998;

William McCall, "Critics Have Nike Stumbling; Shoe Company Blasted for Tolerating Sweatshops," *Chicago Tribune*, October 11, 1998.
43 Matt Krasnowski, "Former Sweatshop Slaves Try to Reform Garment Industry," *Standard-Speaker*, June 27, 1996; "Agent: INS Accused of Blocking Probe of Sweatshops," *Los Angeles Times*, August 10, 1995; Ramachandran, Collins, Su, Cummings, and Ahmad, "The El Monte Sweatshop Slavery Cases," 281.
44 Kenneth Noble, "Workers in Sweatshop Raid Start Leaving Detention Site," *New York Times*, August 12, 1995.
45 Sweatshop Watch, "About Sweatshop Watch," Garment Workers Calendar (1998), Lora Jo Foo Papers, Sophia Smith Collection, Smith College, Northampton, MA; Ramachandran, Collins, Su, Cummings, and Ahmad, "The El Monte Sweatshop Slavery Cases," 282.
46 Kenneth Noble, "U.S. Warns Big Retailers About Sweatshop Goods," *New York Times*, August 15, 1995.
47 Ross, *Slaves to Fashion*, 155–56.
48 Press release, May 20, 1996, National Retail Federation.
49 Ross, *No Sweat*, 10–15.
50 George White and Patrick McDonnell, "Sweatshop Workers to Get $2 Million," *Los Angeles Times*, October 24, 1997.
51 Ramachandran, Collins, Su, Cummings, and Ahmad, "The El Monte Sweatshop Slavery Cases," 283, 289; Connie Kang, "Final $1.2 Million Added to Thai Workers' Settlement," *Los Angeles Times*, July 29, 1999.
52 Smith, "Case Study," 737–71.
53 Frank Swoboda, "Firm Accused of Slave Labor Policy at Plant," *Washington Post*, February 12, 1992.
54 Esbenshade, *Monitoring Sweatshops*, 126–27; Joe Murphy, "Pipe Dreams," *Pacific Daily News*, October 28, 1987.
55 US Congress, House, Committee on Interior and Insular Affairs, Subcommittee on Insular and International Affairs, "Northern Mariana Islands' Garment Industry: Oversight Hearing Before the Subcommittee on Insular and International Affairs of the Committee on Interior and Insular Affairs," House of Representatives, 102nd Congress, 2nd sess., July 30, 1992, 43, Wisconsin State Historical Society, Madison, WI.
56 Floyd Takeuchi, "Saipan Steams and Seams," *Honolulu Star-Bulletin*, November 8, 1989.
57 "Textile Factories Must Clean Up Act," *Pacific Daily News*, November 16, 1987; Al Meyeroff, "Saipan Sweatshops 'Made in USA,'" *San Francisco Examiner*, April 10, 1999; Philip Shenon, "Made in the U.S.A.?—Hard Labor on a Pacific Island/A Special Report: Saipan Sweatshops Are No American Dream," *New York Times*, June 18, 1993; "Citing 'America's Worst Sweatshop': Suit Targets U.S. Retailers, Saipan," Associated Press, January 14, 1999.
58 "Former Sweatshop Worker to Speak at CLU," *Thousand Oaks Acorn*, February 24, 2011; Grevatt, "Lesbian/Gay/Bisexual/Transgender Liberation,"

63–65; "Former Sweatshop Worker Connects with C.U. Activists," *Cornell Daily Sun*, February 26, 2001.
59 Elizabeth Brennan, "Gap Unfazed by Protests over Human Rights," *SF Gate*, January 14, 2000.
60 Leila Salazar, "14 Activists Arrested at GAP Headquarters," email alert to Global Exchange listserve, January 1, 2000.
61 Criminal charges were dropped against the activists in October 2021, who would go on to win a civil suit against the City of Fresno and the owners of the mall. "20 Gap Protesters Arrested Outside Fresno Mall," *SF Gate*, May 8, 2000.
62 Robert Collier and Jenny Strasburg, "Clothiers Fold on Sweatshop Lawsuit / Saipan Workers to Get Millions," *San Francisco Chronicle*, September 27, 2002.
63 Spectar, "Pay Me Fairly, Kathie Lee," 61–92.
64 Barry Beark, "Kathie Lee and the Sweatshop Crusade," *Los Angeles Times*, June 14, 1996.
65 Klein, *No Logo*, 11–26.
66 Charles Bowden, "Keeper of the Fire," *Mother Jones* (July/August 2003).
67 Stephanie Strom, "A Sweetheart Becomes Suspect; Looking Behind Those Kathie Lee Labels," *New York Times*, June 27, 1996.
68 Diane Sawyer, ABC *20/20 Downtown*, May 22, 1995.
69 Rob Howe, "Labor Pains," *People*, June 10, 1996.
70 Steven Greenhouse, "With $7,500 in Cash, Giffords Scramble to Save Face at Sweatshop," *New York Times*, May 24, 1996; Steven Greenhouse, "Live with Kathie Lee and Apparel Workers," *New York Times*, May 31, 1996; Gifford told *People* magazine, "We never saw the donation as a panacea for the sweatshop problem. Frank and I felt a moral and ethical responsibility because they were manufacturing clothing bearing my name. . . . These people were in dire straits, and we had to do something to help." Howe, "Labor Pains."
71 Joana Ramey, "Kernaghan Cheers Gifford Move to Monitor Makers of Her Line," *Women's Wear Daily*, May 23, 1996.
72 "Rep. George Miller to Hold Press Conference with 15 Year Old Honduran Worker," George Miller press release, May 28, 1996; Bob Herbert, "The Wrong Indonesian: In America," *New York Times*, November 1, 1996.
73 Ross, *Slaves to Fashion*, 160–61.
74 Ross, *Slaves to Fashion*, 160; Esbenshade, *Monitoring Sweatshops*, 4–8; Hemphill, "Monitoring Global Corporate Citizenship," 85. Many activists and workers criticized the Forum, which took place in July 1996, as a means for brands to repair their image rather than implanting real standards to improve conditions. Codirector of the Nicaraguan Network Education Fund Katherine Hoyt reported that while three hundred people attended the forum, "retailers, manufacturers, and contractors,

as well as representatives of labor (US and international), consumers, academia, and human rights were all present, but industry dominated." Katherine Hoyt, email message to PeaceNet listserve, August 8, 1996.

75 "Wal-Mart's Shirts of Misery," National Labor Committee (July 1999); "Free Trade's Hidden Secrets: Why We Are Losing Our Shirts," National Labor Committee (1993); "Liz Claiborne / Sweatshop Production in El Salvador," National Labor Committee (1998); Phillips, "Mickey Goes to Haiti and Leaves," 144–63; Stephanie Salter, "Disney's Shame: 30-Cents-an-Hour Sweatshops," *San Francisco Examiner*, September 8, 1996; Armbruster-Sandoval, *Globalization and Cross-Border Labor Solidarity in the Americas*, 19–20.

76 US Congress, "African Growth and Opportunity Act—Resumed," 106th Congress, First Session, Congressional Record, no. 152 (1999), S13657–S13659.

77 Stephen Franklin, "Charles Kernaghan: Labor Activist," *Chicago Tribune*, February 6, 2000.

78 "Quotes on the Impact of the Institute," http://www.globallabourrights .org/, accessed September 20, 2012; "Reebok Disputes Activist Labor Group's Sweatshop Allegations," *Bennington Banner*, July 23, 2005.

79 Bonacich and Appelbaum, "Offshore Production," 141; "Rage Against Sweatshops," *Record-Journal*, December 15, 1997.

80 Krupat, "Rethinking the Sweatshop," 112–27.

81 Spectar, "Pay Me Fairly, Kathie Lee," 66.

82 Khor, "The WTO and Foreign Investment," 304–14; Edelman, "Peasant–Farmer Movements, Third World Peoples, and the Seattle Protests," 109–28.

83 Juliette Beck, "Why We Are Protesting," *Washington Post*, April 16, 2000.

84 Richard Goldstein, "The Birth of a Movement," *Village Voice*, July 25, 2000.

85 Marcus Franklin Dayton, "Woman to Describe Sweatshop Conditions She Endured on Pacific Island of Saipan," *Dayton Daily News*, March 21, 2000.

86 Lindsey Baker, "Former Sweatshop Worker: Rise Against Poor Conditions," *Daily Nebraskan*, November 17, 2000; "Former Sweatshop Worker Connects with C.U. Activists," *Cornell Daily Sun*, February 26, 2001.

87 Iris Young, "From Guilt to Solidarity," *Dissent Magazine* (2003).

88 Steven Greenhouse, "Duke to Adopt a Code to Prevent Apparel from Being Made in Sweatshops," *New York Times*, March 8, 1998.

89 Steven Greenhouse, "Two Protests by Students over Wages for Workers," *New York Times*, January 31, 1999.

90 United Students against Sweatshops, "What's Wrong with the FLA?"; Ross, *Slaves to Fashion*, 163–66; Hemphill, "Monitoring Global Corporate Citizenship," 90.

91 Hemphill, "Monitoring Global Corporate Citizenship," 86; Athreya, "Can Fashion Ever Be Fair?," 18–19. See also Esbenshade, *Monitoring Sweatshops*.
92 United Students Against Sweatshops, "Minutes from the Worker Rights Consortium Founding Conference" (April 2000), http://www.workersrights.org/, accessed August 14, 2012; United Students Against Sweatshops, "Campus Organizing Manual," http://www.campusactivism.org/server-new/uploads/Campus_Org_Manual-05.pdf, accessed March 4, 2025; Workers Rights Consortium, "Our Work," https://www.workersrights.org/our-work, accessed September 18, 2024.
93 Vogeler and Richards, "Madison."
94 "The UW and Sweatshops," *Capital Times*, July 30, 1998; S. L. Bachman, "Stopping Sweatshop Abuses Depends on Students' Activism," *Wisconsin State Journal*, November 28, 1999; "UW to Join Anti-Sweatshop Effort," *Wausau Daily Herald*, February 19, 2000.
95 Moniqua Lane, "Necessary Absurdity," *Arizona Daily Wildcat*, February 22, 2000.
96 Jim Irwin, "Nike Pulls Out of Deal with University," *Columbian*, April 28, 2000.
97 Fred Girard, "Nike at Odds with Michigan," *Detroit News*, April 28, 2000.
98 William McCall, "Critics Have Nike Stumbling; Shoe Company Blasted for Tolerating Sweatshops," *Chicago Tribune*, October 11, 1998.
99 Heidi Schlumpf, "Sole Man," 48–49.
100 Jim Keady, *Nike Sweatshops: Behind the Swoosh*, posted July 28, 2011, YouTube video: https://www.youtube.com/watch?v=M5uYCWVfuPQ.
101 Keady, *Nike Sweatshops*.
102 Steven Greenhouse, "Labor Fight Ends in Win for Students, *New York Times*, November 17, 2009; Todd Finkelmeyer, "Sweating the Big Stuff," *Capital Times*, December 2, 2009; Robyn Blumner, "Students Make Russell Do the Right Thing," *Tampa Bay Times*, November 29, 2009.
103 William Branigin, "Amid Criticism, U.S. Commonwealth Trying to Win Congressional Favor," *Washington Post*, February 22, 1997.
104 DeLay made these statements at a benefit dinner for Willie Tan, the CEO of Tan Holdings Corporation. See also Jeffrey Smith, "The DeLay-Abramoff Money Trail," *Washington Post*, December 31, 2005.
105 *Congressional Record* (Bound Edition), vol. 145 (1999), part 18, United States Government Publishing Office, October 24, 1999; Department of Justice, "Three Plead Guilty to Forcing Women Into Slavery and Prostitution in Northern Mariana Islands," press release, October 5, 1999, https://www.justice.gov/archive/opa/pr/1999/October/466cr.htm.
106 Connie Chung and Charles Gibson, "The Shame of Saipan," 20/20, May 24, 1999.
107 Chung and Gibson, "The Shame of Saipan."

108 Louis Dubose, "Stranger Than Paradise: An Excerpt From 'The Hammer: Tom Delay: God, Money, and the Rise of the Republican Congress,'" *Texas Observer*, September 10, 2004.

109 Susan Schmidt and James V Grimaldi, "Abramoff Pleads Guilty to 3 Counts: Lobbyist to Testify About Lawmakers in Corruption Probe," *Washington Post*, January 4, 2006; Morgan Smith and Aziza Musa, "Hammer, Nailed," *Texas Tribune*, January 11, 2011. After his release from prison, Abramoff released his memoirs, in which he details the high level of organization that went into maintaining a cheap, vulnerable labor source in the CNMI, writing: "The real benefit of the congressional trips was only apparent once the representatives and staff had returned. From the end of the first trip to the Marianas during Easter recess of 1996, we had a permanent cadre on Capitol Hill ready to stop any attacks on the CNMI. Whenever any representative or staff launched an anti-CNMI attack, one of the travelers would detect it early, inform us, and then usually take the lead in the counter assault." Abramoff, *Capitol Punishment*, 81.

110 Anderson, "Kathie Lee's Children," https://mises.org/free-market/kathie-lees-children, accessed March 4, 2025.

111 Nicholas D. Kristof and Sheryl WuDunn, "Two Cheers for Sweatshops," *New York Times*, September 24, 2000.

112 Kristof and WuDunn, "Two Cheers for Sweatshops."

113 Nicholas Kristof, "In Praise of the Maligned Sweatshop," *New York Times*, June 6, 2006.

114 Kristof, "In Praise of the Maligned Sweatshop."

115 Benjamin Powell, "In Defense of 'Sweatshops,'" *Econlib*, June 2, 2008.

116 Irvin Molotsky, "Furor Builds over Sweatshop Exhibit," *New York Times*, September 20, 1997.

4. "AMAZON CRIME"

1 Fashion Revolution, "Fashion Revolution's Black Friday Campaign Calls for an End to Overproduction, Overconsumption and Waste," news release November 1, 2021, https://www.fashionrevolution.org/blackfriday/.

2 "Amazon Protests: 31 Arrested as Extinction Rebellion Targets Retailer," BBC News, November 26, 2021.

3 "Black Friday Protest Hits Amazon," *Toronto Star*, November 27, 2021.

4 Anthony Cuthbertson, "Amazon Black Friday Strikes and Protests Coordinated Around the World," *Independent*, November 27, 2020.

5 Theresa Braine, "It's Amazon Prime Day and a Growing Chorus Is Calling for a Boycott," *New York Daily News*, June 21, 2021; Alex Ledsom, "Amazon Prime Day Boycott: US Workers Chase EU Successes," *Forbes*, October 6, 2020.

6   Dean Moses, "Protesters March into Lobby of Amazon Investor Calling for an End in Facial Recognition Sales to ICE and Police," *Villager*, May 24, 2021.
7   Moses, "Protesters March into Lobby of Amazon Investor"; Kari Paul, "Amazon Shareholders Reject 15 Motions on Worker Rights and Environment," *Guardian*, May 25, 2022.
8   See, among others, Orleck, *"We Are All Fast-Food Workers Now."*
9   "Thai Factory Fire's 200 Victims Were Locked Inside, Guards Say," *New York Times*, May 12, 1993; Bob Herbert, "Terror in Toyland," *New York Times*, December 21, 1994; Denholm Barnetson, "More than 200 Killed, 500 Injured in Thai Factory Fire, *United Press International*, May 11, 1993.
10 Steven Greenhouse, "US Retailers Decline to Aid Factory Victims in Bangladesh," *New York Times*, November 23, 2013; "$40 Million Fund Being Set Up for Victims, Families of Bangladesh Factory Collapse," *Canadian Press*, December 24, 2013; Calum MacLeod and Jayne O'Donnell, "Latest Bangladesh Factory Fire Kills Owner, Seven Others," *USA Today*, May 9, 2013; Julhas Alam, "Bangladesh Factory Collapse Death Toll Hits 1,034," *Associated Press*, May 10, 2013; Marcia Dunn, "Bangladesh Collapse Left Many Amputees," *Associated Press*, June 20, 2013.
11 Nicolas Niarchos, "The Dark Side of Congo's Cobalt Rush," *New Yorker*, May 24, 2021.
12 Siddharth Kara, "Is Your Phone Tainted by the Misery of the 35,000 Children in Congo's Mines?," *Guardian*, October 12, 2018; Annie Kelly, "Apple and Google Named in US Lawsuit over Congolese Child Cobalt Mining Deaths," *Guardian*, December 16, 2019; Michele Fabiola Lawson, "The DRC Mining Industry: Child Labor and Formalization of Small-Scale Mining," Wilson Center, September 1, 2021.
13 Steve Strauss, "'Gig Economy' Is Stressful, but the Freedom Can't Be Beat," *USA Today*, May 8, 2017.
14 Yue Zhang, "Gig Economy Offers More Freedom and Choice," *Independent* (London), December 21, 2021.
15 Mina Haq, "Face of 'Gig' Work Is Female, Empowered," *USA Today*, April 6, 2017.
16 Tom Spiggle, "Gig Workers as Employees: Why America Won't Follow the UK Anytime Soon," *Forbes*, February 26, 2021; David Olive, "What Is Wrong with Uber? Everything," *Toronto Star*, July 3, 2021; "Diary of an Uber 'Sweatshop,'" *Sunday Star*, November 13, 2016; Sally Kohn, "How Amazon Became Santa's Sweatshop," *Daily Beast*, December 11, 2014; John Baber, "Local US Newspaper Exposes Amazon 'Sweatshop,'" *Globe and Mail*, October 5, 2011; Peter Campbell, "Apple Hit By Sweatshop Allegations," *Daily Mail*, July 30, 2013; Michael Sainato, "Amazon Warehouse Workers in Alabama: 'They Work You to Death,'" *American Prospect Blogs*, December 23, 2020. On sexuality and work, see Canaday, *Queer Career*.
17 Pink, *The Climate Change Crisis*, 1–11.

18   "Report: China Emissions Exceed All Developed Nations Combined," BBC News, May 7, 2021.
19   Institute for European Environmental Policy, "More Than Half of All CO2 Emissions Since 1751 Emitted in the Last 30 Years," April 20, 2020, https://ieep.eu/news/more-than-half-of-all-co2-emissions-since-1751-emitted-in-the-last-30-years/, accessed March 4, 2025; World Bank, "CO2 Emissions (Metric Tons Per Capita)—China," data.worldbank.org, accessed November 7, 2022; Office of the United States Trade Representative, Executive Office of the President, "The People's Republic of China," ustr.gov, accessed November 7, 2022; United Nations Environment Programme, "Emissions Gap Report 2022: The Closing Window."
20   Justine Calma, "Amazon's Climate Pollution is Getting Way Worse," *The Verge*, August 1, 2022; Will Evans, "Private Report Shows How Amazon Drastically Undercounts Its Carbon Footprint," *Reveal*, February 25, 2022.
21   David Vetter, "This Is How Much Plastic from Amazon Deliveries Ends Up in the Ocean," *Forbes*, December 15, 2020.
22   Richard Pallot, "Amazon Destroying Millions of Items of Unsold Stock in One of Its UK Warehouses Every Year, ITV News Investigation Finds," June 22, 2021, itv.com, accessed November 8, 2022; Jeff Collins, "Amazon Triples Southern California Delivery Hubs to Get Packages Out Faster," *Orange County Register*, March 26, 2021; People's Collective for Environmental Justice, "Warehouses, Pollution, and Social Disparities: An Analytical View of the Logistical Industry's Impacts on Environmental Justice Communities Across Southern California," April 2021; Sam Levin, "Amazon's Warehouse Boom Linked to Health Hazards in America's Most Polluted Region," *Guardian*, April 15, 2021; Vetter, "This Is How Much Plastic from Amazon Deliveries Ends Up in the Ocean."
23   Vanessa Forti, Cornelis Peter Baldé, Ruediger Kuehr, and Garam Bel, "The Global E-waste Monitor 2020: Quantities, Flows, and the Circular Economy Potential," United Nations University, 2020, 23–25.
24   Lin, Cai, and Li, *The China Miracle*, 299–322; Vogel, *Deng Xiaoping and the Transformation of China*, 693–714; Tantri, "China's Policy for Special Economic Zone," 231–50.
25   Fenwick, "Evaluating China's Special Economic Zones," 377.
26   "80 Killed as Fire Sweeps Through Toy Factory in China," Associated Press, November 20, 1993; "The Tragic Chinese Toy Story," *South China Morning Post*, December 15, 1999.
27   Chan, "Culture of Survival," 163–88; Chan, *China's Workers Under Assault*, 106–33; Kathy Wilhelm, "Abuse by Taiwan, Hong Kong Bosses," *Honolulu Advertiser*, April 3, 1994; "Leading Newspaper Hits South China City for Blast," *United Press International*, August 17, 1993; Mandy Zuo, "Factory Fire Wounds Refuse to Heal," *South China Morning Post*, May 1, 2014.
28   Chan, Selden, and Ngai, *Dying for an iPhone*, 69–80.

29 Ngai and Chan, "Global Capital, the State, and Chinese Workers," 386–87; "Hon Hai Precision," www.forbes.com, accessed November 22, 2022.
30 Chan, Selden, and Ngai, *Dying for an iPhone*, 69–80.
31 George Knowles, "Life for China's Migrant Workers: Dorm That Looks Like Prison," *South China Morning Post*, May 27, 2016; Michael Martina, "China's Dorm Room Discontent Emerges as New Labour Flashpoint," *Reuters*, September 27, 2012; "China: Foxconn Dormitory Beds Shared By 2 Workers, Raised Privacy Concerns," *Nanfang Daily*, August 9, 2006 (translated for Business and Human Rights Resource Centre); Chan, Selden, and Ngai, *Dying for an iPhone*, 57–58, 100–101.
32 Yunxue Deng, "Gender in Factory Life: An Ethnographic Study of Migrant Workers in Shenzhen Foxconn," master's thesis, Hong Kong Polytechnic University, 2012, 59–61; Fincher, *Betraying Big Brother*, 54; Aaron Halegua, "Workplace Gender-Based Violence and Harassment in China: Harmonizing Domestic Law and Practice with International Standards," U.S.-Asia Law Institute, New York University School of Law, 2021, 6; Aaron Halegua, Workplace Gender-Based Violence and Harassment in China, https://globallaborjustice.org/wp-content/uploads/2021/06/Halegua-Workplace-GBVH-in-China-FINAL-2021.06.21-10-am-EST.pdf, accessed March 4, 2025.
33 Chan, Selden, and Ngai, *Dying for an iPhone*, 69–80.
34 Gethin Chamberlain, "Schoolchildren in China Work Overnight to Produce Amazon Alexa Devices," *Guardian*, August 8, 2019.
35 Chan, Selden, and Ngai, *Dying for an iPhone*, 69–80.
36 Gethin Chamberlain, "Underpaid and Exhausted: The Human Cost of Your Kindle," *Guardian*, June 9, 2018; "Rights Group Hits Amazon, Foxconn over China Labor Conditions," *Reuters*, June 10, 2018; Matt Day, "Watchdog Criticizes Conditions at Chinese Factory That Builds Amazon Echo Speakers," *Seattle Times*, June 9, 2018.
37 Brian Merchant, "Life and Death in Apple's Forbidden City," *Guardian*, June 18, 2017.
38 Chan, Selden, and Ngai, *Dying for an iPhone*, 69–80; Juliet Ye, "Foxconn Installs Antijumping Nets at Hebei Plants," *Wall Street Journal*, August 3, 2010; Bruce Blanch, "Foxconn Suicides: 'Workers Feel Quite Lonely,'" BBC News, May 28, 2010.
39 "Workers Threatened Suicide in Chinese Labor Dispute," Associated Press, January 13, 2012.
40 "China Foxconn Workers Riot at Chengdu Restaurant," BBC News, June 8, 2012; Maxim Duncan and Clare Jim, "Foxconn China Plant Closed After 2,000 Riot," *Reuters*, September 23, 2012.
41 Alexei Oreskovic, "Apple's Steve Jobs Finds Foxconn Deaths 'Troubling,'" *Reuters*, June 1, 2010.
42 Scott Nova and Isaac Shapiro, "Polishing Apple: Fair Labor Association Gives Foxconn and Apple Undue Credit for Labor Rights Progress," Eco-

43   nomic Policy Institute Report Briefing Paper #352, November 8, 2012; Chan, Selden, and Ngai, *Dying for an iPhone*, 27, 50.

43   Juliette Garside, "Child Labour Uncovered in Apple's Supply Chain," *Guardian*, January 25, 2013.

44   Tyler Sonnemaker, "Apple Knew a Supplier Was Using Child Labor but Took 3 Years to Fully Cut Ties, Despite the Company's Promises to Hold Itself to the 'Highest Standard,'" *Business Insider*, December 31, 2020.

45   Jenny Chan, interview by author, November 2 and 3, 2022; Ross Eisenbrey, "Don't Be Fooled by Apple's PR: Workers Strike Against Sweatshop Conditions," Economic Policy Institute, November 1, 2013; Bang, "Unmasking the Charade of the Global Supply Contract," 255–322.

46   Jenny Chan, interview by author, November 2 and 3, 2022.

47   Jenny Chan, interview by author, November 2 and 3, 2022.

48   Jenny Chan, interview by author, November 2 and 3, 2022.

49   Jenny Chan and Students and Scholars Against Corporate Misbehavior to John Pepper, "A Public Statement on The Walt Disney Company Annual Meeting of Shareholders," March 6, 2008; Jenny Chan, interview by author, November 2 and 3, 2022.

50   "Disney Sweatshops Alleged," *CNN Money*, August 18, 2005; Boris, "An Interview with Pun Ngai," 129–31, 147; Jenny Chan, interview by author, November 2 and 3, 2022.

51   Chan and SACOM to John Pepper, "A Public Statement on The Walt Disney Company Annual Meeting of Shareholders"; "Chinese Workers Link Sickness to N-Hexane and Apple iPhone Screens," *Guardian*, May 7, 2010; Royston Chan, "Chinese Workers Appeal to Apple over Health Worries," *Reuters*, February 21, 2011.

52   Jenny Chan, interview by author, November 2 and 3, 2022.

53   Jenny Chan, interview by author, November 2 and 3, 2022.

54   Jenny Chan, interview by author, November 2 and 3, 2022.

55   Li Qiang, interview by author (Claudia Liu, translator), June 8, 2023.

56   China Labor Watch, "The Other Side of the Fairy Tales: An Investigation of Labor Conditions at Five Chinese Toy Factories," November 20, 2015, https://chinalaborwatch.org/the-other-side-of-fairy-tales-an-investigation-of-labor-conditions-at-five-chinese-toy-factories/, accessed March 4, 2025; Mark Gurman, "Apple, Foxconn Broke a Chinese Labor Law to Build Latest iPhones," September 8, 2018, www.bloomberg.com, accessed November 16, 2022; China Labor Watch, "Amazon Profits from Secretly Oppressing Supplier's Workers: An Investigative Report on Hengyang Foxconn," June 10, 2018, www.chinalaborwatch.com, accessed November 16, 2022.

57   China Labor Watch, "Three China Labor Watch's investigators released on bail, pending a trial," June 28, 2017, www.chinalaborwatch.com, accessed November 16, 2022.

58. China Labor Watch, "China Labor Watch Urges Amazon to Address Whistleblower's Demands," January 30, 2022, www.chinalaborwatch.com, accessed November 16, 2022.
59. China Labor Watch, "China Labor Watch Urges Amazon to Address Whistleblower's Demands."
60. Li Qiang, interview by author (Claudia Liu, translator), June 8, 2023.
61. Li Qiang, interview by author (Claudia Liu, translator), June 8, 2023.
62. Li Qiang, interview by author (Claudia Liu, translator), June 8, 2023.
63. Tess Riski, "Workers Risking the COVID-19 Outbreak at Amazon's Troutdale Warehouse Signed a Strict Confidentiality Agreement," *Willamette Week*, December 2, 2020, www.wweek.com, accessed December 6, 2022; Spencer Woodman, "Exclusive: Amazon Makes Even Temporary Warehouse Workers Sign 18-Month Non-Competes," *The Verge*, March 26, 2015, www.theverge.com, accessed December 6, 2022.
64. "Protests Intensify Against Amazon's Working Conditions," *Material Handling and Logistics*, December 21, 2018.
65. Meira Gebel, "I'm An Amazon Delivery Driver: I've Had to Pee in Water Bottles and Eat Lunch in My Van to Avoid Getting Penalized," *Business Insider*, March 31, 2021; MWPVL International, "Amazon Global Supply Chain and Fulfillment Center Network," www.mwpvl.com/html/amazon_com.html, accessed November 2, 2022; Spencer Soper, "Inside Amazon's Warehouse," *Morning Call*, August 1, 2015.
66. Soper, "Inside Amazon's Warehouse."
67. Alimahomed-Wilson and Reese, *The Cost of Free Shipping*, 10; Gethin Chamberlain, "Underpaid and Exhausted: The Human Cost of Your Kindle," *Observer*, June 9, 2018; "Protests Intensify Against Amazon's Working Conditions," *Material Handling and Logistics*, December 21, 2018.
68. Michael Sainato, "The Outcry over Deaths on Amazon's Warehouse Floor," *Guardian*, October 18, 2019; Kate Briquelet and Josh Fiallo, "Amazon Employee Who Died on Prime Day Was Hardworking Dad," *Daily Beast*, July 27, 2022.
69. Max Zahn and Sharif Paget, "'Colony of Hell': 911 Calls from Inside Amazon Warehouses," *Daily Beast*, March 11, 2019; Irene Tung, Maya Pinto, and Debbie Berkowitz, "Injuries, Dead-End Jobs, and Racial Inequality in Amazon's Minnesota Operations: A Case Study on the Human Costs of Amazon's Growth," National Employment Law Project, December 2021.
70. Matthew Gault, "Amazon Introduces Tiny 'ZenBooths' for Stressed-Out Warehouse Workers," *Vice*, May 27, 2021; "From Body Mechanics to Mindfulness, Amazon Launches Employee-Designed Health and Safety Program Called WorkingWell Across U.S. Operations," *BusinessWire*, May 17, 2021, www.businesswire.com, accessed November 17, 2022.
71. Gebel, "I'm an Amazon Delivery Driver: I've Had to Pee in Water Bottles and Eat Lunch in My Van to Avoid Getting Penalized," *Business Insider*,

March 31, 2021; "UK Drivers Delivering for Amazon Seek Employee Rights," *Reuters*, October 13, 2021; Branwen Jones, "'I Find Bottles of Urine in My Van'—Delivery Driver," *Western Mail*, April 29, 2022.

72 "Amazon U-Turn on Urinating Drivers," *Daily Telegraph*, April 5, 2021; "Amazon Apologizes for Wrongly Denying Drivers Need to Urinate in Bottles," BBC, April 4, 2021.

73 Luke O'Neil, "Amazon's Denial of Workers Urinating in Bottles Puts the Pee in PR Fiasco," *Guardian*, March 25, 2011; Ken Klippenstein, "Documents Show Amazon Is Aware Drivers Pee in Bottles and Even Defecate En Route, Despite Company Denial," *Intercept*, March 25, 2021.

74 Robert Bell, "Drivers Protest Amazon Work Practices at Center," *Rochester Democrat and Chronicle*, April 6, 2021; Seren Morris, "Amazon Driver Leaves Packages Upside Down to Start 'No More Smiles' Protest," *Newsweek*, April 7, 2021.

75 Annie Palmer, "Nearly One in Five Amazon Delivery Drivers Suffered Injuries in 2021, Study Finds," CNBC, May 24, 2022; KING 5 Staff, "Driver Delivering Amazon Packages Dies When Truck Goes Over Embankment Near Elma," KING 5 News, August 17, 2022; Chelsea Donovan, "7-Year-Old Walking Home From School Hit By Amazon Van in Holly Springs," WRAL News, September 15, 2022; Tony Kurzweil, "Woman Killed in Collision with Amazon Delivery Van in Anaheim," KTLA News, October 27, 2022; Erum Salam, "Police Kill Two Dogs After US Amazon Driver Dies in Apparent Animal Attack," *Guardian*, October 25, 2022.

76 William Thornton, "'Awe-Inspiring' Amazon Center Taking Shape in Bessemer," AL.com, May 10, 2019.

77 Erin Edgemon, "'The Deal Is Done:' Amazon to Bring 1,500 Jobs to Bessemer," AL.com, June 22, 2018; Quick Facts, Bessemer, Alabama, United States Census Bureau, https://www.census.gov/quickfacts/bessemercityalabama, last accessed on October 24, 2022.

78 Isobel Asher Hamilton," Amazon Drops $2 Coronavirus Pay Raise for Warehouse Workers as CEO Jeff Bezos' Fortune Nears $150 Billion," *Business Insider*, June 3, 2020; Abha Bhattarai and Christopher Ingraham, "Workers Call on Walmart, Amazon and Other Retailers to Bring Back Hazard Pay Ahead of Holiday Rush," *Washington Post*, November 23, 2020; Chase Peterson-Withorn, "How Much Money America's Billionaires Have Made During the Covid-19 Pandemic," *Forbes*, April 30, 2021; Spencer Soper, "Amazon Accused of Underreporting COVID Cases Contracted At Work," *Los Angeles Times*, November 30, 2021.

79 "Q&A with Bessemer, AL Amazon Union Organizer Jennifer Bates," *American Postal Worker Magazine*, September–October 2021.

80 Jay Greene, "Amazon Fights Aggressively to Defeat Union Drive in Alabama, Fearing a Coming Wave," *Washington Post*, March 9, 2021; Ryan Bort, "Jennifer Bates on Organizing Amazon's Alabama Union Drive and Taking on Jeff Bezos," *Rolling Stone*, March 29, 2021.

81 Michael Sainato, "Amazon Warehouse Workers in Alabama: 'They Work You to Death,'" *American Prospect*, December 23, 2020.

82 Sainato, "Amazon Warehouse Workers in Alabama."

83 US Senate Budget Committee Hearing on the Income Inequality Crisis in America, "Testimony by Jennifer Bates, Learning Ambassador at Amazon BHM1, Bessemer Alabama," March 17, 2021; Ryan Bort, "Jennifer Bates on Organizing Amazon's Alabama Union Drive and Taking on Jeff Bezos," *Rolling Stone*, March 29, 2021; Steven Greenhouse, "'We Deserve More': An Amazon Warehouse's High-Stakes Union Drive," *Guardian*, February 23, 2021.

84 Chelsea Connor, interview by author, November 15, 2022; William Thornton, "Jefferson County Now Says Traffic Lights Were Changed Near Amazon," *AL.com*, February 7, 2021.

85 US Senate Budget Committee Hearing on the Income Inequality Crisis in America, "Testimony by Jennifer Bates, Learning Ambassador at Amazon BHM1, Bessemer Alabama," March 17, 2021.

86 Charles Bethea, "The Alabama Workers Trying to Unionize an Amazon Fulfillment Center," *New Yorker*, Mark 17, 2021; National Labor Relations Board, "Your Right to Form a Union," https://www.nlrb.gov; Ryan Port, "Jennifer Bates on Organizing Amazon's Alabama Union Drive and Taking on Jeff Bezos," *Rolling Stone*, March 29, 2021; Jay Greene, "Amazon Fights Aggressively to Defeat Union Drive in Alabama, Fearing a Coming Wave," *Washington Post*, March 9, 2021.

87 Retail, Wholesale and Department Store Union, "Black Lives Matter Movement to Lead Caravan in Support Of Bessemer, Al Amazon Workers Seeking Union Representation," news release, March 21, 2021, https://patch.com/alabama/birmingham-al/black-lives-matter-lead-caravan-support-amazon-unionization, accessed March 4, 2025.

88 Annabelle Williams, "Black Lives Matter Helped Inspire Amazon Workers' Push to Unionize In Alabama, Union President Says," *Business Insider*, March 1, 2021; Chelsea Connor, interview by author, November 15, 2022.

89 Annie Palmer, "Amazon Illegally Interfered in Alabama Warehouse Vote, Union Alleges," CNBC News, April 7, 2022.

90 William Thornton, "Mailbox Stirs Controversy in Amazon Union Vote," *AL.com*, February 24, 2021.

91 Natasha Dailey, "Amazon Just Lost Its Bid to Require In-Person Voting for a Union Election in Alabama," *Business Insider*, February 5, 2021; John Logan, "The Legacy of Bessemer: The Amazon Campaign Is a Gift to the Labor Movement," *Labor Online*, April 23, 2021; Lauren Kaori Gurley, "Amazon Sends 'Vote NO' Instructions to Unionizing Employees, Tells Them to Use New Mailbox," *Vice News*, February 24, 2021.

92 Chelsea Connor, interview by author, November 15, 2022.

93 Sebastian Herrera, "Amazon Workers at Alabama Facility Poised to Vote a Second Time on Union Bid," *Wall Street Journal*, February 2, 2022; Anne

D'Innocenzio, "Amazon Workers Try New Tactics to Unionize," Associated Press, February 5, 2022; Scott Heric, "Unfair Labor Practices at Amazon," *Saint Louis/Southern Illinois Labor Tribune*, March 14, 2022; William Thornton, "Amazon, Union Trade Allegations In Bessemer Election: Will There Be a Third Vote?," *AL.com*, April 8, 2022.

94   Chelsea Connor, interview by author, November 15, 2022.
95   Thornton, "Amazon, Union Trade Allegations in Bessemer Election: Will There Be a Third Vote?"
96   Hillary Russ, "Instacart, Amazon Workers Strike as Labor Unrest Grows During Coronavirus Crisis," *Reuters*, March 30, 2020.
97   Alene Tchekmedyian and Genaro Molina, "Amazon Workers March to Jeff Bezos' Mansion, Calling for Higher Wages, Protections," *Los Angeles Times*, October 5, 2020.
98   Avery Hartmans, "The Amazon Worker Who Was Fired After Calling for Better Warehouse Safety Standards Led a Protest in Front of Jeff Bezos' New York City Apartment," *Business Insider*, August 20, 2020; Sebastian Klovig Skelton, "Aggrieved Amazon Employees Organize Protests at Homes of Jeff Bezos," *Computer Weekly*, August 27, 2020; Evan Sully, "A Fired Amazon Employee Led a Protest in Front of Jeff Bezos' $165 Million Beverly Hills Mansion Over Workers' Wages and Job Protections," *Business Insider*, October 5, 2020.
99   Richard Luscombe, "Covid Caused Huge Shortages in US Labor Market, Study Shows," *Guardian*, September 13, 2022.
100 David Shepardson and Nandita Bose, "Biden Meets with Labor Organizer at Amazon After Senate Hearing," *Reuters*, May 5, 2022; Greg Jaffe, "Chris Smalls's Amazon Uprising and the Fight for a Second Warehouse," *Washington Post*, June 12, 2022; "Amazon.Com Union Organizer Meets with Biden at White House," *Reuters*, May 5, 2022; Karen Weise and Noam Scheiber, "Amazon Workers on Staten Island Vote to Unionize in Landmark Win for Labor," *New York Times*, April 1, 2022; "Amazon Objecting to Union's Victory in New York, Alleging Interference," *Reuters*, April 8, 2022; Annie Palmer, "Amazon Loses Effort to Overturn Historic Union Election at Staten Island Warehouse," CNBC News, September 1, 2022.
101 Wilson, "Company Town," 147.
102 Kshama Sawant, interview by author, August 16, 2023.
103 Wilson, "Company Town," 147.
104 Elizabeth Weise, "Amazon's Aggressive Side Shows in Seattle Tax Fight," *Journal and Courier*, May 17, 2018; Wilson, "Company Town," 149–53.
105 Wilson, "Company Town," 153–54; Alana Semuels, "How Amazon Helped Kill a Seattle Tax on Business," *Atlantic*, June 13, 2018; David Streitfeld and Claire Ballentine "Seattle Officials Repeal Tax That Upset Amazon," *New York Times*, June 12, 2018; Devin Coldewey, "Seattle Reverses Controversial Tax Amazon Opposed, Just a Month After Approving It," *TechCrunch*, June 14, 2018; "Amazon's Seattle Tax Revolt," *Wall Street Journal*,

October 28, 2019; Gregory Scruggs, "Amazon's $1.5 Million Political Gambit Backfires in Seattle City Council," *Reuters*, November 10, 2019.

106 David Kroman, "Sawant Revives 'Tax Amazon' Campaign to Address Homelessness," Cascade PBS News, February 12, 2020, https://www.cascadepbs.org/2020/02/sawant-revives-tax-amazon-campaign-address-homelessness, accessed March 4, 2025.

107 Mai Hoang, "The Sawant Recall Election Is Relatively Small, but Its Audience Is Huge," Cascade PBS News, November 20, 2021, https://www.cascadepbs.org/news/2021/11/sawant-recall-election-relatively-small-its-audience-huge, accessed March 4, 2025; Mai Hoang, "Kshama Sawant Says Failed Recall Attempt Emboldened Her," Cascade PBS News, February 17, 2022, https://www.cascadepbs.org/news/2022/02/kshama-sawant-says-failed-recall-attempt-emboldened-her, accessed March 4, 2025; Kshama Sawant, interview by author, August 16, 2023.

108 Alex Halverson, "Amazon Replaces Microsoft as Seattle Area's Top Corporate Giver," *Puget Sound Business Journal*, May 17, 2022.

109 Dennis Green, "New York City Will Be Bathed with Orange Light in Support of Its Bid for Amazon's $5 Billion Headquarters," *Business Insider*, October 18, 2017; Shannon Liao, "The Eight Most Outrageous Things Cities Did to Lure Amazon for HQ2," *The Verge*, October 19, 2017.

110 Ivan Pereira and Lisa Colangelo, "Activists, Unions Protest HQ2 Plan," *Newsday*, November 27, 2018; Brittany Shoot, "On Cyber Monday, New Yorkers Protest Amazon's New HQ2 with a 'Day of Action,'" *Fortune*, November 26, 2018; Jacob Passy, "Community Activists Stage Cyber Monday Protests in Fight Against Amazon's HQ2," *Market Watch*, November 26, 2018.

111 Jessica Tyler, "'Amazon Has Got to Go': Protesters Swarmed City Hall as New York's City Council Held a Contentious Hearing About Amazon's HQ2 Deal," *Business Insider*, December 12, 2018.

112 Kate Taylor, "New Yorkers Are Storming One of Amazon's Stores in Protest of HQ2," *Business Insider*, November 26, 2018.

113 "Amazon East HQ: Incentives from, Benefits for, Chosen Cities," *Fort Worth Business Press*, November 13, 2018; Ivan Pereira and Lisa Colangelo, "Activists, Unions Protest HQ2 Plan," *Newsday*, November 27, 2018; Pat Garafalo, "How Amazon, Google, and Other Companies Exploit NDAs," *New York Times*, June 29, 2021.

114 Joseph Pisani, "Amazon, in Stunning Reversal, Dumps NYC as New HQ Site," *Denver Post*, February 14, 2019.

115 Bill de Blasio, "The Path Amazon Rejected," *New York Times*, February 16, 2019.

116 Joan Verdon, "Warehouse Workers, Many from New Jersey, Rally to Get Amazon to Improve Working Conditions," *NorthJersey*, December 13, 2017.

117 Lauren Aratani, "New Jersey Urged to Enforce 'Code of Conduct' for Amazon Workers," *Guardian*, December 12, 2018.

118 Elizabeth Weise, "Amazon's Annual Meeting Draws Protests from Pilots and Drag Queens," *USA Today*, May 30, 2018; Verdon, "Warehouse Workers, Many From New Jersey, Rally to Get Amazon to Improve Working Conditions"; Aratani, "New Jersey Urged to Enforce 'Code of Conduct' for Amazon Workers."

119 Liz Sawyer, "Workers Protest Conditions at Amazon's Shakopee Center," *Star Tribune*, December 14, 2018.

120 Ibrahim Hirsi, "Meet Three Somali-American Women Fighting for Better Work Conditions at Amazon," Minnesota Public Radio, July 15, 2019; Steve Karnowski, "Amazon Minnesota Warehouse Workers Plan 'Prime Day' Strike," *St. Cloud Times*, July 10, 2019; Caitlin O'Kane, "Muslim Amazon Employees Say They Fear Taking Time to Pray at Work, Are Discriminated Against In Several Ways," CBS News, May 9, 2019; Irene Tung, Maya Pinto, and Deborah Berkowitz, "Injuries, Dead-End Jobs, and Racial Inequity in Amazon's Minnesota Operations," National Employment Law Project, December 2021.

121 Dan Herbeck, "Grand Island Not Owned by Senecas, Arcara Rules," *Buffalo News*, June 21, 2002; "Grand Island Introduced to Massive Project Olive," *Niagara Frontier Publications*, March 7, 2020; David Reilly, interview by author, November 14, 2022.

122 David Reilly, interview by author, November 14, 2022.

123 Sam Sharpe, "The Subsidy Gamble: New York State Is Betting Big on Tesla," *Dismal Science*, March 14, 2020; Dave Reilly and Nicole Gerber, "Project Olive Does Not Fit Grand Island's Comprehensive Plan," public remarks to Grand Island Town Board, July 2020; David Reilly, interview by author, November 14, 2022.

124 The Coalition for Responsible Economic Development for Grand Island, "What It Means to Be a Community: Reflections on the Successful Campaign to Stop Amazon's Warehouse on Grand Island, NY," August 13, 2020.

125 David Reilly, interview by author, November 14, 2022.

126 David Reilly, interview by author, November 14, 2022.

127 Sarah Grace Taylor, "Nearly $1M Pours in from Each Side in Seattle Councilmember Sawant's Recall," *Seattle Times*, December 2, 2021, www.seattletimes.com, accessed November 22, 2022.

128 Charles Bolinger, "OSHA Cites Amazon Facilities for Ergonomic Violations," *Edwardsville Intelligencer*, February 1, 2023.

129 Siddharth Kara, "How 'Modern-Day Slavery' in the Congo Powers the Rechargeable Battery Economy," by Terry Gross, *Fresh Air*, PBS, February 1, 2023; Sainato, "The Outcry over Deaths on Amazon's Warehouse Floor"; Chan, Selden, and Ngai, *Dying for an iPhone*, 69–80; Gebel, "I'm An Amazon Delivery Driver: I've Had to Pee in Water Bottles and Eat Lunch in My Van to Avoid Getting Penalized."

130 Heather Somerville, "Elon Musk Moves to Texas, Takes Jab at Silicon Valley," *Wall Street Journal*, December 8, 2020.

CONCLUSION

1. "Domestics Should Organize," *Pittsburgh Courier*, September 11, 1937.
2. Ramachandran, Collins, Su, Cummings, and Ahmad, "The El Monte Sweatshop Slavery Cases"; Shenon, "Made in the U.S.A.?"; Greenhouse, "Live with Kathie Lee and Apparel Workers"; Keady, Nike Sweatshops.
3. Rick Romell, "Foxconn Groundbreaking Date Changed Again to Accommodate Schedules of Trump, Others," *Milwaukee Journal Sentinel*, June 21, 2018; "Fact Check: Taxpayers Have Already Spent Money on Foxconn's Wisconsin Campus," *Chicago Tribune*, February 1, 2019; Nilay Patel, "A Former Foxconn Executive Tries to Explain What Went Wrong in Wisconsin," *The Verge*, April 19, 2022.
4. Thaslima Begum and Redwan Ahmed, "Bangladesh Garment Workers Fighting for Pay Face Brutal Violence and Threats," *Guardian*, November 15, 2023.
5. McKenna Schueler, "Moms, Disney Fans Call on Disney World to Rescind Support for Proposed Child Labor Rollbacks in Florida," *Orlando Weekly*, February 1, 2024; Terry Castleman, "Garment Workers in SoCal Are Paid 'As Little as $1.58 Per Hour,' Labor Department Says," *Los Angeles Times*, April 4, 2023; Michael Sainato, "Republicans Continue Effort to Erode US Child Labor Rules Despite Teen Deaths," *Guardian*, October 20, 2023; The Conversation, "States Are Loosening Restrictions on Child Labor," *US News*, June 26, 2023; Karl Ebert, "Children Hired to Work Graveyard Shifts Cleaning Slaughterhouses, Labor Department Says," *USA Today*, November 13, 2022; Francisco Uranga and Erin Douglas, "As Texas Swelters, Local Rules Requiring Water Breaks for Construction Workers Will Soon Be Nullified," *Texas Tribune*, June 16, 2023.
6. Haleluya Hadero, "Amazon Argues That National Labor Relations Board Is Unconstitutional, Joining SpaceX and Trader Joe's," *Associated Press*, February 16, 2024.
7. Brooks, *Unraveling the Garment Industry*, xx.
8. Li Qiang, interview by author (Claudia Liu, translator), June 8, 2023.
9. Kshama Sawant, interview by author, August 16, 2023.
10. Schneiderman, "A Cap Maker's Story," 935–38.

BIBLIOGRAPHY

ARCHIVES

FKP	Florence Kelley Papers, Manuscripts and Archives Division, New York Public Library
FMC	Fromkin Memorial Collection, Golda Meir Library, University of Wisconsin-Milwaukee, Milwaukee, WI
JLOP	Jessie Lloyd O'Connor Papers, Sophia Smith Collection of Women's History, Neilson Library, Smith College, Northampton, MA
LFPC	Lectures of Frances Perkins Collection, Kheel Center Labor and Management Microfilm Collections, Catherwood Library, Cornell University, Ithaca, NY
LWSP	League of Women Shoppers Papers, Sophia Smith Collection of Women's History, Neilson Library, Smith College, Northampton, MA
MCBP	Mary Cornelia Barker Papers, Manuscript, Archives, and Rare Book Library, Robert W. Woodruff Library, Emory University
NCLR	National Consumers' League Records, Manuscript Division, Library of Congress, Washington, DC
PWTUL	Papers of the Women's Trade Union League and Its Principal Leaders, Schlesinger Library, Radcliffe Institute, Harvard University, Cambridge, MA
RCLM	Records of the Consumers' League of Massachusetts, 1891–1955, Radcliffe Institute, Harvard University, Cambridge, MA
WGRPC	Walter Goldwater Radical Pamphlet Collection, Special Collections Library, Peter J. Shields Library, University of California, Davis

PRIMARY SOURCES

Oral Histories and Interviews

Jenny Chan, interview by author, November 2, 3, 2022
Chelsea Connor, interview by author, November 15, 2022

Mary Domsky-Abrams, interview by Leon Stein, date unknown, https://trianglefire.ilr.cornell.edu

Max Hochfield, interview by Leon Stein, January 20, 1957, https://trianglefire.ilr.cornell.edu

Florence Mason, interview by Sybil Shainwald, February 1972, folder 39, box 2, Thomas Brooks/Colston Warne Collection, Consumer Movement Archives, Kansas State University, Manhattan, KS

Eraclio Montanaro, interview by Leon Stein, February 3, 1958, https://trianglefire.ilr.cornell.edu

Li Qiang, interview by author (Claudia Liu, translator), June 8, 2023

David Reilly, interview by author, November 14, 2022

Kshama Sawant, interview by author, August 16, 2023

Colston Warne, interview by Sybil Shainwald, April 1971, folder 59, box 2, Thomas Brooks/Colston Warne Collection, Consumer Movement Archives, Kansas State University, Manhattan, KS

Ed Weston, interview by Robert Friedheim in 1946, folder 6, box 1, Robert Friedheim Seattle General Strike Collection, University of Washington Libraries, Seattle, WA

Archival Collections

Archive of American Minority Cultures, W. S. Hoole Special Collections Library, University of Alabama, Tuscaloosa, AL

Fromkin Memorial Collection, Golda Meir Library, University of Wisconsin-Milwaukee, Milwaukee, WI

Great Britain. Parliament. House of Lords. *Fifth Report of the Select Committee on the Sweating System* (1890)

Ida M. Tarbell Collection, Special Collections Pelletier Library at Allegheny College, Meadville, PA

Industry Collection, Birmingham Public Library Archives, Birmingham, AL

Kheel Center for Labor-Management Documentation and Archives, Cornell University, Ithaca, NY
    LECTURES OF FRANCES PERKINS
    AMALGAMATED CLOTHING WORKERS OF AMERICA PAPERS

Library of Congress, Washington, DC
    AMERICAN LIFE HISTORIES: MANUSCRIPTS FROM THE FEDERAL WRITERS' PROJECT, 1936–1940
    NATIONAL CONSUMERS' LEAGUE PAPERS
    WOMEN'S TRADE UNION PAPERS

Margaret Dreier Papers, Special Collections, University of Florida, Gainesville, FL

Mary Cornelia Barker Papers, Manuscript, Archives, and Rare Book Library, Robert W. Woodruff Library, Emory University

Pamphlet Collection, Wisconsin Historical Society, Madison, WI
Robert Friedheim Seattle General Strike Collection, University of Washington Special Collection Library, Seattle, WA
Schlesinger Library, Radcliffe Institute, Harvard University, Cambridge, MA
    CONSUMERS' LEAGUE OF MASSACHUSETTS
    PAPERS OF THE WOMEN'S TRADE UNION LEAGUE AND ITS PRINCIPAL LEADERS
Sophia Smith Collection of Women's History, Smith College, Northampton, MA
    JESSIE LLOYD O'CONNER PAPERS
    LEAGUE OF WOMEN SHOPPERS RECORDS
    LORA JO FOO PAPERS
Thomas Brooks / Colston Warne Collection, Consumer Movement Archives, Kansas State University, Manhattan, KS
Walter Goldwater Radical Pamphlet Collection, Special Collections Library, Peter J. Shields Library, University of California, Davis
Wellesley College Archives, Margaret Clapp Library, Wellesley College, Wellesley, MA

Contemporary Published Sources

Abramoff, Jack. *Capitol Punishment: The Hard Truth About Washington Corruption from America's Most Notorious Lobbyist*. 1st ed. WND Books, 2011.
Blanshard, Paul. *Labor in Southern Cotton Mills*. New Republic Press, 1927.
Henry, Alice. *The Trade Union Woman*. D. Appleton, 1915.
Mailly, William. "The Triangle Trade Union Relief." *American Federationist* (July 1911), 544–47.
Mary. "Factory Thoughts." *Voice of Industry*. June 12, 1846.
Mitchell, Therese. *Consider the Woolworth Workers*. League of Women Shoppers, 1940.
Mitchell, Therese, and Jane Filley. *Consider the Laundry Workers*. League of Women Shoppers, 1937.
Nestor, Agnes. "I Became a Striker." In *America's Working Women: A Documentary History—1600 to the Present*. Edited by Rosalyn Baxandall, Linda Gordon, and Susan Reverby. Vintage Books, 1976.
National Consumers' League. "The Consumer's Control of Production: The Work of the National Consumers' League." Supplement to the *Annals of the American Academy of Political and Social Science* (1909).
"Observations of Lowell by an Associationist, 1846." In *Lowell History: Visitor Observations 1827–1913. Voice of Industry*. University of Massachusetts. https://libguides.uml.edu/.
Patten, Simon. *The Consumption of Wealth*. T. and J. W. Johnson, 1899.
The Poetry and Brief Life of a Foxconn Worker: Xu Lizhi (1990–2014). Translated by friends of the Nao project and published to libcom.org. https://libcom.org/article/poetry-and-brief-life-foxconn-worker-xu-lizhi-1990-2014.

Sanville, Florence L., Josephine Goldmark, Curt Miller, James H. McKenney, James T. Bixby, Alice Lakey, et al. "The Consumer's Control of Production: The Work of the National Consumers' League." *Annals of the American Academy of Political and Social Science* 34 (1909), 1–3, 583.

Tung, Irene, Maya Pinto, and Debbie Berkowitz. "Injuries, Dead-End Jobs, and Racial Inequality in Amazon's Minnesota Operations: A Case Study on the Human Costs of Amazon's Growth." National Employment Law Project, December 2021.

Vale, Rena. *Against the Red Tide*. Standard Publications, 1953.

Government Documents

United States. Congress. Senate. *Budget Committee Hearing on the Income Inequality Crisis in America, One Hundred and Seventeenth Congress, First Session*, 2021 (statement Amazon worker Jennifer Bates).

United States. Congress. Senate. Senate Finance Subcommittee on Fiscal Responsibility and Economic Growth Public. *Hearing on Promoting Competition and Economic Growth in the Technology Sector, One Hundred and Seventeenth Congress, First Session*, 2021 (statement of Amazon worker Courtenay Brown).

United States. General Accounting Office. Efforts to Address the Prevalence and Conditions of Sweatshops: Report to the Chairman, Subcommittee on Commerce, Consumer and Monetary Affairs, Committee on Government Operations, House of Representatives, November 1994.

Newspapers and Periodicals

Abbeville Press and Banner
AL.com
Al Jazeera
Allentown Democrat
America's Textile Reporter
American Mercury
American Postal Worker Magazine
American Prospect
Arizona Daily Wildcat
Associated Press
Atlanta Constitution
Atlanta Semi Weekly Journal
Atlantic
Baltimore Sun
Bennington Banner
Berkshire Eagle
Brooklyn Citizen

Buffalo Commercial
Buffalo Evening News
Buffalo News
Bulletin
BusinessWire
Butler County Press
Cairo Bulletin
Canadian Press
Capital Times
Casper Daily Tribune
Charlotte News
Chicago Daily Tribune
Chicago Tribune
Columbian
Columbus Telegram
Commonwealth College Fortnightly
Computer Weekly
Constitutional Review
Consumers Union Reports
Cornell Daily Sun
Corp Watch
Counterattack: Facts to Combat Communism
Crisis
Crosscut
Daily Beast
Daily Labor Report
Daily Mail
Daily Nebraskan
Daily Telegraph
Dallas Morning News
Day Book
Econlib
Economist
Edwardsville Intelligencer
Evening Star
Evening World
Forbes
Fort Worth Business Press
Globe and Mail
Good Housekeeping
Guardian
Harper's
Holiday Magazine
Honolulu Advertiser

Honolulu Star-Bulletin
Independent
Intercept
In These Times
Joplin Globe
Journal and Courier
Journal of Business Ethics
Journal of the American Bankers Association
Knoxville Journal
Nation
New York Evening Journal
New York Times
New York Times Magazine
New York Tribune
New Yorker
Newark Evening Star
Niagara Frontier Publications
NorthJersey
Observer
Ocala Evening Star
Orange County Register
Orlando Weekly
Oshkosh Northwestern
Outlook
Pacific Daily News
People
Philadelphia Inquirer
Pittsburgh Courier
Pittsburgh Press
Popular China
Progressive Woman
Puget Sound Business Journal
Record
Record-Journal
Reuters
Reveal
Richmond News Leader
Rochester Democrat and Chronicle
Rolling Stone
Saint Louis/Southern Illinois Labor Tribune
Saint Louis Star
Saint Paul Echo
San Francisco Chronicle

San Francisco Examiner
Seattle Times
Seward Daily Gateway
SF Gate
Smithsonian Magazine
South China Morning Post
Spokane Daily Chronicle
Sports Business Journal
Standard-Speaker
Star Tribune
St. Cloud Times
Student Outlook
Sun
Sunday Star
Tampa Bay Times
TechCrunch
Texas Observer
Texas Tribune
Thousand Oaks Acorn
Time
Topeka State Journal
Toronto Star
United Automobile Worker
United Press International
US News
USA Today
Vassar Miscellany
Verge
Vice News
Villager
Village Voice
Wall Street Journal
Washington Herald
Washington Post
Washington Times
Wausau Daily Herald
Western Mail
Willamette Week
Will Maupin's Weekly
Wisconsin State Journal
Woman Shopper
Women's Wear Daily
Working Woman

SECONDARY SOURCES

Abramoff, Jack. *Capitol Punishment: The Hard Truth About Washington Corruption from America's Most Notorious Lobbyist*. WND Books, 2011.

Adamson, Christopher. "Punishment After Slavery: Southern State Penal Systems, 1865–1890." *Social Problems* 30, no. 5 (1983): 555–69.

Albrect, Donald. *World War II and the American Dream: How Wartime Building Changed a Nation*. MIT Press, 1995

Alimahomed-Wilson, Jake, and Ellen Reese, eds. *The Cost of Free Shipping: Amazon in the Global Economy*. Pluto Press, 2020.

Altenbaugh, Richard J. *Education for Struggle: The American Labor Colleges of the 1920s and 1930s*. Temple University Press, 1990.

Anderson, William L. "Kathie Lee's Children." *Free Market* 14, no. 9 (1996), https://mises.org/free-market/kathie-lees-children.

Armbruster-Sandoval, Ralph. *Globalization and Cross-Border Labor Solidarity in the Americas: The Anti-Sweatshop Movement and the Struggle for Social Justice*. Routledge, 2005.

Arnesen, Eric, ed. "Women's Trade Union League." In *Encyclopedia of U.S. Labor and Working-Class History*. Routledge, 2007.

Athreya, Bama. "Can Fashion Ever Be Fair?" *Journal of Fair Trade* 3, no. 2 (2022): 18–19.

Baker, Ella, and Marvel Cooke. "The Slave Market." *The Crisis* 42 (1935), 331, 340.

Baker, Kelly J. *Gospel According to the Klan: The KKK's Appeal to Protestant America, 1915–1930*. University Press of Kansas, 2011.

Bang, Naomi Jiyoung. "Unmasking the Charade of the Global Supply Contract: A Novel Theory of Corporate Liability in Human Trafficking and Forced Labor Cases." *Houston Journal of International Law* 35, no. 2 (2013): 255–322.

Bao, Xiaolan. "How Did Chinese Women Garment Workers in New York City Forge a Successful Class-Based Coalition during the 1982 Contract Dispute?" PhD diss., State University of New York, 2005.

Bao, Xiaolan. "Sweatshops in Sunset Park: A Variation of the Late-Twentieth-Century Chinese Garment Shops in New York City." In *Sweatshop USA: The American Sweatshop in Historical and Global Perspective*. Edited by Daniel E. Bender and Richard A. Greenwald. Routledge, 2003.

Beaudry, Mary C., and Stephen A. Mrozowski. "The Archeology of Work and Home Life in Lowell, Massachusetts: An Interdisciplinary Study of the Boott Cotton Mills Corporation." *IA: Journal of the Society for Industrial Archeology* 14, no. 2 (1988): 1–22.

Belmont, Alva. "Work of the Woman's Party for the First Five Years." *Equal Rights* XIII, May 15, 1926, 109–10.

Bender, Daniel E. *Sweated Work, Weak Bodies: Anti-Sweatshop Campaigns and Languages of Labor*. Rutgers University Press, 2004.

Bender, Daniel E., and Richard A. Greenwald. *Sweatshop USA: The American Sweatshop in Historical and Global Perspective*. Routledge, 2003.

Benson, Susan Porter. *Counter Cultures: Saleswomen, Managers, and Customers in American Department Stores, 1890–1940*. University of Illinois Press, 1986.

Black, Henry Campbell. "The Enemy Within Our Gates: Bolshevism's Assault Upon American Government." *Constitutional Review* 3, no. 1 (1919): 76.

Blee, Kathleen M. *Women of the Klan: Racism and Gender in the 1920s*. University of California Press, 1991.

Bluestone, Barry. Foreword to *Beyond the Ruins: The Meanings of Deindustrialization*. Edited by Jefferson Cowie and Joseph Heathcott. Cornell University Press, 2003.

Bonacich, Edna, and Richard Appelbaum. "Offshore Production." In *Sweatshop USA: The American Sweatshop in Historical and Global Perspective*. Edited by Daniel E. Bender and Richard A. Greenwald. Routledge, 2013.

Boris, Eileen. *Home to Work: Motherhood and the Politics of Industrial Homework in the United States*. Cambridge University Press, 1994.

Boris, Eileen. "An Interview with Pun Ngai." *New Labor Forum* 15, no. 2 (2006): 129–31, 147.

Boris, Eileen, and Annelise Orleck. "Feminism and the Labor Movement: A Century of Collaboration and Conflict." *New Labor Forum* 20, no. 1 (2011): 33–41.

Brecher, Jeremy. *Strike!: The True History of Mass Insurgence in American from 1877 to Present*. Straight Arrow Books, 1972.

Brooks, Ethel Carolyn. *Unraveling the Garment Industry: Transnational Organizing and Women's Work*. University of Minnesota Press, 2007.

Broughton, Chad. *Boom, Bust, Exodus: The Rust Belt, the Maquilas, and a Tale of Two Cities*. Oxford University Press, 2015.

Bruere, Martha Bensley. "What Is to Be Done?" In *Out of the Sweatshop: The Struggle for Industrial Democracy*. Edited by Leon Stein. Quadrangle/New Times Book, 1977.

Byerly, Victoria Morris. *Hard Times Cotton Mill Girls: Personal Histories of Womanhood and Poverty in the South*. Cornell University Press, 1986.

Cahill, Cathleen. "'Our Democracy and the American Indian': Citizenship, Sovereignty, and the Native Vote in the 1920s." *Journal of Women's History* 32, no. 1 (2020): 41–51.

Canaday, Margot. *Queer Career: Sexuality and Work in Modern America*. Princeton University Press, 2023.

Carson, Jenny. *A Matter of Moral Justice: Black Women Laundry Workers and the Fight for Justice*. University of Illinois Press, 2021.

Carson, Jenny. "'Taking on Corporate Bullies': Cintas, Laundry Workers, and Organizing in the 1930s and Twenty-First Century." *Labor Studies Journal* 35, no. 4 (2010): 453–79.

Chan, Anita. *China's Workers Under Assault: The Exploitation of Labor in a Globalizing Economy*. M. E. Sharpe, 2001.

Chan, Anita. "Culture of Survival: Lives of Migrant Workers Through the Prism of Private Letters." In *Popular China*. Edited by Perry Link, Richard Madsen, and Paul Pickowicz. Rowman and Littlefield, 2002.

Chan, Jenny, Mark Selden, and Pun Ngai. *Dying for an iPhone: Apple Foxconn and the Lives of China's Workers*. Haymarket Books, 2000.

Chang, Gordon. *Ghosts of Gold Mountain: The Epic Story of the Chinese Who Built the Transcontinental Railroad*. Houghton Mifflin, 2019.

Cobble, Dorothy Sue. "Labor Feminists and President Kennedy's Commission on Women." In *No Permanent Waves: Recasting Histories of U.S. Feminism*. Edited by Nancy A. Hewitt. Rutgers University Press, 2010.

Cobble, Dorothy Sue. *The Other Women's Movement: Workplace Justice and Social Rights in Modern America*. Princeton University Press, 2004.

Cohen, Karl. "Toontown's Reds: HUAC's Investigation of Alleged Communists in the Animation Industry." *Film History* 5, no. 2 (1993): 190–203.

Cohen, Lizabeth. *A Consumers' Republic: The Politics of Mass Consumption in Postwar America*. Knopf, 2003.

Cohen, Robert. *When the Old Left Was Young: Student Radicals and America's First Mass Student Movement, 1929–1941*. Oxford University Press, 1993.

Collins, Jane L. *Threads: Gender, Labor, and Power in the Global Apparel Industry*. University of Chicago Press, 2003.

Cowie, Jefferson. *The Great Exception: The New Deal and the Limits of American Politics*. Princeton University Press, 2016.

Cowie, Jefferson. *Stayin' Alive: The 1970s and the Last Days of the Working Class*. New Press, 2010.

Cudd, Ann E., and Nancy Holmstrom. *Capitalism, For and Against: A Feminist Debate*. Cambridge University Press, 2011.

Davis, Angela. *Women, Race and Class*. Vintage Books, 1983.

Deng, Yunxue. "Gender in Factory Life: An Ethnographic Study of Migrant Workers in Shenzhen Foxconn." Master's thesis, Hong Kong Polytechnic University, 2012.

Denning, Michael. *The Cultural Front: The Laboring of American Culture in the Twentieth Century*. Verso, 1998.

Desai, Manisha. "Transnational Solidarity: Women's Agency, Structural Adjustment, and Globalization." In *Women's Activism and Globalization: Linking Local Struggles and Global Politics*. Edited by Nancy A. Naples and Manisha Desai. Taylor and Francis, 2002.

Deutsch, Christopher Robert. "Against the Red Tide: Rena M. Vale and the Long Red Scare in California." Master's thesis, California State University, 2010.

Deutsch, Tracey. *Building a Housewife's Paradise: Gender, Politics, and American Grocery Stores in the Twentieth Century*. University of North Carolina Press, 2010.

Dreier, Peter. "Florence Kelley: Pioneer of Labor Reform." *New Labor Forum* 21, no. 1 (2012): 70–76.

Dublin, Thomas. "Women, Work, and Protest in the Early Lowell Mills: 'The Oppressing Hand of Avarice Would Enslave Us.'" *Labor History* 16 (1975): 99–116.

DuBois, Ellen Carol. *Suffrage: Women's Long Battle for the Vote*. Simon and Schuster, 2020.

Dumenil, Lynn. *The Second Line of Defense: American Women and World War I*. University of North Carolina Press, 2017.

Dye, Nancy Schrom. *As Equals and as Sisters: Feminism, the Labor Movement, and the Women's Trade Union League of New York*. University of Missouri Press, 1980.

Edelman, Marc. "Peasant–Farmer Movements, Third World Peoples, and the Seattle Protests Against the World Trade Organization, 1999." *Dialectical Anthropology* 33, no. 2 (2009): 109–28.
English, Beth Anne. *A Common Thread: Labor, Politics, and Capital Mobility in the Textile Industry*. University of Georgia Press, 2006.
Esbenshade, Jill Louise. *Monitoring Sweatshops: Workers, Consumers, and the Global Apparel Industry*. Temple University Press, 2004.
Farley, Lin. *Sexual Shakedown: The Sexual Harassment of Women on the Job*. Warner Books, 1980.
Farmer, Brian R. *American Conservatism: History, Theory and Practice*. Scholars Press, 2005.
Farrell-Beck, Jane, and Jean Parsons. *Twentieth Century Dress in the United States*. Fairchild, 2007.
Featherstone, Liza. *Students Against Sweatshops*. Verso, 2002.
Fenwick, Ann. "Evaluating China's Special Economic Zones." *Berkeley Journal of International Law* 2, no. 2 (1984): 376–97.
Fincher, Leta Hong. *Betraying Big Brother: The Feminist Awakening in China*. Verso, 2021.
Fink, Leon. *Sweatshops at Sea: Merchant Seamen in the World's First Globalized Industry, from 1812 to the Present*. University of North Carolina Press, 2011.
Finnegan, Margaret Mary. *Selling Suffrage: Consumer Culture and Votes for Women*. Columbia University Press, 1999.
Fisher, Harry. *Comrades: Tales of a Brigadista in the Spanish Civil War*. University of Nebraska Press, 1998.
Flexner, Eleanor, and Ellen F. Fitzpatrick. *Century of Struggle: The Woman's Rights Movement in the United States*. Belknap Press of Harvard University Press, 1996.
Flink, James J. *The Automobile Age*. MIT Press, 1990.
Frager, Ruth A. *Sweatshop Strife: Class, Ethnicity, and Gender in the Jewish Labour Movement of Toronto, 1900–1939*. University of Toronto Press, 1992.
Fraser, Jill Andresky. *White-Collar Sweatshop*. Norton, 2001.
Fraser, Steve. *The Age of Acquiescence: The Life and Death of American Resistance to Organized Wealth and Power*. Hachette, 2015.
Garson, Barbara. *The Electronic Sweatshop: How Computers Are Transforming the Office of the Future into the Factory of the Past*. Simon and Schuster, 1988.
Ginsburg, Ruth Bader. "Muller v. State of Oregon: One Hundred Years Later." *Willamette Law Review* 45 (2008): 359–70.
Glickman, Lawrence B. *Buying Power: A History of Consumer Activism in America*. University of Chicago Press, 2009.
Glickman, Lawrence B. "The Strike in the Temple of Consumption: Consumer Activism and Twentieth-Century American Political Culture." *Journal of American History* 88, no. 1 (2001): 99–128.
Gordon, Jennifer. *Suburban Sweatshops: The Fight for Immigrant Rights*. Belknap Press of Harvard University Press, 2005.
Green, Hardy. *The Company Town: The Industrial Edens and Satanic Mills That Shaped the American Economy*. Basic Books, 2010.

Greenwald, Richard A. "'The Burning Building at 23 Washington Place': The Triangle Fire, Workers and Reformers in Progressive Era New York." *New York History* 83, no. 1 (2002): 55–91.

Grevatt, Martha. "Lesbian/Gay/Bisexual/Transgender Liberation: What's Labor Got to Do with It?" *Social Policy* 31, no. 3 (2001): 63–65.

Griffith, Barbara S. *The Crisis of American Labor: Operation Dixie and the Defeat of the CIO*. Temple University Press, 1988.

Halegua, Aaron. *Workplace Gender-Based Violence and Harassment in China: Harmonizing Domestic Law and Practices with International Standards*. US–Asia Law Institute, New York University School of Law, 2021.

Hancock, Ange-Marie. *The Politics of Disgust: The Public Identity of the Welfare Queen*. New York University Press, 2004.

Hancock, Christin Lee. "Black Women and Suffrage: A History of Political Freedom and Race in the United States." In *Religion, Women of Color, and the Suffrage Movement: The Journey to Holistic Freedom*. Edited by Simon Mary Asese Aihiokhai. Lexington Books, 2022.

Hapke, Laura. *Sweatshop: The History of an American Idea*. Rutgers University Press, 2004.

Hargrave, Lindsay, and Carolyn Kitch. "*Life* on Campus: *Life* Magazine's 'College Girl' as an Ordinary and Ideal Symbol of America in the 1930s." *Journalism History* 47, no. 2 (2021): 170–88

Hays, Sharon. *Flat Broke with Children: Women in the Age of Welfare Reform*. Oxford University Press, 2003.

Heller, Rita R. "The Women of Summer: The Bryn Mawr Summer School for Women Workers, 1921–1938." PhD diss., Rutgers University, 1986.

Hemphill, Thomas. "Monitoring Global Corporate Citizenship: Industry Self-Regulation at a Crossroads." *Journal of Corporate Citizenship* 14 (2004): 85.

Hill, Rebecca. "The History of the Smith Act and the Hatch Act: Anti-Communism and the Rise of the Conservative Coalition in Congress." In *Little "Red Scares": Anti-Communism and Political Repression in the United States, 1921–1946*. Edited by Robert Goldstein. Routledge, 2016.

Hollis, Karyn L. *Liberating Voices: Writing at the Bryn Mawr Summer School for Women Workers*. Southern Illinois University Press, 2004.

Howlett, Charles F. *Brookwood Labor College and the Struggle for Peace and Social Justice in America*. Edwin Mellen Press, 1993.

Hunter, Tera W. *To 'Joy My Freedom: Southern Black Women's Lives and Labors After the Civil War*. Harvard University Press, 1997.

Hyman, Paula E. "Immigrant Women and Consumer Protest: The New York City Kosher Meat Boycott of 1902." *American Jewish History* 70, no. 1 (1980): 91–105.

Jacobs, Meg. *Pocketbook Politics: Economic Citizenship in Twentieth-Century America*. Princeton University Press, 2005.

Jacoby, Robin Miller. "The Women's Trade Union League and American Feminism." *Feminist Studies* 3, no. 1/2 (1975): 126–40.

Jones, Jacqueline. *Labor of Love, Labor of Sorrow: Black Women, Work, and the Family from Slavery to the Present*. Basic Books, 1985.

Katz, Daniel. *All Together Different: Yiddish Socialists, Garment Workers, and the Labor Roots of Multiculturalism*. New York University Press, 2011.

Kessler-Harris, Alice. *Out to Work: A History of Wage-Earning Women in the United States*. Oxford University Press, 1982.

Kessler-Harris, Alice. *In Pursuit of Equity: Women, Men, and the Quest for Economic Citizenship in 20th Century America*. Oxford University Press, 2001.

Khor, Martin. "The WTO and Foreign Investment: Implications and Alternatives for Developing Countries." *Development in Practice* 6, no. 4 (1996): 304–14.

Kingsley, Charles. *Cheap Clothes and Nasty*. W. Pickering, 1950.

Kinville, John E. *The Grey Eagles of Chippewa Falls: A Hidden History of a Women's Ku Klux Klan in Wisconsin*. Arcadia Publishing, 2020.

Klein, Naomi. *No Logo: No Space, No Choice, No Jobs*. Macmillan, 2002.

Krupat, Kitty. "Rethinking the Sweatshop: A Conversation About United Students Against Sweatshops (USAS) with Charles Eaton, Marion Traub-Werner, and Evelyn Zepeda." *International Labor and Working-Class History*, no. 61 (2002): 112–27.

Kuhn, Moritz, Moritz Schularick, and Ulrike I. Steins. "Income and Wealth Inequality in America, 1949–2016." *Journal of Political Economy* 128, no. 9 (2020): 3469–3519.

Lasch-Quinn, Elizabeth. *Black Neighbors: Race and the Limits of Reform in the American Settlement House Movement, 1890–1945*. University of North Carolina Press, 1993.

LaVille, Helen. *Cold War Women: The International Activities of American Women's Organisations*. Manchester University Press, 2002.

Leach, William. *Land of Desire: Merchants, Power, and the Rise of a New American Culture*. Vintage Books, 1993.

Leberstein, Stephen. "Shooting Rabid Dogs: New York's Rapp–Coudert Attack on Teachers Unions." In *Little "Red Scares": Anti-Communism and Political Repression in the United States, 1921–1946*. Edited by Robert Goldstein. Routledge, 2016.

Lichtenstein, Nelson, and Judith Stein. *A Fabulous Failure: The Clinton Presidency and the Transformation of American Capitalism*. Princeton University Press, 2023.

Liebhold, Peter, and Harry R. Rubenstein. "Bringing Sweatshops into the Museum." In Daniel E. Bender and Richard A. Greenwald. *Sweatshop USA: The American Sweatshop in Historical and Global Perspective*. Routledge, 2003.

Lin, Justin Yifu, Fang Cai, and Zhou Li. *The China Miracle: Development Strategy and Economic Reform*. Chinese University of Hong Kong Press, 2003.

Lorence, James J. *The Unemployed People's Movement: Leftists, Liberals, and Labor in Georgia, 1929–1941*. University of Georgia Press, 2009.

Malone, Samantha. "Domestic Work in the United States: Gender, Immigration, and Personhood." *Georgetown Journal of Law and Modern Critical Race Perspectives* 10, no. 1 (2018): 65–88.

Marglin, Stephen Alan, ed. *The Golden Age of Capitalism: Reinterpreting the Postwar Experience*. Oxford University Press.

Martin, Charles H. "Southern Labor Relations in Transition: Gadsden, Alabama, 1930–1943." *Journal of Southern History* 47, no. 4 (1981): 545–68.

May, Vanessa H. *Unprotected Labor: Household Workers, Politics, and Middle-Class Reform in New York, 1870–1940*. University of North Carolina Press, 2011.

McCammon, Holly J. "The Politics of Protection: State Minimum Wage and Maximum Hours Laws for Women in the United States, 1870–1930." *Sociological Quarterly* 36, no. 2 (1995): 217–49.

Meeropol, Michael. *Surrender: How the Clinton Administration Completed the Reagan Revolution*. University of Michigan Press, 1998.

Miklós, András. "Exploiting Injustice in Mutually Beneficial Market Exchange: The Case of Sweatshop Labor." *Journal of Business Ethics* 156, no. 1 (2019): 59–69.

Milkman, Ruth. "Preface." In *The Cost of Free Shipping: Amazon in the Global Economy*. Edited by Jake Alimahomed-Wilson and Ellen Reese. Pluto Press, 2020.

Miller, Arthur. "The University of Michigan." *Holiday Magazine* (1953), 70.

Miller, Stephen. *The New Deal as a Triumph of Social Work: Frances Perkins and the Confluence of Early Twentieth Century Social Work with Mid-Twentieth Century Politics and Government*. Palgrave Macmillan, 2015.

Minchin, Timothy. "Shutdowns in the Sun Belt: The Decline of the Textile and Apparel Industry and Deindustrialization in the South." In *Life and Labor in the New New South*. Edited by Robert H. Zieger. University Press of Florida, 2012.

Moody, Kim. *On New Terrain: How Capital is Reshaping the Battleground of Class War*. Haymarket Books, 2017.

Moore, John Robert. "Senator Josiah W. Bailey and the 'Conservative Manifesto' of 1937." *Journal of Southern History* 31, no. 1 (1965): 21–39.

Moore, Leonard J. "Historical Interpretations of the 1920s Klan: The Traditional Review and the Populist Revision." *Journal of Social History* 24, no. 2 (1990): 341–57.

Naison, Mark. *Communists in Harlem During the Depression: Blacks in the New World*. Grove Press, 1984.

Ngai, Pun, and Jenny Chan. "Global Capital, the State, and Chinese Workers: The Foxconn Experience." *Modern China* 38, no. 4: 383–410.

Norwood, Stephen H. *Strikebreaking and Intimidation: Mercenaries and Masculinity in Twentieth-Century America*. University of North Carolina Press, 2002.

Opdycke, Sandra. *Jane Addams and Her Vision for America*. Prentice Hall, 2012.

Opler, Daniel J. *For all White-Collar Workers: The Possibilities of Radicalism in New York City's Department Store Unions, 1934–1953*. Ohio State University Press, 2007.

Opler, Daniel. "Monkey Business in Union Square: A Cultural Analysis of the Klein's-Ohrbach's Strikes of 1934–35." *Journal of Social History* 36, no. 1 (2002): 149–64.

Orleck, Annelise. *Common Sense and a Little Fire: Women and Working-Class Politics in the United States, 1900–1965*. University of North Carolina Press, 1995

Orleck, Annelise. "The Needle Trades and the Uprising of Women Workers: 1905–1919." In *City of Workers, City of Struggle: How Labor Movements Changed New York*. Edited by Joshua B. Freeman. Columbia University Press, 2019.

Orleck, Annelise. *Rethinking American Women's Activism*. Routledge, 2015.

Orleck, Annelise. *"We Are All Fast-Food Workers Now": The Global Uprising Against Poverty Wages*. Beacon Press, 2018.

Orleck, Annelise. "'We Are That Mythical Thing Called the Public': Militant Housewives during the Great Depression." *Feminist Studies* 19, no. 1 (1993): 147–72.

Pastorello, Karen. *A Power Among Them: Bessie Abramowitz Hillman and the Making of the Amalgamated Clothing Workers of America*. University of Illinois Press, 2008.

Phillips, Lisa A. W. "Mickey Goes to Haiti and Leaves: Disney's Transnational Quest for Cheap Labor in the Post–Cold War Era." *International Labor and Working-Class History* 101 (2022): 144–63.

Pink, Ross Michael. *The Climate Change Crisis: Solutions and Adaption for a Planet in Peril*. Palgrave Macmillan, 2018.

Powell, Benjamin. *Out of Poverty: Sweatshops in the Global Economy*. Cambridge University Press, 2014.

Procter, Ben H. *William Randolph Hearst: Final Edition, 1911–1951*. Oxford University Press, 2007.

Rader, Katherine. "Delineating Agriculture and Industry: Reexamining the Exclusion of Agricultural Workers from the New Deal." *Studies in American Political Development* 37, no. 2 (2023): 146–63.

Ramachandran, Gowri, Audrey B. Collins, Julie Su, Scott Cummings, and Muneer Ahmad. "The El Monte Sweatshop Slavery Cases." *Southwestern Journal of International Law* 23, no. 1 (2017): 281.

Reagan, Leslie J. *When Abortion Was a Crime: Women, Medicine, and Law in the United States, 1867–1973*. University of California Press, 1997.

Remus, Emily. *A Shoppers' Paradise: How the Ladies of Chicago Claimed Power and Pleasure in the New Downtown*. Harvard University Press, 2019.

Revised Laws of Massachusetts (1902). Reprinted in *Landmark Briefs and Arguments of the Supreme Court of the United States: Constitutional Law*, vol. 16. University Publications of America, 1975.

Rohe, William M., and Harry L. Watson. *Chasing the American Dream: New Perspectives on Affordable Homeownership*. Cornell University Press, 2007.

Ross, Andrew. *No Sweat: Fashion, Free Trade and the Rights of Garment Workers*. Verso, 1997.

Ross, Robert J. S. *Slaves to Fashion: Poverty and Abuse in the New Sweatshops*. University of Michigan Press, 2004.

Saez, Emmanuel, and Gabriel Zucman. "Wealth Inequality in the United States Since 1913: Evidence from Capitalized Income Tax." *Quarterly Journal of Economics* 131, no. 2 (2016): 519–78.

Schlumpf, Heidi. "Sole Man." *U. S. Catholic* 66, no. 10 (2001): 48–49.

Schneiderman, Rose. "A Cap Maker's Story: Rose Schneiderman." *Independent* 58 (1905): 935–38.

Schofield, Ann. "The Uprising of the 20,000: The Making of a Labor Legend." In *A Needle, a Bobbin, a Strike: Women Needleworkers in America*. Edited by Joan M. Jensen and Sue Davidson. Temple University Press, 1984.

Shor, Francis Robert. *Dying Empire: U.S. Imperialism and Global Resistance*. Routledge Press, 2010.

Sklar, Kathryn Kish. *Florence Kelley and the Nation's Work: The Rise of Women's Political Culture, 1830–1900*. Yale University Press, 1995.

Smith, Erin Geiger. "Case Study: Does I v. the Gap, Inc.: Can a Sweatshop Suit Settlement Save Saipan?" *Review of Litigation* 23, no. 3 (2004): 737–71.

Smith, Lillian Eugenia. *Killers of the Dream*. Norton, 1994.

Spectar, J. M. "Pay Me Fairly, Kathie Lee: The WTO, the Right to a Living Wage, and a Proposed Protocol." *New York Law School Journal of International and Comparative Law* 20, no. 1 (2000): 61–92.

Stansell, Christine. *The Feminist Promise: 1792 to the Present*. Modern Library, 2011.

Stein, Leon. *Out of the Sweatshop: The Struggle for Industrial Democracy*. Quadrangle/New York Times Books, 1977.

Stevens, Elbert E. "The Great Open Shop Conspiracy." *Labor Digest* 13, no. 3 (1921): 6.

Storrs, Landon R. Y. *Civilizing Capitalism: The National Consumers' League, Women's Activism, and Labor Standards in the New Deal Era*. Gender and American Culture. University of North Carolina Press, 2000.

Storrs, Landon R. Y. "Left-Feminism, the Consumer Movement, and Red Scare Politics in the United States, 1935–1960." *Journal of Women's History* 18 (2006): 40–67.

Storrs, Landon R. Y. "Red Scare Politics and the Suppression of Popular Front Feminism: The Loyalty Investigation of Mary Dublin Keyserling." *Journal of American History* 90, no. 2 (2003): 491–524.

Storrs, Landon R. Y. *The Second Red Scare and the Unmaking of the New Deal Left*. Princeton University Press, 2013.

Tantri, Malini L. "China's Policy for Special Economic Zone: Some Critical Issues." *India Quarterly* 68, no. 3 (2012): 231–50.

Taylor, Ronald B. *Sweatshops in the Sun: Child Labor on the Farm*. Beacon Press, 1973.

Traxel, David. *Crusader Nation: The United States in Peace and the Great War, 1898–1920*. Knopf Doubleday, 2007.

Tuttle, Carolyn. *Mexican Women in American Factories: Free Trade and Exploitation on the Border*. University of Texas Press, 2012.

Vapnek, Lara. *Breadwinners: Working Women and Economic Independence, 1865–1920*. University of Illinois Press, 2009.

Vogel, Ezra. *Deng Xiaoping and the Transformation of China*. Harvard University Press, 2013.

Vogeler, Ray, and Harry Richards. "Madison: Sitting Down for Justice." *Against the Current* 86 (2000), https://againstthecurrent.org/atc086/p940/.

Von Drehle, David. *Triangle: The Fire that Changed America*. Atlantic Monthly Press, 2003.

Ware, Susan. *Beyond Suffrage: Women in the New Deal*. Harvard University Press, 1981.

Ware, Susan. *Holding Their Own: American Women in the 1930s*. American Women in the Twentieth Century. Twayne, 1982.

Warne, Clinton L. "The Consumer Movement and the Labor Movement." *Journal of Economic Issues* 7, no. 2 (1973): 307–16.

Webber, Michael J., and David L. Rigby. *The Golden Age Illusion: Rethinking Postwar Capitalism*. Guilford Press, 1996.

Weiler, N. Sue. "The Uprising in Chicago: The Men's Garment Workers Strike, 1910–1911." In *A Needle, a Bobbin, a Strike: Women Needleworkers in America*. Edited by Joan M. Jensen and Sue Davidson. Temple University Press, 1984.

Whalen, Carmen Teresa. "Sweatshops Here and There: The Garment Industry, Latinas, and Labor Migrations." *International Labor and Working-Class History*, no. 61 (2002): 45–68.

Wilson, Katie. "Company Town: What Happens to a City and Its Democracy When Amazon Dominates?" In *The Cost of Free Shipping: Amazon in the Global Economy*. Edited by Jake Alimahomed-Wilson and Ellen Reese. London: Pluto Press, 2020.

Zimmerman, Joan G. "The Jurisprudence of Equality: The Women's Minimum Wage, the First Equal Rights Amendment, and Adkins v. Children's Hospital, 1905–1923." *Journal of American History* 78, no. 1 (1991): 188–225.

INDEX

Italic page numbers refer to figures

5th Amendment, 70
9 to 5, 79–80
14th Amendment, 39
15th Amendment, 51
19th Amendment, 40, 49, 51
1909 Uprising. *See* Uprising of 20,000 (New York City)
20/20, 99–100, 106

Abad, Carmencita "Chie," 92–93, 96, 99–100, 153
Abercrombie & Fitch, 91
abortion, forced, 1, 7, 78, 92, 105, 150
Abramoff, Jack, 105–6, 181n109
Abramowitz Hillman, Bessie, 30–31
Acheson, Dean, 73
activism. *See* anti-sweatshop activism; civil rights activism; labor feminism
Addams, Jane, 18–19, 21, 23, 31–32
Adidas, 98
Adkins v. Children's Hospital (1923), 41
Adler, Stella, 49
Afghanistan, 108
AFL-CIO, 79, 92
Africa, 85, 107. *See also individual countries*
African Methodist Episcopal Zion Church, 27
agricultural industry, 6, 15, 53, 72, 79, 84, 150; farmworkers, 2, 68, 76, 149
Alabama, xiv, 15, 43, 69; Bessemer, 130–39, 141, 146, 148, 153; Birmingham, 28

Alabama Power, 43
A.L.A. Schechter Poultry Corp. v. United States (1935), 63
Amalgamated Clothing and Textile Workers Union, 83
Amalgamated Clothing Workers of America (ACWA), 32, 65
Amazon, 3, 151–52, 154–57; Bessemer (AL) warehouse, 130–39, 141, 146, 148, 153; HQ2, 139, 141–46; Kindles, 4; Project Olive (Grand Island, NY), 144–46, 148; shareholder activism, 69; Staten Island (NY) warehouses, 136, 138, 146, 153; sweatshop conditions, 6–8, 11–12, 109–48
Amazon Labor Union (ALU), 137–38
Amazon Prime Day, 9, 110, 127–28, 131, 144
American Association of University Women, 46
American Bankers' Association, 44
American Civil Liberties Union, 60
American Dream, 106
American Federation of Labor (AFL), 21, 25, 52–53, 60, 79, 92, 166n124. *See also* AFL-CIO
American League for Peace and Democracy, 71
American Liberty League, 72
American Mercury, 60, 71
American Plan, 43. *See also* open shops
American Red Cross, 20, 35, 51

American Right, 11, 74
Anderson, Mary, 40–41, 44–46, 49, 108, 156
Anderson, William, 106–7
Ann Taylor (company), 92, 125
anti-Americanism, 43
Anti-Nazi League, 71
anti-sweatshop activism, xiii–xv, 2, 7–9, 152–57; and the global assembly line, 11–12, 109–48; and the global justice movement, 11, 77–108; and labor feminism, 10, 13–46; in the Popular Front, 10–11, 47–76; women's role in, 12
apparel industry, 2, 78, 83, 92–105, 113, 151. *See also* garment workers
Apparel Industry Partnership (AIP), 96–97
Apple, 3, 12, 111, 122, 156; iPhones, 4, 112, 115, 119–20; sweatshop conditions, 113–14, 117, 120, 123, 124, 126, 130, 151
Arizona, 102; Tucson, 141
Armbruster-Sandoval, Ralph, 84
Asia, 78, 85, 89, 107, 115. *See also individual countries*
Associated Waist and Dress Manufacturers, 25
Athreya, Bama, 101
Auburn University, 106
Auchter, Thorne, 81
automotive industry, 72

Ballinger, Jeff, 86, 96
Ballmer, Steve, 139
Bandow, Doug, 105
Bangladesh, 7, 91, 97, 106, 112, 151–52; Dhaka, 111
Baraka, Ras, 143, 153
Barker, Mary Cornelia, 70, 173n104
Barnard College, 28
Bas, Nikki, 93, 108
Bates, Jennifer, 132–33
Beard, Mary, 59
Beaudry, Mary, 3
Beck, Juliette, 99
Behind the Swoosh, 103
Belmont, Alva Vanderbilt, 27, 36, 41
Benjamin, Medea, 85–86, 96, 108

Bezos, Jeff, 109–10, 114, 125, 129, 131–34, 137–39, 145, 147
Biberman, Herbert, 70
Biden, Joe, 108, 133, 138, 156
birth control, 7, 17, 79
Black Friday, 9, 109–10, 138, 143
Black Lives Matter (#BLM) movement, 110–11, 134
Blackrock, 110
Black Women's Agenda, 88
Blanck, Max, 34, 36–37
Blatch, Harriet Stanton, 18
Bluestone, Barry, 83
Bolshevism, 43
Bonus March, 54
Borden Dairy Company, 69
Boris, Eileen, 8, 23
Bowden, Charles, 94
boycotts, 9–12, 25, 56, 59, 61, 75, 103, 110, 116
Brandeis Brief, 39–40
bread and roses, 29–30
Briggs, Barbara, 97
British Parliament, 2
Brooks, Ethel, 154–55
Brookwood Labor College, 45
Brown, Courtenay, 6
Brown University, 102
Bruere, Martha Bensley, 34–35
Bryn Mawr College, 28, 42, 45
Bryn Mawr Summer School for Women Workers in Industry, 44–46, 53
BUM International, 90
Bush, George H. W., 82
Bush, George W., xiii, 108

California, 22, 71, 88, 96, 115, 130, 150–51; El Monte, 77, 84, 89–90, 92, 98, 154; Los Angeles, 58, 139, 150; San Francisco, 55, 75, 87, 89, 93, 147
California Lutheran University, 93
California Senate Factfinding Subcommittee on Un-American Activities (CUAC), 72
California State University, Fresno, 93
Calvin Klein (company), 91, 151

Canada, 82, 141, 144; Alberta, 64
Cannon, Katie Geneva, 66
capitalism, xv, 24, 75–76, 78, 103, 105, 108, 116, 121; civilizing, 9; and ethical consumption, 29; gendered, 41, 85; naturalization of, 14; organizing against, 54; racialized, 44; sweatshop capitalism, 34, 91, 149
carbon emissions, 111, 114–15
Caroti, Arturi, 36
Carson, Jenny, 62, 65
Catholics, 27, 35, 44, 48, 67, 103
Cato Institute, 105
Catt, Carrie Chapman, 49
celebrity, 48, 59, 88, 94, 96–98, 111
Chan, Jenny, 4, 117, 121, 123
Chan, Ka Wai, 116
Chicago strike (1910–1911), 24, 30–34, 38, 46, 153
child labor, 1, 3, 18, 23, 49, 59, 94–96, 106, 108, 112–13, 118, 120–21, 125–26, 146, 149, 156; activism against, 17–19, 21, 24, 29, 56–57; regulation of, 26, 40–41, 43, 63, 78, 81, 150–52; and sweatshop definition, 6, 16
Children's Place, 111
China, 88, 139; gig economy in, 113; manufacturing for US companies, 91, 114; Shenzhen, 3–4, 116–17, 141, 151; sweatshops in, 7, 84, 116–26, 132, 151–53, 155; workers from, 15, 91, 138, 146, 155
China Labor Watch (CLW), 124–25, 138
China Miracle/Dream, 116
Chinese Communist Party, 116
Chipotle, 136
Christmas, 9, 13–14, 19, 46, 116, 142
Chung, Connie, 106
CIA, 79
Cintas, 84
Civilian Works Administration, 53
civil rights, 10–11, 20–21, 45–46, 53, 70, 73, 76, 94, 134, 150
civil rights activism, 10–11, 20–21, 45–46, 53, 73, 76, 134, 150

Civil War (US), 15
class, 141; class consciousness, 55; class segregation, 17, 23; cross-class alliances, 7, 12–46, 51–52, 56, 67–68, 88; middle class, 8–10, 19–21, 23, 29, 34, 36, 42, 49, 56, 58, 62, 69, 75–79, 83, 150–51; precariat, 11; upper class, 21, 23, 29, 36, 42; working class, 15, 17–18, 20–21, 23, 26, 35, 40–42, 52, 59, 66, 79, 83, 106, 130, 139, 152–55
class-action lawsuits, 1, 91, 153
climate change, 11, 110–11, 114, 142
Clinton, Bill, 82, 90, 96, 105
closed shops, 26, 72
coal industry, 15, 71, 141, 147
Coalition for Responsible Economic Development for Grand Island (CRED4GI), 144–45, 154
cobalt industry, 112, 126, 146, 151
Cobble, Dorothy Sue, 17
CODEPINK, 85, 108
Cold War, 85. *See also* House Committee on Un-American Activities (HUAC, Dies Committee); Red Scare
collective action, xv, 9, 24–25
collective bargaining, 72
college students, 10, 20, 22, 76, 110, 118, 125, 168n23; anti-sweatshop activism by, xiii–xv, 12, 28, 31, 42, 53–54, 86–87, 93, 98–104, 107–8, 120–24, 138, 152–53, 156–57; antiviolence activism, 79
Collier, Nina, 68
Colón, Maria, 84
Columbia University, 28, 75
Coman, Katharine, 31
Commonwealth of the Northern Mariana Islands (CNMI), 104, 106, 181n109; Saipan, 1–2, 6–8, 10, 91–93, 95, 98, 100, 105, 117, 150, 152–53
communism, 44, 54, 65, 69, 70–74, 76, 79, 170n61. *See also* Red Scare
Communist Party USA (CP), 55, 70–72
Congress of Industrial Organizations (CIO), 53–54, 71, 79, 168n23. *See also* AFL-CIO
Connecticut, 84

INDEX **213**

Connor, Chelsea, 136
Conservative Manifesto, 73
construction industry, 15, 81, 84, 141, 175n13
consumer activism, 79, 155; and labor feminism, 13–46; and the Popular Front, 11, 55–62, 68–70, 73–76. *See also* League of Women Shoppers (LWS); National Consumers' League (NCL); New York Consumers' League; white labels
Consumers' League of New York, 13, 38–39
Consumer's League of Providence, Rhode Island, 28
Consumers' Research (CR), 69–70, 171n80
Consumers Union (CU), 171n80
convict leasing, 15
Cornell University, 20, 79, 99
corporate households, 3
COVID-19 pandemic, 11, 109, 128, 131, 133, 136–38
Cowie, Jefferson, 76
Croker, Edward, 34
Cuba, 86
Cullors, Patrisse, 134
Cyber Monday, 9, 110, 142

Danaher, Kevin, 85
de Blasio, Bill, 141–43
debt peonage, 15, 89, 91
deindustrialization, 82–83, 104, 130, 144, 146, 150
DeLay, Tom, 105–6
delivery drivers, 7, 13, 60, 126, 128–30, 132–33, 138–39, 147, 149, 151
Dell, 113, 117, 123
Democratic Party, 73, 76–77; New Democrats, 82
Democratic Republic of the Congo (DRC), 112–14, 126, 146, 151
Department Store Employees Union, 48
department stores, 13–14, 17, 47–48, 50, 55, 57, 60–61, 69, 72, 114
deportation, 12, 85, 92, 150
deregulation, 43, 94, 113

Diaz, Wendy, 95–96, 153
Dies, Martin, 69–73. *See also* House Committee on Un-American Activities (HUAC, Dies Committee)
Dies Committee. *See* House Committee on Un-American Activities (HUAC, Dies Committee)
Dillard's, 151
direct action, 93, 100
diseases, 19–20, 81, 108, 115, 123
Disney, 59, 72, 97, 122, 124–25, 151; Hong Kong Disneyland, 121
dispatch workers, 118–20
domestic violence, 21
domestic workers, 6, 53, 62–63, 66–68, 74–76, 84, 113, 129, 149–50, 153, 155
Domestic Workers' Union (DWU), 67, 74, 171n71
Dominican Republic, 83
Domsky-Abrams, Mary, 33, 37
Donovan, Raymond, 81, 175n13
Dorr, Rheta Childe, 40
Dotson, Donald, 81
Dreier, Mary, 27, 34
Du Bois, W. E. B., 45
Ducker, Rebecca, 59
Duke University, 100
Du Pont, 72
Dutcher, Elizabeth, 27

Eastern European Jewish immigrants, 7, 27, 33, 44
eBay, 112
Economic Policy Institute, 120
elites, 8–10, 14, 17–18, 20, 27–28, 32, 36, 40, 42–43, 45, 51, 72
El Salvador, 83–84, 95
Elsesser, Rikee, 75
Engels, Friedrich, 20
England, 2, 117; London, 2. *See also* Great Britain; United Kingdom
environmental protections, 82, 85, 110, 121, 148, 150
Equal Employment Opportunity Commission (EEOC), 81

Equality League of Self-Supporting Women, 18
Equal Rights Amendment, 40–41
errand boys, 13
ethics, 56, 125, 178n70; ethical consumption, 10, 14, 17, 20, 29, 57, 86; ethically produced goods, 8, 20, 59, 95. *See also* white labels
Etsy, 112
European Union, 114
e-waste, 115
Extinction Rebellion, 109
extraction industries, 3, 15, 114, 117

Facebook, 111, 147. *See also* Meta
Factory Investigation Commission (FIC), 38, 154
factory towns, 83
factory workers, 47, 49–50, 138, 145; and anti-sweatshop activism, xiv, 1, 30–31, 44, 55, 86, 91, 99–100; working conditions, 1–12, 15–16, 19–20, 24–26, 33–40, 56, 63, 77–78, 82, 84–107, 111, 113–14, 116–28, 146, 149–54
fair-labor labels, 9
Fair Labor Standards Act (1938), 52–53, 151
fair trade, 85
Farmer, Frances, 49
farmworkers, 2, 68, 76, 149
fascism, 54, 167n7, 168n23
Fashion Industry Forum, 96
FBI, 70, 72
Federal Theater Project, 71
Federal Writers' Project, 67, 71
Federated Press, 71
feminism, 7, 12, 71, 74, 79, 82, 85, 88; labor, 10, 13–46, 68. *See also* Women's Liberation Movement
Feminist Majority, 88
Fidelity, 110
Fight for $15 campaign, 111
Filley, Jane, 64
Fisher, Harry, 167n7
Fisher-Price, 111
FLA, 100–102, 120
flexibility, 2, 4, 64, 79, 94, 101, 113, 147

Florida: Miami, 59
Floyd, George, 134
Foo, Lora Jo, 89
forty-hour workweek, 48, 64, 78
Foxconn, 4–5, 7, 12, 116–22, 125–26, 128, 141, 151, 153
Foxconn People, 5
Fraser, Steve, 16
The Freeman, 74
The Free Market, 106
free trade, 11, 82–83, 85, 88, 93, 97, 99, 108, 114, 150, 155
free trade zones, 83

The Gap, 1, 91–94, 96, 98, 99
garment workers, 11, 18, 44, 108; and anti-sweatshop activism, xiv, 10, 14, 24, 27, 30–32, 36, 45, 112, 153–55; working conditions, 1–2, 7–8, 16, 20, 25–26, 30–32, 47–48, 55–56, 77–79, 84, 89–97, 111–14, 149, 151–52. *See also* apparel industry
general strikes, 25, 55, 166n124
Georgia, 141; Atlanta, 55–56, 59–60, 70–71, 173n104; Greensboro, 54
Gershwin, Leonore, 59
Gianaris, Michael, 142, 153
G. I. Bill, 79
Gifford, Frank, 95, 178n70
Gifford, Kathie Lee, 94–98, 105–6, 111, 123, 150, 178n70
gig economy, 11, 108, 113
Gilded Age, 10, 15, 146; New, 78, 147
Gingrich, Newt, 78
Ginsburg, Ruth Bader, 40
Glickman, Lawrence, 23
global assembly line, 35, 88, 98–99
Global Exchange, 2, 11, 85–88, 92, 96–99, 107–8, 153, 155
Global Fashion Factory, 95, 104
Global Justice Movement, 11, 77–108, 110, 153
Global South, 6, 83, 101, 150
Global War on Terror, 108
Goldmark, Josephine Clara, 39
Gonzalez, Lydda, 98
Goodyear Tires, 69, 171n77

INDEX **215**

Google, 111, 113, 117, 132, 147
Gou, Terry, 117
Grand Island, NY, 144–46, 148
Great Britain, 2, 21. *See also* England; United Kingdom
Great Depression, 10, 46, 49, 52–54, 56, 62, 74, 76, 113, 150
Great Exception, 8, 152
Great Migration, 62
Great Recession, 111, 139
Green, William, 60
Guatemala, 84
Guess?, 90, 98, 125
Gulley, Ken, 131

Haifeng, Hua, 125
Haiti, 97
Hapke, Laura, 5
Harding, Warren, 45
Harris, Isaac, 34, 36–37
Harris, Kamala, 138
Hasbro, 111, 124
Hawes, Elizabeth, 49
Hays, Aline Davis, 59–60, 70
Hays, Arthur Garfield, 60
Hearst, William Randolf, 73, 168n37, 173n98
Heaven's Gate, 88
Heller, Rita, 45
Hellman, Lillian, 59, 70, 75
Heng, Su, 125
Henry Street Settlement House, 21
Herndon, Angelo, 71, 168n23, 173n104
Highlander Folk School, 45
Hirsch, Michael, 164n88
H&M, 3
Hochfield, Esther, 33
Hollings, Fritz, 97
Hollywood, 11, 72; blacklist, 70
Honduras, 84, 94–95, 97–98, 103, 106
Hong Kong, 116, 121–22, 124–25, 148
House Committee on Un-American Activities (HUAC, Dies Committee), 69–73, 76

Housing for All, 139
Hoyt, Katherine, 178n74
Hull House, 18, 21, 31–32, 71
human rights, 1, 85, 91, 96, 100, 102–4, 106, 110, 112, 120, 126, 178n74
human trafficking, 90, 105

Illinois, 18; Chicago, 16, 21–22, 38, 43, 45, 55–56, 58–59, 65, 71, 160n22, 168n37. *See also* Chicago strike (1910–1911)
Immigration and Naturalization Service (INS), 89–90
indentured servitude, 1, 5, 91
independent contractors, 11–12, 83, 113, 129–30
India, 114, 126
Indiana League of Women Voters, 45
Indonesia, 86–88, 103, 103–4, 150, 152
Institute for European Environmental Policy, 114
International Labor Rights Forum, 101
International Ladies Garment Workers Union (ILGWU), 27, 29, 35, 37, 53, 80
Iraq, 108
Italian immigrants, 25, 27, 44
Ivanka Trump (brand), 125

Jackson, Bo, 130
Japan, 116, 126
JCPenney, 91, 151, 155
Jessica McClintock (company), 91
Jewish people, 34–35; Eastern European Jewish immigrants, 7, 27, 33, 44
JFK8, 137–38, 154
Jim Crow, 51
Jobs, Steve, 120
Johnson, Sam, 77
Joint Relief Committee, 35
Jones, Dora Lee, 67
Jordan, Michael, 86–87, 94–95, 105, 111

Kader Factory, 111, 116
Kansas, 63
Kara, Siddharth, 112

Keady, Jim, 87, 102–3
Kelley, Florence, 18–21, 23, 39, 42, 46
Kendall and Kylie, 125
Kentucky: Harlan County, 71
Kernaghan, Charles, 94–98, 121, 124
Kessler-Harris, Alice, 7, 52
Kingsley, Charles, 2
Klarreich, Kathie, 85
Klein, Naomi, 84, 94
Klein's, 48, 55
Knight, Phil, 86–88, 95, 102, 103, 140, 152
Kretzu, Leslie, 103
Kristof, Nicholas, 106–7, 113
Krugman, Paul, 83
Ku Klux Klan (KKK), 44, 51

labor feminism, 10, 13–46, 68
labor laws, 36, 60, 64, 101, 105, 149; activism for, 9, 15, 18–19, 22, 38–44, 54, 67, 68, 78; anti-discrimination, 79; attacks on, 14, 26, 70–73, 140, 150–51; child labor, 26, 40–41, 43, 63, 78, 81, 150–52; and the global assembly line, 1–2, 155; New Deal, 41, 48, 52–53, 57, 62–63, 70–76, 79, 81–82, 150; non-disclosure, 142; protective legislation, 39–44, 51, 55, 62, 154; and unions, 14, 26; violations of, 6, 37, 47–48, 91–92, 118, 120–21, 125, 132, 146, 151, 152, 168n37, 173n98. *See also* class-action lawsuits; *individual legislation and court cases*
LaGuardia, Fiorello, 48
Lasch-Quinn, Elizabeth, 23
Latin America, 78, 82–85, 89. *See also individual countries*
laundry industry, 22, 47, 62–65, 67–68, 84, 149–50, 152–55, 168n23
League of Women Shoppers (LWS), 8, 82, 88, 97, 153–57, 160n22; "Household Occupation in the District of Columbia," 68; National Legislation Committee, 68; and the Popular Front, 11, 48–76; *The Woman Shopper*, 60–61, 75, 171n80
League of Women Voters, 45, 72
Lemlich, Clara, 25, 46, 157

Levi Strauss and Company, 91
liberalism, 54, 56, 70–71, 105, 147, 171n80
Liberty of Contract, 14–15, 26, 106, 113, 149–50, 156
living wage, 19, 31, 75, 78, 143, 169n45, 171n79
Liz Claiborne (company), 91, 97
Lizhi, Xu, 4
Lochner, Joseph, 39, 152
Long 20th Century, 7
Lowell, Josephine Shaw, 18
Lowell Mill Girls, 3–4
Lowell Offering, 3–4
Ludwig von Miles Institute, 106
Lumpkin, Beatrice, 54, 168n23

Macy's, 77, 105
"Made in the USA" labels, 1, 91
Mailly, William, 35
Mak, Karin, 121
maquiladoras, 82
Mariana Islands. *See* Commonwealth of the Northern Mariana Islands (CNMI)
Martinez, Rosa, 83
Marymount University's National Consumer Sweatshop Surveys, 8
Massachusetts, 18; Boston, 22; Lowell, 3–4
Mattel, 124
Matthews, J. B., 69–72, 171n80
May's Department Store, 69
McCarthy, Joseph, 73
McCormick, Robert, 73
McDonald's, 6, 84, 100, 151
meatpacking industry, 81
Meeropol, Michael, 82
Mellon, Andrew, 44
Meta, 111, 147. *See also* Facebook
#MeToo movement, 118
Metropolitan Opera House, 36
Mexican American War, 3
Mexico, 3, 82, 98
Meyer, Fred, 90
Microsoft, 113, 117, 119, 139–40
Milkman, Ruth, 7

INDEX   **217**

Miller, Arthur, 53
Miller, Frieda, 49, 156
Miller, George, 77, 96
Mingfang, Tang, 125, 157
minimum wage, 6, 26, 32, 39, 41, 52–53, 62–66, 68, 81, 86, 92, 95, 100, 111, 150, 152
Minnesota, 63, 128; Minneapolis, 55, 134, 143
misogyny, 7, 82. *See also* welfare queen trope
Mitchell, Therese, 64
Moller, Kristen, 85
Montanaro, Eraclio, 33
Montgomery Ward, 90
Moody, Kim, 84
Morehead v. New York, 63
Morello, Tom, 98
Morgan, Anne, 27–29, 36, 155
Morris, Vivian, 67
Mrozowski, Stephen, 3
Ms. Foundation for Women, 88
MTV, 98
Muller, Curt, 39, 152
Muller v. Oregon (1908), 39–42, 62, 152
Musk, Elon, 147

National Association for the Advancement of Colored People ((NAACP), 23, 35
National Association of Clothiers, 26
National Basketball Association (NBA), 86, 97, 103
National Consumers' League (NCL), 38–39, 49, 55–56, 59, 68–69, 71, 82, 97, 108, 138, 154, 156–57; ethical consumption campaigns, 13–15, 18–29, 43–47, 57, 64; legal campaigns, 38–39, 41, 53
National Domestic Workers Alliance, 84
National Labor Committee, 97–98, 107, 121
National Labor Relations Act (1935, Wagner Act), 53, 70, 72, 168n37, 173n98
National Labor Relations Board (NLRB), 70, 81, 133, 152, 171n80
National Negro Congress, 68
National Organization for Women, 88

National Recovery Administration, 52
National Retail Federation (NRF), 90
National Urban League, 63
National Women's Party, 40–41, 49
neoliberalism, 142, 150
Nestor, Agnes, 16, 21–22, 46, 155
Network Education Fund, 178n74
New Deal, 39, 85, 90, 152; labor reform in, 29, 41, 48, 52–57, 62–63, 70–76, 79, 81–82, 150
New Deal liberals, 54
New Gilded Age, 78, 147
New Jersey, 6, 60, 63–64, 74, 127, 143; Newark, 34, 143
Newman, Pauline, 38
Newspaper Guild, 59
New York Building Department, 37
New York Bureau of Fire Prevention, 38, 154
New York City, 18, 75, 97, 103, 124, 139, 141; anti-sweatshop activism in, 13–14, 20–46, 47–48, 55–60, 64–69, 153–54; Bronx, 66–67, 113; Brooklyn, 27, 63, 69, 143; Lower East Side, 25; Queens, 143; Staten Island, 136, 138, 146, 153; sweatshops in, 1–2, 7–8, 33–38, 78, 95–96, 150, 152, 155. *See also* Uprising of 20,000 (New York City)
New York City Committee of Safety, 42
New York City Council, 38
New York Consumers' League, 18, 29
New York Department of Labor, 38
New York Shirtwaist Makers Union, 25
New York State, 38, 63, 68; Buffalo, 13, 145; Grand Island, 144–46, 148; Long Island, 142
New York State Hotel Association, 63
New York Supreme Court, 48
Ngai, Pun, 4, 117
Niemen Marcus, 77
Nike, 86–88, 93, 96, 98, 102–5, 111, 130, 140–41, 150, 152
Nintendo, 117
Nordstrom, 151
North American Free Trade Agreement (NAFTA), 82, 96, 98–99
North Carolina, 87, 130
Northwestern University, 31, 42

Norwood, Stephen, 28
"No Sweat" campaign, 90
No Tax on Jobs campaign, 140

Oakland City Council, 108
Obama, Barack, 133
Ocasio-Cortez, Alexandria, 142, 153
Occupational Safety and Health Administration (OSHA), 81, 88, 92, 146, 175n11
Occupy Wall Street (OWS), 110–11
O'Connor, Jessie Lloyd, 71, 172n87
Ohio, 65, 146; Columbus, 13; Etna, 127
Ohrbach, Nathan, 48
Ohrbach's, 48, 50, 55
Omar, Ilhan, 143, 154
open shops, 26, 43
Oregon, 39, 42, 62, 102, 140, 152
O'Reilly, Leonora, 18, 21, 155
Orleck, Annelise, 7, 23, 46
Oshkosh B'Gosh, 91
outsourcing, 62, 84, 94, 104
overtime labor, 4–5, 88, 101, 118–21, 123, 125
overtime pay, 6, 53, 65–66, 79, 92

Park, Doug, 146
Parker, Dorothy, 70
Paul, Alice, 41
Penaloza, Nancy, 96
Pennsylvania, 18, 63; Allentown, 127; Pittsburgh, 16, 55, 75
Perkins, Francis, 29, 37–39, 42, 45–46, 49, 108, 156
Personal Responsibility and Work Opportunity Reconciliation Act (PRWORA), 82
Philippines, 7, 91–92
political power, 20, 42, 79, 108
Polo Ralph Lauren, 91
Popular Front, 10–11, 47–76, 85, 99, 153–54
Posetta, Rose, 53
Powell, Benjamin, 107
pregnancy, 78–79, 92, 95, 97, 101, 120, 150
Pride at Work, 93
Pro America, 74
Progressive Era, 6, 10, 49, 51–54, 59–60, 153–55; labor feminism in, 13–46

protective legislation, 39–44, 51, 55, 62, 154. *See also Muller v. Oregon* (1908)
Protestants, 35, 44, 67
Public Citizen, 110
purchasing power, 9, 59, 155

Qiang, Li, 124, 126, 155

race, 44–45, 71; and Amazon, 130, 134; and anti-sweatshop activism, 9, 11, 18, 23, 62, 65, 68, 153; and class, 23–24, 79, 150; and labor, 5, 7, 15–16, 26–27, 39, 52, 62–68, 79, 81–82, 84–85, 107, 114–15, 150; and the Popular Front, 51–52, 54; racial uplift, 14; and state's rights, 51; and suffrage, 18, 49, 51. *See also* racial segregation; racism; white supremacy
racial segregation, 17, 23–24, 51, 79
racism, xiii, 27, 51, 82. *See also* Jim Crow; Ku Klux Klan (KKK); southern strategy; welfare queen trope
Rader, Katherine, 52
Rage Against the Machine, 98
railroad industry, 15–16, 39, 162n40
Raises, Rights, and Respect Campaign, 81
Rajal, Angel, 126–27
Rana Plaza Building, 111–12
Randolph, A. Philip, 45
Reagan, Ronald, 81–82
Red Scare, 43–45, 71, 73, 79; Second, 69, 74. *See also* Cold War; House Committee on Un-American Activities (HUAC, Dies Committee)
Reebok, 97–98
REI, 136
Reich, Robert, 90, 96, 100
Reilly, Dave, 144–45
Republican Party, 73, 77, 82, 99
restaurant workers, 155
Retail, Wholesale and Department Store Union (RWDSU), 132
Reuther, Walter, 45
Richardson, Darryl, 132–33
Right to Work states, 26, 147
Riis, Mary Phillips, 59

Robeson, Paul, 72
Robins, Margaret Dreier, 21, 27, 31–32, 45
Robins, Mary Dreier, 21, 27
Roosevelt, Eleanor, 11, 170n60
Roosevelt, Franklin Delano, 38, 45
Rosie the Riveters, 49
Russell Athletics, 98, 103, 105
Russian immigrants, 25, 30
Russian Revolution, 43
Rust Belt, 144

Sabran, Rose, 34
Sacco, Nicola, 70
Sadisah, 86
safety standards, 6, 10, 37–38, 78, 81, 85, 116, 137–38, 146
Saint John's University, 102
Sako Factory, 100
Salasky, Karen, 127
Salazar, Leia, 93
Sanger, Margaret, 45
Santa Clara County v. Southern Pacific Railroad (1886), 39
Sawant, Kshama, 139–41, 146, 153, 155–56
Sawyer, Diane, 95
Schlink, F. J., 171n80
Schneiderman, Rose, 18, 21, 36–38, 46–47, 155–56
Schofield, Ann, 24, 29
Scott, Miriam Finn, 29
Sears, 77, 111
seasonal workers, 11, 13, 133
Seattle City Council, 139–40, 155
Seattle General Strike (1919), 166n124
Seattle WTO protest (1999), 99, 102, 110
second shift, 40, 154
Seo Fashions, 95
September 11, 2001, attacks, xiii
settlement house movement, 21–23
sexism, xiii, 3, 40, 79
sexual violence, 1, 7, 12, 62, 77–79, 81–82, 88, 98, 118, 126, 146, 150. *See also* #MeToo movement
Shakopee Amazon Fulfillment Center, 143–44

SHEIN, 3
Shepard, Alice Lesser, 75, 173n105
shop girls, 13
Simpson, O. J., 88
Singapore, 116
SK Fashions Factory, 77, 84, 89, 104
Sklar, Kathryn Kish, 8
slavery, 3, 5–6, 39; aftermath of, 15, 23–24; contemporary, 89–91, 105, 108, 126, 151, 154; term used in labor activism, 62, 66–67, 87, 113, 122, 153
Smalls, Christian, 137–38, 156
Smeal, Eleanor, 88
Smith, Jaclyn, 94
Smith College, 28
Smithsonian National Museum of American History, 98, 108; *Between a Rock and a Hard Place*, 77–78, 89
socialism, 20, 25, 27, 32, 54–55, 72, 140
Social Security, 66, 68, 150
solidarity, xv, 4, 101, 120, 134, 138, 154; cross-class feminist, 7, 9–10, 12, 13–46; in the Popular Front, 11, 47–76; transnational, 2, 85, 88–89, 98, 104
Solomon, Eugene, 25–26
Sondergaard, Gale, 70
South Carolina, 97
southern strategy, 51
Southern Summer School for Women Workers in Industry, 45, 70
South Korea, 100
Space Jam, 87
SpaceX, 152
special economic zones (SEZs), 116–17, 139
Spectar, Jem, 99
Stanford University, 87
Stanton, Elizabeth Cady, 18
Starbucks, 136, 139–40
Starr, Ellen, 32
steel industry, 68, 72, 81, 130
Steghagen, Emma, 32
Stein, Leon, 6
Storrs, Landon, 8, 68
Strauss, Steve, 113

students. *See* college students
Students and Scholars Against Corporate Misbehavior (SACOM), 121–24, 138, 153, 157
Su, Julie, 89, 108, 156
subcontracting, 2, 87, 91, 100, 104, 123, 178n74
suffrage, 3, 17–18, 21–24, 28–29, 40, 49, 51, 59, 71
suicide, 3–5, 117–22, 128, 146
Sukaesih, Cicih, 86, 96
supply chains, 7, 11, 14, 104, 121, 126, 139, 146
surveillance, 3, 113, 128, 132
sweated labor, 2, 10, 31, 56, 63, 87, 90–91, 108, 126, 147, 153
Sweatshop Watch, 2, 7, 11, 89–93, 95, 98, 106–8, 121, 153–54, 156

Taft, Helen, 20, 59, 156, 162n22
Taft, William Howard, 20
Tan Holdings Corporation, 91–92
Tarbell, Ida, 59
Target, 1, 91
temperance, 17
Tennessee, 45, 147; Nashville, 142
Tesla, 113, 145, 147, 151
Texas, 77, 107, 147, 151
Texas Tech University: Free Market Institute, 107
Thailand, 77, 89, 106–7, 111, 116, 150, 154
Thrasher, Sara Marie, 132
Tipaldo, Joseph, 63, 152
Tollison, Byron, 132
Tommy Hilfiger (company), 1, 91, 151
Toshiba, 117
Toys "R" Us, 111
Trader Joe's, 152
Traub-Werner, Marion, 87
Triangle Shirtwaist Company fire (1911), 2, 7, 10, 24, 33–38, 59, 77, 111, 138, 154
T. Rowe Price, 110
Trump, Donald, 133, 151
Tufts University, 85
Tulipshare, 110
Twitter/X, 103, 129, 142, 147

Uber, 2, 11, 19, 113–14, 147
Ukraine, 25
UN Environment Programme, 114
Union of Needletrades, Industrial and Textile Employees (UNITE), 91, 95
unions, 9, 18, 48, 79, 112, 151, 154; and Amazon, 109, 132–38, 143, 146–47, 152–53, 156; attacks on, 43, 73–74, 78, 81–84, 150; gender in, 15, 21–22, 24–25, 29, 40, 45, 53; and the global justice movement, 85, 89, 94–95, 101, 103; and labor feminism, 14, 21–22, 24–27, 31, 33–37, 46; and Liberty of Contract, 14, 149; and the Popular Front, 53–76. *See also* closed shops; open shops; *individual unions*
United Garment Workers, 31
United Hebrew Trades, 35
United Kingdom, 109, 115, 128, 143. *See also* England; Great Britain
United Methodist Church, 87
United Students Against Sweatshops (USAS), 87, 98–104, 107–8, 120–21, 123, 153
university apparel, xiii–xiv, 87, 92, 98–104, 107–8, 120–21, 123, 153, 154
University of Arizona, 102
University of California system, 92
University of Chicago, 31
University of Dayton, 99
University of Michigan, 53, 102
University of Nebraska, 100
University of North Carolina, 87
University of Oregon, 102, 140, 152
University of Wisconsin, 101
University of Wisconsin-Milwaukee, 101
Uprising of 20,000 (New York City), 24–25, 27–29, 34, 36, 53, 62, 155, 157
US Agency for International Development (USAID), 83
US Chamber of Commerce, 52
US Congress, 20, 44, 77, 79, 82, 89, 91–92, 95–96, 106, 143; Senate, 6, 97, 105, 132–33. *See also* House Committee on Un-American Activities (HUAC, Dies Committee)
US Department of Justice, 73, 105

INDEX **221**

US Department of Labor (DOL), 90, 92, 146, 151; Women's Bureau, 40, 49, 68, 156
US Department of State, 79
US Department of the Interior, 92, 105
US Supreme Court, 14, 20, 39–41, 63, 81, 149

Vale, Rena, 71–72
Vanzetti, Bartolomeo, 70
Vassar College, 14, 27–28
Vietnam, 88
Virginia, 143
Von Maur, 151
Vulcan, 140
vulnerability, 7, 12, 56, 75, 85, 98, 114, 147, 150, 181n109

wages, 1, 5, 105, 107, 119, 126, 131–32, 134, 149; back, 65, 90, 101, 154; calls to raise, 9, 12, 27, 30, 56, 58, 69; cuts to, 4, 16; gendered, 40–41, 52–53, 66–67, 82; living wage, 19, 31, 75, 78, 143, 169n45, 171n79; low, xiii, 4, 14, 16, 40, 43, 47, 57, 62, 66–67, 82–84, 88–89, 97, 103, 113; minimum wage, 6, 26, 32, 39, 41, 52–53, 62–66, 68, 81, 86, 92, 95, 100, 111, 150, 152; overtime wages, 6, 53, 65–66, 79, 92; piece-based, 2, 31; racialized, 66–67, 82; wage theft, 90, 93, 120, 125, 150
Wagner Act. *See* National Labor Relations Act (1935, Wagner Act)
Walker, Alice, 88
walkouts, 9, 16, 31, 65, 86, 137
Walmart, 6, 84, 94–97, 105–6, 111, 124, 130, 148, 150, 155–56
Walsh, Marty, 138
Walter, Alice, 88
Washington, DC, 20, 28, 41, 54–55, 63–65, 67–68, 85, 105, 130, 142, 153
Washington State: Seattle, 45, 46, 99, 102, 110, 131, 139–41, 143, 146–47, 152, 155, 166n124
Weiler, Sue, 32
welfare, 82, 84, 96, 105, 141
welfare queen trope, 82
Wellesley College, 28, 31, 42

Wharton School of Business, 17
White, Reggie, 87
white labels, 20–21, 57, 90, 147
white supremacy, 7, 11, 18, 44, 51–52, 54, 68–69, 76. *See also* Jim Crow
Wilson, Katie, 139
Wilson, Woodrow, 51
Wintek, 123
Wisconsin, 45, 101, 151; Menomonee, 28; Milwaukee, 19, 61, 101
Wisconsin Summer School, 45
Wise, Louise Waterman, 59
Wise, Stephen W., 25, 34, 36–38, 46, 59
Women's Liberation Movement, 79. *See also* feminism
women's studies, xiv
Women's Trade Union League (WTUL), 8, 10, 14–15, 21–41, 44–47, 49, 53, 55–57, 62, 65, 67–68, 71, 74, 82, 108, 154–56
Wood, Peggy, 49
Woodward, Helen, 74
Woolworth Department Store, 60
Worker Rights Consortium (WRC), 101–2, 121, 154
workers' compensation, 6, 66, 68
workers' rights, 8, 110; and Freedom of Contract, 14–15
Works Progress Administration, 53, 71
World Trade Organization (WTO), 85, 104, 116; 1999 Seattle protest, 99, 102, 110
World War I, 43, 49, 51, 62, 108, 172n87
World War II, 49, 73, 78, 173n105

x. *See* Twitter/x
xenophobia, 7, 16, 44

Young Communist League, 167n7
Young Men's Christian Association (YMCA), 28
Young Women's Christian Association (YWCA), 66–67
YouTube, 103

Zhao, Li, 125
Zheng, Yue, 113
Zugsmith, Leane, 75

www.ingramcontent.com/pod-product-compliance
Lightning Source LLC
Chambersburg PA
CBHW021854230426

43671CB00006B/390